Creative Careers:

Real Jobs in Glamour Fields

Career Books from Wiley Press

Bridges To Success: Finding Jobs and Changing Careers, Austin &
Vines
Creative Careers: Real Jobs in Glamour Fields, Blake & Bly
Dream Jobs: A Guide to Tomorrow's Top Careers, Bly & Blake
Getting Noticed: A Manager's Success Kit, Kravetz
High Tech Job Finder: A Guide to America's 100 Hottest Communities,
Marrs & Marrs
Not Just A Secretary: Using the Job to Get Ahead, Morrow & Lebov
Résumés that Work, Foxman & Polksy

Wiley Press books are available at quantity discounts when used to promote products or services. For information please write to Special Sales Department, John Wiley & Sons.

Creative Careers:

Real Jobs in Glamour Fields

GARY BLAKE AND ROBERT W. BLY

The Wiley Press
JOHN WILEY & SONS, INC.
New York • Chichester • Brisbane • Toronto • Singapore

Library of Congress Cataloging in Publication Data:

Blake, Gary.
  Creative careers.

    Includes index.
    1. United States—Occupations. I. Bly, Robert W.
II. Title.
HF5382.5.U5B56   1985   331.7'02'0973   84-29093
ISBN 0-471-81560-8

Printed in the United States of America

10 9 8 7 6

The most difficult thing in life is to make money doing what you most like to do.

—Henri Cartier-Bresson

Acknowledgments

It is impossible to survey career opportunities in one field—much less *ten* fields—without a lot of help. This help includes not only people who sit still while we ask them questions about what they do, but also people who check facts, read drafts, and make sure that we keep talking to the experts in each field until we achieve a balanced point of view.

In particular, we'd like to thank Elizabeth Perry and Judy Wilson, our editor and publisher, for encouraging us to write this book and for making us feel a part of the Wiley family.

We also thank Joe Gennaro for his research and editorial assistance on our chapter covering careers in the movie industry.

Thanks also to Jennifer Levy, Channa Taub, Sue Shapiro, Cynthia Kirk, Eve Blake, Tom Okada, Alix Coleman, Steve Price, Bob Ullman, Howard DeFelice, Louis Scheeder, Julie Cornfield, Richard Curtis, Julia Strohm, Jean Blake, Adele Gross, Gail Rentsch, Dominick Abel, Jon Isear, Andras Kron, Joel Bernard, Richard Douglass, Mike Buglio, Harrald Boergen, Ron Capozzoli, Kim Warner, Amy Bly, Dave Mosel, Janice Remer, Phil Caso, Rosemarie Santini, Bruce Whigham, Dick Fox, Steven Scharf, Mark Lewis, Stuart Samuels, and everyone else who took the time to help us learn about their business.

Introduction

Theater . . . Film . . . Television . . . Music . . . Advertising . . . Publishing . . . Travel and Tourism . . . Finance . . . Gourmet Food . . . Photography. Many people dream about working in these glamorous industries. For those of you who want to turn your dreams into reality, we've written this book to help you break into any of these ten glamour fields and find success and satisfaction in a job you enjoy.

Of course, these are no ordinary careers. From Broadway to Wall Street, from Hollywood to Madison Avenue, they represent ten of the most exciting, talked-about businesses in the work world. For generations, people have sacrificed time, money, and security for a chance to make movies or work in the theater or break into the music business.

Most of these careers are alluring because of their visibility, the chance they give you to be in the spotlight. Other attractions are, of course, the work itself and the people you'd be working with, both of which are often more colorful and creative than the usual nine-to-five type of job.

We won't kid you. If you want a safe, secure job with a steady paycheck and reasonable hours, most of these fields are not for you. Getting the job you want will be tough, and becoming a star will be even tougher. But if you want to try, the advice, information, and resources in this book can tip the odds of success in your favor.

How did we select these particular careers? We simply asked ourselves—and dozens of friends, colleagues, and acquaintances—what jobs they considered the most fun, exciting, artistic, and creative—in a word, glamorous.

Creative Careers: Real Jobs in Glamour Fields is intended as a
practical guide for career changers and job seekers who dare to
dream. In each field, we cover both the "superstar" jobs as well
as the entry-level jobs that don't require the artistic talents of
a prodigy or the luck of a lottery winner. We attempt to
describe these careers with a mixture of excitement, soberness,
and sense; what has emerged, we hope, is a realistic, helpful
guide for people who want to land the job of their dreams.

Each chapter provides a brief history and background information on a particular industry. The chapters then give you in-
depth career tips and guidance: an overview of the types of
jobs available in the field; qualifications and training required
to break into each area; the type of personality you need to fit
into each job; how to write the best cover letters and résumés;
how to turn a phone call into a job interview and an interview
into a job; typical salary levels in each area; how to advance to
the top job spots; how to uncover hidden job opportunities or
create your own.

In addition, each chapter contains numerous lists of resources: employment agencies; top companies in each field;
training programs and schools; professional societies and
trade associations; reference books, industry directories, and
trade journals; glossaries of technical terms; and other resources to get you started in your job search.

Here's a chapter-by-chapter preview of the book:

- **Advertising.** The excitement and glory in this field are in
  "big-league, front-line" advertising—handling major television and print campaigns for national brands. This chapter tells where to find and how to get a job with the giant
  agencies that handle such prominent accounts. It also
  focuses on two of the top jobs in advertising: copywriting
  and account management.
- **Book publishing.** Have you ever yearned to be a part of the
  book world? This chapter identifies the key positions at
  publishing houses and details how you can work your way
  up to become the editor of a major book by a top author. It
  includes interviews with top editors, a list of major publishers, and a thorough description of the publishing process.

- **The financial world.** Do you want to make million-dollar deals and grow rich beyond the dreams of avarice? Then a career in finance is for you. We provide an overview of the many hidden job opportunities in finance, from investment banking and trading to operations management and venture capital. And we also cover two of the most popular and lucrative careers—stockbroker and the financial planner—in even greater detail.
- **Gourmet food.** Everyone secretly believes he or she has an unbeatable recipe or harbors a vision of what constitutes the perfect restaurant. We survey the world of gourmet food, focusing on restaurateurs and gourmet caterers. The chapter shows you how people have bridged the gap between the dreams and realities of marketing their gourmet creations.
- **Movies.** Maybe you're not the next Brando or Bergman. But there are still plenty of exciting opportunities for you in the movie business, from stunt person and extra to special-effects expert and sound man. This chapter tells you where the jobs are in the movie business and how to break in.
- **Music.** A hit record can turn a performing artist into an instant millionaire. But many of the most successful people in the business—promoters, managers, producers, record-company executives, publishers—can't sing a note. We'll take you inside the major record companies, studios, music publishers, and entertainment firms to show you how the music business works and where you can fit in.
- **Photography.** Practically everyone who has ever taken a snapshot has fantasized about capturing images the way the pros do. We discuss several opportunities in photography—assistant photographer, still-life photographer, wedding photographer—and provide in-depth interviews with people in these fields. Although the pace is fast and the work erratic, photography is a career that never loses its fascination.
- **Television.** Cable may be easier to break into, but network television is the big time. If you've set your sights on working for one of the big three—ABC, NBC, or CBS—we'll

tell you the best way to land a spot in production, programming, promotion, sales, or any of a half dozen other
career opportunities in network television. We also provide profiles of all three networks.
- **Theater.** Although we can't pretend to help you become
  the next Harold Prince, Neil Simon, Michael Bennett, or
  Tommy Tune, we have described ways of breaking into
  apprenticeships at theaters across America as well as on
  and off Broadway. We also show you how to apply your
  perseverance, who to apply to, and how to parlay your
  experience to a permanent post in this most glamorous of
  fields.
- **Travel and tourism.** This field is larger than any other
  discussed in the book. For most people, travel itself is a
  broadening, exciting experience, and the related work can
  be equally rewarding. We focus on entry-level positions in
  the airline, hotel, and cruise industries, paying special
  attention to the travel wholesaler. We'll tell you how to
  find a position that will satisfy your craving for faraway
  places.

Although study in any of these fields is, of course, recommended, you don't need an advanced degree or technical
training to succeed. We show you how liberal-arts majors and
other nonspecialists can break into these fields and rise to the
top.

We aren't Pollyannas, though. These ten fields are highly
competitive, and we've tried to identify realistic starting
places for people who believe that they would enjoy participat-
ing in them even if they never get to be the superstars.

Creative Careers is a mixture of fact and opinion, of sober,
hardheaded advice coupled with hopes and dreams. We believe
the jobs in these fields will go to the people who want them, are
willing to compete for them, have the resources to find work.

Reading this book may be the first step toward an exciting
career, with the help of patience, luck, timing, ambition, and a
bit of talent.

We've tried to show you the doors to the glamour job of your
dreams. Only you can choose to open those doors.

Good luck!

Contents

Advertising

Fairfax Cone, founding partner of one of the largest ad agencies in the world, once remarked, "The inventory of an advertising agency goes down in the elevator every night."

This was his way of saying that *people* are an advertising agency's most valuable asset. And it's true, more so than in any other business.

Manufacturers, for example, can gain a leg up on the competition by holding the patents to new technology. Distributors can gain a competitive edge by keeping more stock on the shelves. But in advertising, the only real advantage one agency has over the next is its people—and the quality of the advertising they produce. That's just one of many reasons why advertising is so exciting—and so rewarding, both financially and in terms of self-satisfaction.

According to the American Association of Advertising Agencies (better known as the 4 A's), an advertising agency is "a service company that earns its income from planning, creating, producing and placing printed advertisements and broadcast commercials for its clients." In other words, when "Monday Night Football" and "Hill Street Blues" are interrupted by pitches for Perdue Chickens, Coca-Cola, AT&T, or Texas Instruments computers, people who work in ad agencies are responsible for writing, filming, and placing these commercials on the air.

This wasn't always the case. According to Stephen Fox, author of *The Mirror Makers*, advertising agencies were first formed in the mid-1800s to buy space in newspapers for advertisers. The agencies, usually one- or two-man operations,

1

actually worked for the newspapers; they would solicit ads, obtain (but not prepare) copy from the advertiser, and send it along to the paper, where it would be typeset and placed in the appropriate issue. Ads were written by the advertiser and designed by the newspaper's layout director; the agency did neither. When Daniel Lord, an advertising agent, gave unsolicited advice to a client on how to improve his ad, the client told Lord to mind his own business.

Lord, operating in the 1870s, was one of the earliest agencies. The first was opened by Volney Palmer in Philadelphia in 1843. One of the earliest advertised products was Lydia Pinkham's Vegetable Compound, which claimed to be "the positive cure for all female complaints."

The first major ad agency, N. W. Ayer, was started in 1868 with $250. Ayer set the agency's fee as 15 percent of the cost of the space. Although Ayer's fee was based on space costs, as were the fees of Lord, Palmer, and others whose sole function was to buy space, Ayer did more than just place ads. The agency wrote and designed the ads and advised their clients on how to make their campaigns most effective.

The first major consumer packaged good was Ivory soap (a *packaged good* is a brand-name product wrapped in a package and sold off the shelf). Ivory was launched in 1882 with the advertising slogan "99 44/100% pure."

Today's big ad agencies do much more than just buy space or write slogans; the *full-service* ad agency, as defined by the 4 A's, provides "all the services necessary to handle the total advertising function." In addition to the writing, design, and placement of ads and commercials, these services can include everything from market research and planning, to sales promotion and package design, to public relations and television programming.

Few industries offer the broad range of exciting jobs that advertising does. Depending on your position, you might hobnob with top corporate executives at 21, Four Seasons, and other famous New York lunch spots . . . be part of the team that plans the winning strategy in the advertising war between McDonald's and Burger King (or Federal Express and Emery, or AT&T and MCI, or Pepsi and Coca-Cola) . . . supervise the shooting of lavish commercials with beautiful models in far-away places . . . or maybe even write a slogan so memorable that it goes beyond advertising to become a permanent part of the culture (such as Morton's "When it rains, it pours" or Wendy's "Where's the beef?"). Whatever your interest—writing or designing, business planning or working with clients, print or TV, research or management—there's a glamour job for you in advertising.

There are more than four thousand full-service agencies in the United States, with thousands of smaller agencies offering such specialty services as art and copy, direct marketing, media buying, and financial advertising, with each filling a niche in the marketplace. Although both types of agencies can be profitable, the trend is for major advertisers to concentrate their accounts at large, full-service agencies.

In advertising, the biggest accounts are packaged goods marketed nationwide—Crest, Diet Coke, Charmin toilet paper, Ivory soap, and other low-price products you can buy off the shelf at the supermarket or drugstore to eat, drink, or rub on your body. These accounts usually have the biggest budgets and go to the biggest agencies (although some product areas, such as airlines and automobiles, can command even bigger budgets than packaged goods). They also run the most expensive, elaborate campaigns. If you want to gain status and wealth in the ad-agency business, you need to be working at one of the top twenty or so agencies on a major-packaged-goods or other large account. This chapter will tell you how to get there in style.

Arriving at the top in advertising is a real accomplishment because the field is so competitive. The personnel director at one of the top twenty agencies reported that he recently chose seven people to fill seven openings—from a pool of *fifteen hundred* applicants! "Standards are high and the competition is tough," writes Victor G. Bloede in "The Full-Service Agency," a 4 A's pamphlet, "so when you succeed in the agency business, you know you've made it in the major league."

The competition *is* fierce. It's not enough to be talented, to create advertising that wins client approval and boosts sales, or to do your job to the best of your ability. Advertising people—especially those in entry-level jobs—are willing to do anything to get in and get ahead. Even at the bottom, they frequently put in twelve-hour days from Monday to Friday and come in on the weekends as well. In this competitive field, career comes before leisure, and the demanding schedule forces one to choose between leading a normal social life and having a successful advertising career.

If you thrive on this type of competition and put work above home life, the agency business—with its constant deadlines and hectic pace—might be for you. Conversely, if you prefer a balance between work and home, and you consider your family and your leisure time important, the fast pace of big-agency life might not suit you. There are alternatives, of course. You can work on the "client side," in the advertising or marketing department of a manufacturer, where the pace may be slower and the hours less demanding. Or you can work in a small agency, where, away from the mainstream of Madison Avenue, the competition may not be quite so cutthroat.

Madison Avenue is the avenue in Manhattan that runs parallel between Park Avenue and Fifth Avenue, from Twenty-third Street up to River Drive in Harlem. But when applied to advertising, the term *Madison Avenue* refers to the major ad agencies clustered in midtown Manhattan. Most of the agencies are actually located not on Madison Avenue itself but on the streets nearby: J. Walter Thompson and McCann-Erickson are on Lexington Avenue, Ogilvy & Mather on Forty-eighth Street, Grey on Third Avenue, Ted Bates in Times Square.

Although many cities have active advertising communities, New York City is still the hub of the advertising industry. Of the top ten agencies in the world, seven have their headquarters in New York. The New York Yellow Pages lists more than twelve hundred firms under "advertising agencies"—the most of any city in the United States. And 70 percent of the commercials produced in this country are filmed in New York. (In 1983, the New York Mayor's Office of Film, Theater, and Broadcasting issued 1,742 permits for shooting commercials outdoors in New York. And, of course, that figure doesn't include commercials filmed indoors in studios.)

New York City, television, advertising . . . all three conjure up images of glamour: bright lights, fame, attention, big money. In reality, the advertising business mixes glitter with nitty-gritty, dash with dog work. Here's how Creative Group Head Karen Cole Winters describes it in her book *Your Career in Advertising:*

> There are moments in advertising that are absolutely exhilarating: the first time you make a presentation and the client loves your campaign ideas; seeing your first TV spot on the air; traveling to some exotically distant city or country for an "on location" commercial. But it's not glamorous standing around a sound stage watching an actress pour dog food out of a can. It's not glamorous pasting typewritten copy on storyboards at two o'clock in the morning. And it's not glamorous sitting in a smoke-filled meeting room for eight hours.
>
> For all the fantasies that it creates for the public, advertising is itself a business of reality. There are high moments and low moments, but most of the time it's like any other business. If you go into advertising expecting a constant whirl of fun and excitement, you will probably be disappointed.[1]

This may clash with your own image of the ad-agency business, but image and reality are often two different things.

For example, the advertising business is famous for its legendary "three-martini lunches." But a recent *Adweek* survey of top agency executives revealed that very few of them drink martinis or have elaborate dining habits. Carl Spielvogel, CEO of Backer & Spielvogel, says his favorite lunch is tuna fish at his desk; his second choice is lunch in the agency dining room. Keith Reinhard, CEO of Needham, Harper & Steers, likes to order in McDonald's Chicken McNuggets or a pastrami sandwich. And Jay Chiat, chairman of Chiat/Day, says, "I don't go on business lunches unless someone makes me."

(To be fair, there are still a few gourmands to be found among top agency people. Maryellan Flynn, a vice president at Grey Advertising, says she likes asparagus and fish at the King Cole Room, fettuccine at Orsini's, and bay scallops at Smith & Wollensky. And most days you'll find Al Hampel, president of D'Arcy MacManus Masius, lunching at the prestigious Four Seasons or Perigord East.)

For most ad-agency people, however, lunch is not a big part

of their day. To be precise, lunch and other breaks account for
only 7.2 percent of the average advertising employee's time,
according to George Tibball, president of STG Marketing Communications.

Tibball surveyed agency people to find out just what they do
during the 2,080 hours (40 hours a week multiplied by fifty-two
weeks) they get paid for each year. According to Tibball, here's
how the average employee spends his or her time:

> 1,300 hours doing "billable work" (work on projects that
> will generate income for the agency)
>
> 140 hours on new business development
>
> 50 hours on agency self-promotion
>
> 200 hours attending internal agency meetings
>
> 150 hours nonbillable time (lunch, breaks, etc.)
>
> 240 hours vacation, personal, sick days, holidays

Even the way agency people spend "billable time" may
surprise you. Most laypeople picture an ad agency filled with
row after row of cubicles in which artists, writers, and illustrators spend their days frantically writing and drawing advertisements. In fact, it's safe to say that more time goes into the
planning and development of advertising strategies and campaigns than the actual writing or production.

The top jobs in advertising are directly linked to the big-
name, best-selling products. Packaged goods is traditionally
the top product area. Other big-money product areas you can
aim for include fast food, pharmaceuticals, financial services,
automobiles, communications (phones, express package delivery services), airlines, and computers.

High-tech—computers, software, telecommunications, office
automation systems—is one of the fastest-growing, hottest
areas of advertising. In 1980, high-tech was this country's
tenth largest industry. It is expected to grow to number two
(behind petroleum) by the year 2000. Bob Corriveau, a senior
vice president at Ingalls Associates, says that high-tech copywriters can earn $10,000 a year more than copywriters who are
generalists.

Another growth area is direct marketing, which includes direct mail, mail-order advertising, and telemarketing. Almost every large general advertising agency has formed a direct-marketing division, either by developing one internally or buying a direct-marketing ad agency. Direct-marketing writers and account executives, once thought of as second-class citizens in the advertising world, are now in heavy demand and short supply. And their salaries—also $10,000 or more above those of generalists—reflect the need for their services.

We've already touched upon some of the positions that exist at advertising agencies—copywriter, artist, account executive. Now let's take a closer look at these jobs and the qualifications and skills required to fill them.

CAREERS IN ADVERTISING

The jobs described below are unique to advertising. But keep in mind that ad agencies, like other businesses, have accountants, personnel directors, office managers, bookkeepers, secretaries, and administrative assistants on staff. In addition to being rewarding in themselves, these positions can sometimes lead to one of the jobs listed below (although working your way up from secretary or mail-room attendant is a tough route to take).

Here, in alphabetical order, are the main jobs in advertising:

- **Account executive.** "The account executive is the link—sometimes the executive errand boy, and sometimes the creative facilitator—between the agency and the client," writes Neil Holbert in "Careers in Marketing," a monograph published by the American Marketing Association. "The account executive must know both the *workings of his agency and the client's products and needs,* and the human dynamics that enable the two things to interact successfully."

  The account executive is the liaison between the agency and its client, the advertiser. The account executive helps the advertiser develop his yearly marketing and advertising plan; communicates the client's strategy to the artists, writers, creative directors, and TV producers who will create the actual ads and commercials; and oversees the work to make sure it is completed correctly and on time.

Account executives are primarily *businesspeople*. Their forte is solving the client's business problems and making sure ideas and work flow smoothly between agency and advertiser.

The job requires the ability to make decisions, take the initiative, and sell one's ideas. Desirable personality traits include charm, diplomacy, and tact.

To prepare for a career as an account executive, take courses in business, advertising, and marketing. An MBA will increase your chances of getting a job.

One way to break into the field is to start with a job on the client side as an assistant product or brand manager, then make the move to the agency business after you have a few years' experience. This isn't the most common route, but you should consider it if you have trouble getting an agency job right out of school. Starting annual salaries average $15,000-$18,000. Senior account executives earn $100,000 or more.

- **Art director.** Art directors design ads and commercials. They're the experts in graphic design, typography, photography, illustration, color, and cinematography. A good art director can carry his or her design ideas from initial concept to finished ad with taste and style. In addition to their design tasks, art directors are responsible for choosing outside vendors—television directors, film-production houses, photographers, illustrators, airbrushers—who help the agency to produce the finished ad or commercial.

Most art directors study graphic arts in school, but a bachelor's degree is not a prerequisite. The main thing agencies look for in an art director is the ability to create and express exciting, original advertising ideas with visuals. A good way to sharpen this talent is to get experience working in a graphic-arts studio or the layout department of a retail store or newspaper. Beginning artists can expect to earn a salary of $10,000 to $15,000 a year.

Entry-level artists move from trainee to assistant art director to art director to executive art director. From there, you can go on to become a creative director—a big step up in prestige and managerial responsibility, with a salary of $60,000 a year or more.

- **Copywriter.** The copywriter writes the words for ads and commercials and is responsible for overall themes as well. He or she must combine the communications skills of a professional writer with the persuasiveness of a top salesman in order to write copy that motivates consumers to buy a product.

  Copywriters deal with a broad range of facts and ideas, so a liberal-arts education is the recommended course of study. Many ad-agency copywriters gained their initial experience writing for other media—magazines, newspapers, mail-order catalogs, technical publications, public-relations, or corporate-communications departments. A short stint doing some type of selling is also helpful, for many writers know how to communicate but have little experience in persuasion. Junior copywriters earn starting salaries in the high teens. Senior writers earn $50,000 to $80,000—more if they become creative directors.

- **Creative director.** The creative director oversees all agency activities pertaining to the creation of ads and commercials. He or she supervises writers, art directors, TV producers, illustrators, and photographers.

  The job of creative director requires a combination of creativity, sound judgment, and "people skills." Creative directors are among the best-paid people in advertising; many have healthy six-figure salaries plus expense accounts, bonuses, corner offices, and other perks.

- **Marketing researcher.** The marketing research department conducts studies designed to show who the buyers are for a product; the reasons they buy this type of product; how they react to the product and its package and price; and whether the advertising gets its message across to these buyers and motivates them to buy the product. By finding out what makes the consumer tick, market researchers provide information that helps the account executives, copywriters, and art directors to produce more effective advertising.

  Market research involves designing surveys, doing field

research, analyzing the results, and preparing research reports for agency and client staff. The job requires good analytical and communications skills, an undergraduate degree to get started, and a Ph.D. to rise to the top of the department. Salaries range from the low twenties to six figures depending on your level of experience.

- **Media people.** The media department gets the ads into the papers and magazines and the commercials onto television and radio.

There are two separate jobs in this area: media planning and media buying.

The *media buyer* is the person who buys space in the print media and time on broadcast media. But the job goes way beyond the writing of purchase orders and contracts. The media buyer is a negotiator who deals with the networks and other media to get the best space and time at the lowest possible price.

An effective media buyer can save the agency's clients thousands—even hundreds of thousands—of dollars by getting a good deal. This negotiation is so important that there are a number of companies that specialize in buying media for various clients (both agencies and advertisers).

The *media planner* works with the account executive to plan the client's yearly advertising schedule. The account executive tells the media planner the nature of the advertising campaign and the type of buyer at which it is aimed. The planner, an expert in all media, selects the blend of print, broadcast, and outdoor media that reaches the greatest number of potential customers at the lowest possible cost.

The aspiring media person must combine negotiating skills with sound judgment and the ability to analyze the statistics the media use to describe their viewers and readers. Undergraduate courses in English, math, statistics, marketing, and economics help. Some ad-agency media people started out selling ad space for consumer magazines, local newspapers, or trade journals.

Media buying and planning are of equal importance, but planners tend to rise in salary and title faster than buyers (many of whom become planners themselves). The head of the media department is the media director, and most media directors are former planners.

Although copywriters and account executives are more likely to land a position in top management, media offers a slightly more accessible career path than the creative department or account management. The starting salaries are low, but if you have determination, commitment, and patience, you can find a satisfying career in this area.

After a few years at low pay ($20,000–$30,000), your salary will rise along with your level of responsibility. You'll have contact with high-level management at both the agency and the client's company. And there is some glamour in being wined and dined by the networks, major newspapers, and consumer magazines that are competing with each other for your media dollars. The head of the media department can earn $85,000 a year and more.

- **Print production manager.** The print production manager supervises the mechanical production of ads, sales brochures, and other printed advertising material. This person must be knowledgeable in all phases of print production, from typography and mechanical paste-up to color separations and binding techniques.

  The print production manager buys outside services and materials as needed, and works with these vendors—printers, engravers, mat services, photostat houses, retouchers, typographers—to make sure things are done correctly each step of the way. The print production manager also acts as a consultant to the creative department, advising them on what works in print and what doesn't. The job is essentially one of quality control for printed communications.

  The best training for this job is to work for a printer, graphic-design studio, typesetter, bookbinder, or other business involved in some facet of producing printed material. According to Adweek's 1984 salary survey, the average print production manager earns $27,000 a year.

- **Traffic manager.** The traffic manager is like the foreman in an industrial plant: His job is to keep the work flow moving on schedule and to make sure all projects are done on time.

But, unlike the foreman, the traffic manager has no authority to *order* workers to get moving, since traffic managers rank low on the organizational chart, behind creative directors, copywriters, art directors, and account executives. So the traffic manager has to get people moving through friendly persuasion rather than direct order. It's a delicate task that requires tact and diplomatic skills (a writer or artist under deadline pressure can be rather temperamental and disagreeable).

The traffic manager keeps a schedule of all ongoing projects and tracks their progress from the assignment of job numbers to the completion of the work. At all times, he or she must know who is working on a particular project and how far behind (or ahead of) schedule they are. The job teaches teamwork and organization, and can be a stepping-stone to a position as print production manager or even account executive. No special training is required, but work experience with a printer or art studio helps. Starting salary: $11,000-$15,000 a year.

• **TV producer.** The TV producer supervises the production of commercials in much the same way the print production manager supervises the printing of ads and brochures. He or she works closely with the copywriter and art director to help plan the shooting of their storyboards (a *storyboard* is the script of a commercial laid out in comic-strip form; *shooting* is advertising jargon for the filming or taping of a commercial). He or she selects a director and TV production company, and helps the casting director choose the performers.

During the shooting, the TV producer works with the TV production-company crew (set designer, director, editor, musicians, and sound people) to make sure things are done right. He or she also handles the detail work, dealing with contracts, unions, residuals, film studios, municipalities (to get permits for outdoor shooting), and—of course—the client. The TV producer has to be extremely well organized, because producing television involves a greater number of technical details than the printing of an ad or circular.

Most agency TV producers have backgrounds in graphic arts, music, photography, dramatics, film or videotape production, or broadcast television. A technical knowledge of film and videotape production is helpful. Salary range: $20,000 to $40,000 a year and up.

All of these jobs are exciting and rewarding. But if you want to make it to the top in advertising, your best bet is to aim for a spot as either a copywriter or an account executive. These positions have three advantages over the others.

First, they are the best-paying. Account executives in managerial positions and copywriters who become creative directors earn the top salaries in advertising—salaries in the hundreds of thousands of dollars.

Second, they require the least formal training or technical skill. An art director must study art; a TV producer needs technical knowledge of film production. But the only prerequisites for becoming an account executive or copywriter are the ability to think, sell, and communicate.

Third, if you plan to head an agency empire or build your own, you'll be in good company. Virtually every top agency in business today is headed by a former copywriter or account executive; media buyers, art directors, and market researchers rarely rise to the top.

With this in mind, let's take a more detailed look at these two glamour jobs of advertising—account executive and copywriter.

ACCOUNT MANAGEMENT: THE BUSINESS SIDE

The account-management department is responsible for the business side of the agency's activities.

People in account management serve as the liaison between the client and the service departments within the agency (media, market research, traffic, creative). The job of account management is to make sure the client's projects are planned and executed effectively, accurately, on budget, and on time.

Entry-level people in account management start as trainees. Trainees spend their days learning the business and handling a variety of low-level chores.

After the training period is completed, the trainee becomes an assistant account executive. In this position, he or she assists a full-fledged account executive in handling one or more of the agency's accounts. The assistant is there to provide the account executive with whatever support he or she needs—everything from setting up a conference room and running a slide projector to writing reports and doing product research.

The next step for the assistant is to become an account executive, or AE. The AE has total responsibility for handling a particular portion of the agency's business. A single AE may handle a small account, but teams of AEs manage the large accounts.

The account supervisor manages the team of AEs assigned to an account. Although the AEs can meet with the client and do fairly high-level work on their own, the account supervisor is ultimately responsible. Account supervisors are usually given the additional title of "vice president" to reflect their level of authority and responsibility.

In a large agency with many big accounts and an equal number of account supervisors, the account supervisors report to a management supervisor. And in the biggest agencies, the management supervisor might report to an executive management representative, who, in turn, reports directly to the president.

As you can see, large agencies have well-defined career paths for people in account management. But the number of levels of management and the job titles may differ from agency to agency, so ranks and titles are not absolute. From this point on, we will use the term *account executive* to refer to anyone in account management.

David Mosel, an executive recruiter and former account executive with Young & Rubicam and McCann-Erickson, talks about the AE's job:

"The account executive is the quarterback, the coordinator,

the communicator, the deadline-meeter. But he's not just a glorified messenger. He's the guy that knows the client's business, market by market. He's the businessman. The more he's able to solve the marketing problems, the more of a hero he's going to be.

"The AE is responsible for everything that goes on at the agency—*everything*. If the commercial doesn't get on the air, it's the AE's responsibility. The client doesn't want to talk to the producer or the writer or the media department. He wants to talk to *you*."

Mosel advises aspiring account executives to shoot for the big agencies handling packaged-goods accounts. "As young people entering advertising, you want to go into packaged goods if you can. You'll take something else to get the experience, but you'll move toward packaged goods.

"The biggest advertising budgets are for supermarket and drug products. And you get jobs where the volume is. With packaged goods, you're going to have more job opportunities.

"The big agencies—the top ten or twenty—are where the action is. Don't go to small agencies. That's not where the action is, that's not where the business is, and that's where the insecurity is highest. Small agencies don't have the sophisticated tools to handle big packaged-goods accounts."

An account executive working on a major national brand at a big agency probably has more responsibility than anyone else in advertising, with the possible exception of the head of the agency. With this responsibility comes high visibility and, with advancement, a salary that can reach into the six-figure range.

If you're already packing your bags for the next plane out to Madison Avenue, hold up a minute. First go through the following list and see if you've got what it takes to succeed as an AE:

1. **Education.** A bachelor's degree is required. And for working on packaged-goods accounts, most agencies look for an MBA as well. A good start is to take courses that will aid you in the ad business—debate, public speaking, theater, marketing, writing, accounting, broadcast production.

2. **Looks.** AEs are the agency's most visible people. So while

it's acceptable for a writer or artist to look like a reject from "Creature Feature," the account executive must be presentable.

You don't really have to be an Adonis or fashion model to be an account executive. But you probably won't succeed unless your appearance is generally pleasing and professional. "The pretty people make it in advertising," observes one agency insider. "If they've got brains, they *really* make it!"

3. **Personality.** Adjectives that describe the personality of the ideal account executive include: friendly, personable, tactful, aggressive, tenacious, determined, dogged, dedicated, resilient, reasonable, firm, extroverted, and steady.

Account executives spend most of their days working with others, so they have to get along with people. You need an even temperament and the patience to handle demands from all sides—agency management, the creative department, and the client. And, like all ad-agency employees, you must be able to work well under pressure.

4. **Skills.** Verbal and organizational skills are a must. You have to juggle a lot of details and make sure all the people involved understand what is being done and why.

Skill in sales is also vital. Account executives are responsible for soliciting new business as well as managing current accounts. At some agencies, one group of account executives handles new business while another works on existing business. At other agencies, account executives split their time between ongoing clients and new-business solicitations.

As you progress, knowledge of a client's business also becomes crucial. Rookie account executives can learn about the product on the job. But when an ad agency hires a senior account manager to work on the Chrysler account, they expect to be buying decades of automotive-account experience with their money.

5. **Training.** There are a number of ways to prepare yourself for a career as an account executive who works on big accounts at top agencies.

One way is to learn the advertiser's business from the inside. Get an entry-level position with a manufacturer of packaged goods. Spend a year or two working as a marketing representative, salesman, assistant product or brand manager, or market researcher. This experience will give you the business experience and product knowledge that agencies look for when hiring account executives.

Another route is to get a position in a training program at a big agency and work your way up. A number of the top agencies offer formal training programs in account management (for a listing of these programs, see pages 43-44).

If you can't get into the account-management training program, try for the media-training program or for an entry-level media job (such as media clerk). Agencies often promote media people to account-management positions.

Finally, if the competition for the top jobs is too stiff right now, settle for a small or medium-size agency. Stay there a year or two to get some experience; then, when you reapply to the big agency, you'll have an edge over applicants with no agency experience.

THE COPYWRITER: THE CREATIVE SIDE

The copywriter is an idea person. He or she dreams up the words, the slogans, the jingles, and sometimes the visual images that appear in the ads and commercials you read and see every day.

Copywriting is creative, but it's different than other forms of creative writing. Novels entertain; magazine articles give information; but the copywriter has a tougher job: He or she has to write words that *sell*.

Copywriters work side by side with art directors and creative directors in the *creative department*. While account management handles the business side, the creative department is responsible for the actual writing and design of ads and commercials.

Beginning writers start as trainees, then move up to the

position of junior copywriter. Junior copywriters get to write, but they handle the minor projects—product data sheets, broadsides, circulars, newspaper inserts.

Once they become full-fledged copywriters, they get to work on "major-league copy"—print advertising and television campaigns for the agency's big accounts. The next step up for a copywriter is to become a *copy supervisor*, which involves supervising the work of a team of writers. The copy supervisor is high enough up the organizational ladder to be eligible for a vice presidency.

A copy supervisor can go on to become an associate creative director and then a full-fledged creative director. As we mentioned, the creative director is responsible for all creative work in the agency and supervises writers, artists, illustrators, and photographers.

There may be many creative directors in the agency. They are supervised by a director of creative services. The director oversees major creative tasks (such as the design of a new campaign or theme) and sets the overall tone, style, and "philosophy" of the agency's creative work. The director of creative services reports directly to the agency president.

The higher up you go on this ladder, the more you'll supervise others and the less you'll write. So while the position of creative director tempts copywriters with a prestigious title, more authority, and a six-figure salary, many writers prefer to stay writers, because they would rather write than manage.

How do you gain skill in copywriting? First, you need the skills of the general writer: the ability to write clear, concise, interesting prose. The best way to gain these skills is simply to *write*—for your local newspaper, your college literary magazine, a trade journal, a church bulletin. Many copywriters started out as novelists, newspaper reporters, free-lance magazine writers, poets, proofreaders, or editors. Others worked as advertising managers, salespeople, or as writers for the advertising departments of manufacturers or department stores.

As you master the basics of writing, hone in specifically on copywriting. Keep files of articles on advertising and of ads, sales letters, and brochures that catch your eye. Study the files. What makes a given ad effective or ineffective? Pinpoint copywriting techniques that work and use them in your own writing.

Put together a notebook of your own copy samples. At first, these will be "speculative" ads: ads you've written on your own rather than for a real client. Once you get some experience, you can add clippings of your published ads to the book. The book is your *portfolio*— a collection of your copywriting samples that demonstrates your ability to prospective employers.

One quick way of building a portfolio is to create new ads for existing products. Paste published ads for these products on the lefthand pages of your book. Rewrite the published ads to make them better, and put your improved versions on the facing righthand pages. This before-and-after format can make a dramatic presentation of your ability to outdo the pros.

Every copywriter needs a portfolio. One that contains published ads is best, but many beginners have gotten their first job by showing a portfolio of speculative ads.

Although you should look neat, clean, and professional on your job interview, appearance on the job is not as important for the writer as it is for the account executive. In many creative departments, artists and writers wear casual clothes (jeans, sports shirts, tennis shoes) and save their single three-piece suit for the occasional client meeting. "If you're a writer or artist, you can be more crazy," complains one account executive. "They call it 'creative.' "

However, a business suit is still the appropriate attire for job interviews. Once you get the position, you'll quickly catch on to the agency's dress code.

A broad liberal-arts education is the best training for copywriters, because their job is to combine specific product knowledge with general knowledge of people, places, events, and the world at large to come up with advertisements that sell the product by making it relevant to the consumer's life. The liberal arts allow students to soak up knowledge in such varied and useful fields as creative writing, journalism, poetry, human relations, management, marketing, economics, psychology, and history—all recommended fare for aspiring copywriters.

Specific courses in copywriting can also be valuable, depending on the teacher. Look for courses where the teacher has had professional copywriting experience; you can only learn this skill from someone who knows the field. By doing all the homework assignments, you can build a portfolio of copy to present to prospective employers. Many students have gotten copywriting jobs after completing such courses and putting together sample books of their assignments.

Education doesn't end with college, however. The best copywriters continue to be students throughout their lives and are interested in practically everything. They read books, trade journals, magazines, newspapers; see plays and films; visit galleries, museums, historical sites; keep extensive clipping files of information on all sorts of subjects. They also read popular magazines and watch TV to see what other advertisers are doing and to keep up with the tastes of the general public.

For decades, copywriters have studied what works and what doesn't work in advertising, and many have written books describing their discoveries and techniques. Reading books on advertising and copywriting can give you in a few hours what it took these people decades to learn.

In particular, read any of the books by David Ogilvy, John Caples, Rosser Reeves, Claude Hopkins, or James Webb Young. Other books of interest may be found in the bibliography at the end of this chapter.

Copywriters also study *people*—how they behave; what they do; what they look like; what they eat, wear, and buy. As a copywriter, every person you meet is a potential source of information for your next campaign, and you're always listening to what people say, hoping to capture a comment that could turn into a great slogan or headline.

Many writers prefer to lead solitary lives, hunched over the typewriter banging out the Great American Novel. But the ad-agency copywriter is a team player, working closely with account executives, art directors, and creative directors. "Advertising isn't a business for loners, for prima donnas, and I wish that more people . . . would understand this," writes advertising consultant Whit Hobbs in *Adweek* (7 December 1981). "This is a very tough, complicated business, and again and again it has been proved that the more effectively people work together to create advertising, the more successful the advertising."

Although it's unusual for agencies to offer training programs for copywriters, many big agencies will hire novices and train them informally. If you can't get in as a copywriter, you can start as a secretary or administrative assistant. But be warned: That's a tough route to take, and the chances of your actually moving up to a copywriter's position are slim.

Most agencies want their secretaries to *remain* secretaries; only a few will give secretaries the opportunity to write copy part-time and then advance to a full-time copywriting job. The majority of agencies prefer to hire writers from outside the agency, and they rarely promote clerical staff.

WHERE THE BUCKS ARE

Copywriting and account management are lucrative professions.

Your starting salary may be low, but after a few years you'll be taking home respectable (if not astronomical) paychecks. And if you become a superstar, your salary could soar into the mid-six figures, exceeding the paychecks of many corporate presidents and CEOs.

According to *Adweek* magazine's "1984 Annual Salary Survey," the median 1983 salary for full-fledged account executives (not trainees, assistants, or supervisors) was $30,500; for copywriters, $28,300. In the top 10 percent, the average account executive earned $40,800, the average copywriter $51,200.

The survey also pinpointed some interesting trends:

- Account executives start at higher salaries than copywriters. But senior copywriters usually make more than account executives of equal experience.
- The bigger the agency or account is, the more the account executive, copywriter, or creative director makes. An account executive at a $150-million agency earns, on aver-

age, one-third more than his or her counterpart at a $5-million agency.

- Writers and AEs are paid the most in East and West Coast agencies, the least in the Midwest and South.
- The best-paid people in the advertising industry are not AEs or writers but *independent* (free-lance) *television directors*. A typical director's fee ranges from $7,500 to $13,000 for one day's shooting; top directors—such as Bob Giraldi and Joe Sedelmaier—earn more than a million dollars a year. These directors are hired by various agencies to direct commercials on a per-project basis.
- On the agency side, top creative directors can earn $300,000 to $400,000 a year and more. Top account-management salaries, while in the six figures, can't match this.
- Copywriting salaries are going up twice as fast as those for account executives. From 1981 to 1984, the compensation for copywriters increased 26 percent, as opposed to a mere 13 percent for AEs. (In 1981, *Advertising Age* reported that account executives were more in demand than writers. Nowadays the opposite is true.)

Dick Wasserman, a vice president at Needham, Harper & Steers, wrote up the results of his own salary survey in an article in *Advertising Age* (14 June 1984). To get his data, Wasserman went to Jerry Kindman, a New York CPA who, along with his two partners, handles the tax returns of some three thousand advertising people each year. Two-thirds of his clients are writers or artists, and one-third account executives.

Kindman compiled average salary figures for his account-management clients according to the number of years they'd spent in the business:

Experience	Annual salary
Beginners	$15,000–$18,000
1–2 years	$16,000–$20,000
3–4 years	$18,000–$25,000
5–7 years	$25,000–$32,000
7–10 years	$35,000–$45,000
10–15 years	$35,000–$80,000
15–25 years	$45,000–$150,000

He drew up the same chart for creative people as well:

Experience	Annual salary
Beginners	$11,000–$15,000
1–2 years	$15,000–$25,000
3–4 years	$18,000–$30,000
5–7 years	$25,000–$35,000
7–10 years	$35,000–$50,000
10–15 years	$40,000–$80,000
15–25 years	$50,000–$200,000

Wasserman drew a few interesting conclusions from Kindman's figures and from the results of other surveys he made:

- To move beyond the $40,000-a-year category, a copywriter must have success in writing commercials as well as print advertising. A *reel* (sample film reel or videotape) of five good commercials is a must for copywriters who want to move up in the world of big-agency advertising.
- Once they get beyond the beginner level, copywriters earn more than AEs.
- Although agencies don't come right out and say it, they do prefer to hire younger people. Kindman said he couldn't recall having a client over fifty. The agency business is oriented toward youth and is a difficult job market for older people looking to begin a new career.
- High salaries go to copywriters and creative directors who are willing to work in branch offices outside New York or on certain types of accounts that no one else wants to handle (such as cigarettes).

Whatever your choice—copywriter or account executive—the pay is good, the business exciting, the job challenging and rewarding. Best of all, it doesn't take highly specialized training, skill, or technical knowledge to break in. Now, let's take a look at how to launch your career in advertising.

GETTING STARTED

Although many advertising greats never got past high school, nowadays an undergraduate degree is needed to land most account-management or copywriting jobs. A recent survey of three hundred advertising professionals showed that three-quarters had a bachelor's degree or higher.

Most advertising executives recommend that aspiring writers and AEs, whatever their major, take a good mix of courses in English literature and composition, journalism, speech, business administration, math, social sciences, economics, psychology, accounting, marketing, and advertising. The best preparation is to blend this academic training with job experience in a career allied with or related to advertising—sales, media, print production, journalism, photography.

However, advertising is gaining popularity as a major course of study in its own right. In 1983, 15,892 students majored in advertising at eighty-six colleges and universities throughout the country. These programs graduated 4,942 students at the end of the 1982–83 academic year.

Michigan State University, with 1,208 students and twelve full-time professors, has the largest degree program in advertising. The course of study includes accounting, marketing, math, computer science, writing, psychology, sociology, media planning, consumer behavior, management, and research. In addition, the senior class is divided into "agencies" that compete for a real-life account and develop a campaign that the company will use (in 1984, the client was K-Mart).

Other schools with full-fledged advertising majors include Texas Tech University, the University of Alabama, Louisiana State University, and Boston University. A more complete listing of degree programs in advertising can be found at the end of this chapter.

Be aware that many advertising executives are skeptical of academia's ability to prepare students for life in the "real world" of advertising. So while a college education in advertising may have a lot to offer, it won't necessarily make you a more attractive candidate to potential employers.

In addition to these academic programs, several of the top

agencies have formal in-house training programs for account management, media, art, copywriting, and market research (also listed at the end of the chapter). Unfortunately, there are a limited number of openings in these programs; a survey of the largest twenty agencies revealed that twelve have formal training programs for which, all together, they hire only 145 new trainees each year.

When you've completed your basic training and are ready to offer yourself to the working world, you'll need to write a great résumé and a sharp cover letter. Remember, there are hundreds (maybe thousands) of people like you competing for the job you want. Sure, you're bright, well educated, and willing to work hard. But they are, too. And many are far more experienced. So you need a sharp, no-nonsense résumé and a hard-selling cover letter to set you apart from the crowd.

This isn't as awesome a task as it sounds. One personnel director reports that of the eight thousand résumés he receives each year, two-thirds contain typos, spelling mistakes, or grammatical errors. So if you proofread your résumé thoroughly and have a few other people take a look at it, you're already ahead of two-thirds of the pack!

Although having a letter-perfect résumé is important, it's not enough to land you a job interview. You also need a cover letter that is persuasive enough to convince the employer to see you.

In an article for *Free Enterprise* magazine (October 1975), free-lance copywriter Don Hauptman stresses the need to use "tailored letters"—individual letters tailored to the particular agency or job advertised. "The tailored letter focuses on the *specifics* of the position in question," says Hauptman. "It tells what the applicant can do for the employer."

Such a letter is far more effective than using a form letter or just popping your résumé in the mail with no cover letter. According to a study by the California Employment Development Department, 46 percent of tailored letters result in job interviews, as opposed to only 2 percent of résumés mailed without cover letters.

Hauptman observes that the biggest fault of most cover letters is their failure to address the needs and interests of the

employer, or the job description, qualifications, and responsibilities as stated in the help-wanted ad. He cites as an example
the experience of the head of a high-tech firm who advertised
for an administrative assistant in the local paper. Of two
hundred replies he received, only four letters even alluded to
the qualifications and duties outlined in the ad!

The cover letter—especially one sent to a busy creative
director or agency president—should *sell* you to the agency. Be
aggressive. You should know you're the best candidate for the
job; let the reader know it, too. You should end the letter by
promising to follow up with a phone call in a week or so to set
up an appointment. Take this situation, for example: The
advertising manager of an industrial firm wanted to write
copy for a big ad agency. But the ad agency's help-wanted ad
strictly stated, "We will only consider copywriters with *agency*
experience—no others need apply."

The ad manager had no agency experience and was infuri-
ated by this bit of snobbery. His powerful letter, reprinted
below, turned his lack of experience into an asset and resulted
in a job interview:

Dear Creative Director:

Your *Adweek* classified says you're looking for a copywriter
with agency experience.
   Why?
   I'm a writer on the client side. The product managers I
work for aren't interested in slick, pretty ads that win
creative awards. They demand (and I give them) copy and
concepts that generate leads, create awareness, and increase sales.
   Rather than build a portfolio of splashy four-color advertisements, I've built campaigns that achieve marketing
objectives within set budgets.
   Now, the average agency copywriter may write more ads
than I do. But my book will show you that I do first-rate
work. And if that's not enough, I challenge you to try me
out on a few assignments and see if I don't top every
agency-experienced writer that applies for this position.

Sincerely,

Joe Doakes

Of course, a compelling cover letter is no guarantee of an interview. Mail-order companies are happy to get one or two orders for every hundred direct-mail packages they send out; as a job seeker, you can expect similar results. You're doing great if you get a handful of "yes, come in and see us" calls in response to a mailing of several dozen letters.

Don't be discouraged by this low response rate; it only takes one good response to result in a job. Instead, be persistent. Keep writing letters, and you'll eventually get a response and some interviews.

When you go on interviews, your style in person should match that of your letters—professional and polite, but aggressive and ready to sell. Be punctual. Look like a businessperson: Wear a suit; be clean and neat; if you're a man, keep hair short. Do a little research about the agency—its size, major clients, and track record—before the interview.

Copywriters, of course, must bring their portfolios. Account executives can bring whatever they think will best show their qualifications—marketing plans they've written, a portfolio of campaigns they've supervised, market research studies they've conducted, even letters of praise from happy clients.

Don't be a wallflower. Ask the interviewer a lot of questions about his or her agency and the help they need in the department you'd want to work in. And tell the interviewer why you're the right person for the job.

Always send a thank-you note after every interview. So few people do this that it really sets you apart from the crowd and can turn a maybe into a yes.

If you don't get the job, try to analyze why. Listen to the creative director's critique of your portfolio or the account supervisor's analysis of your background and the experience you lack. If you hear the same comments from a number of different interviewers, a change might be in order. Perhaps you need to improve your copywriting samples, or get more experience, or take a couple of courses. Be realistic about whether you are qualified for the job you seek.

On the other hand, don't be disappointed when the first few interviews don't result in a job offer. We've talked to beginning agency people who said it took them a year or more to get their first job! Even an experienced writer or AE can spend two to six months on the street before finding an agency whose needs fit his or her experience.

So don't despair. Be patient, and if you were meant to work in advertising, you will get that job. However, many people find that the competitive, frantic pace is *not* for them, that they would really be happier in another type of business or writing job.

Recognize, too, that the advertising business is a business where contacts make a difference; it helps if you have a friend or relative in a position of authority at a major agency. If you're fortunate enough to have such a contact, take full advantage of it.

MOVING UP

Some industries frown upon job-hopping. But not so advertising. A lot of people in the business—account executives, creative directors, even headhunters and agency heads—actually *encourage* job-hopping in the early years of a career, because it gives you a broad range of experience and boosts your salary.

A 1974 study conducted by the 4 A's showed a 31-percent annual turnover rate in advertising. More recently, Judd Falk, an executive-search firm, estimated the 1982 turnover rate to be between 30 and 35 percent.

In their "1984 Adweek Salary Survey," *Adweek* even outlined a career path designed to make your job-hopping more productive and profitable.

First, they recommend you start in a big agency to get training and earn the most money you can at the entry-level and junior positions. After you've soaked up an education at the big agency's expense, move to a smaller agency. When you make this move, you'll get a more senior position, more money, and more managerial experience.

If the small agency doesn't grow, switch back to a big agency—this time at the level of account supervisor, creative director, or department head. Look for a big increase in salary when you do.

This sounds logical and may work for some people. In truth, however, there is no surefire formula for success. You have to follow your instincts and grab opportunities as they arise.

It *is* true that strategically shifting from big agency to small agency and back can hasten your progress up the managerial and salary ladders. Here are a few observations to help you shift at the right time and to the right place:

- Big agencies offer many paths for career advancement. But you can be quickly dead-ended at a small agency. "Getting a good position with a small agency is no big deal," said one former small-agency writer. "After all, if you take a job with a five-man agency, you're already in the number-five spot the day you start. And the owner isn't likely to ever let you get to number one."

- The biggest advantage of working for a small agency is that you'll get to handle a broader range of tasks. Small agencies can't afford to hire a specialist for every job, so their employees wear many different hats. A copywriter, for example, might also meet with the client, help plan the advertising schedule, supervise photographers and artists, and even get involved with media buying and printing. This education will be valuable to you later on—for instance, it will give you an understanding of how other departments work when you take a more specialized job at a big agency.

- Most small agencies concentrate on print advertising. And most creative directors look for a solid foundation in print before they'll train you in TV. So by working at a small agency, you can quickly build a portfolio of good-quality print ads. You'll also learn to write brochures, catalogs, and direct-mail pieces—skills that may help you get a job with a larger agency.

- For the most part, only the big agencies have the money, resources, and manpower to service major national accounts. You need to work on these accounts if you want to gain prestige and status in the advertising community.

- With some exceptions, only the major agencies do any substantial work in television. And you need TV experience to break out of the $40,000-a-year mold and earn the top salaries.

● The small-agency job market is less competitive. Most people would rather work at big agencies on big accounts; and smaller agencies often have trouble attracting and holding onto talented writers, artists, account executives, and media people. So if the big-agency game is unpalatable, you can still find happiness—albeit with less money and status—at one of the thousands of fine small agencies operating throughout the United States. The choice is up to you.

Required Reading for Aspiring Ad Executives

Books
Here are some books you can read to dig deeper into the advertising business. The list includes a mix of textbooks, how-to books, autobiographies, memoirs, and history books. Enjoy!

Arlen, Michael J. *Thirty Seconds.* New York: Farrar, Straus & Giroux, 1980. Chronicles the making of one of the thirty-second commercials in AT&T's "Reach out and touch someone" campaign. An entertaining inside look at the world of big-league advertising.

Bly, Robert W. *The Copywriter's Handbook: A Step-by-Step Guide to Writing Copy That Sells.* New York: Dodd, Mead, 1985. A guide to writing effective ad copy, plus advice on career opportunities in copywriting.

Caples, John. *How to Make Your Advertising Make Money.* Englewood Cliffs, N.J.: Prentice-Hall, 1983. Caples, master of the hard sell, reveals secrets and techniques for creating advertising campaigns that get results.

Cummings, Barton A. *The Benevolent Dictators: Interviews with Eighteen Ad Agency Greats.* Chicago: Crain Books, 1984. Insights into the lives of eighteen industry leaders and how they ran their great agencies.

Dunn, S. W. and A. M. Barban. *Advertising: Its Role in Modern Marketing.* Hinsdale, Ill.: The Dryden Press, 1978. A readable textbook that presents a comprehensive overview of the advertising business.

Eicoff, Alvin. *Or Your Money Back.* New York: Crown, 1982. Eicoff, one of the masters of the late-night mail-order TV commercial, presents his unorthodox views on how to create successful TV advertising.

Fox, Stephen. *The Mirror Makers: A History of American Advertising and Its Creators.* New York: William Morrow, 1984. The best history of advertising ever written. Absolutely fascinating.

Kornfeld, Lewis. *To Catch a Mouse, Make a Noise Like a Cheese.* Englewood Cliffs, N.J.: Prentice-Hall, 1983. A book on advertising by a successful advertiser who *hates* advertising agencies. Kornfeld gives the reader a shocking look at what some agencies are doing *wrong.*

Nash, Edward L. *Direct Marketing: Strategy, Planning, Execution.* New York: McGraw-Hill, 1982. One of the most recently published books on direct marketing, a fast-growing segment of the advertising industry.

Ogilvy, David. *Confessions of an Advertising Man.* New York: Atheneum, 1963. Opinions and tips on how to be a great advertising professional, by one of the giants of the industry. Lively and opinionated.

Ogilvy, David. *Ogilvy on Advertising.* New York, Crown, 1983. More Ogilvy advice on how to be a great advertising professional. Covers some of the same ground as *Confessions* but also presents much new material. Well worth reading.

White, Hooper. *How to Produce an Effective TV Commercial.* Chicago: Crain Books, 1981. Explains all you need to know about producing TV commercials. A great introduction to novices with little or no broadcast experience.

Young, James Webb. *A Technique for Producing Ideas.* Chicago: Crain Books, 1940. 'A successful ad man tells how he comes up with advertising ideas. A slim but inspirational volume.

Directories

These directories list ad agencies, advertisers, TV production houses, art studios, and other advertising-related companies. They contain all the names and addresses you need to begin your job search. So get started!

Adweek/Art Directors' Index, 820 Second Ave., New York, NY 10017; (212) 661-8080. A directory listing illustrators, designers, filmmakers, photographers, artists, printers, copywriters, and audiovisual producers who serve the advertising industry.

The Creative Black Book, Friendly Publications, 401 Park Ave. So., New York, NY 10016; (212) 228-9750. A directory of typographers, audiovisual producers, illustrators, artists, model agencies, photographers, printers, TV producers and editors, ad agencies, and other organizations serving the advertising industry.

The Standard Directory of Advertisers, National Register Publishing Company, 3004 Glenview Rd., Wilmette, IL 60091; (312) 256-6067. Lists 17,000 companies that spend $30,000 a year or more on advertising. Each listing includes the company name and address, key personnel, products manufactured, and the size of the ad budget.

The Standard Directory of Advertising Agencies, National Register Publishing Company, 3004 Glenview Rd., Wilmette, IL 60091; (312) 256-6067. Lists 4,400 advertising agencies alphabetically. Indexed by state. Each listing includes the agency's name and address, number of employees, year founded, approximate annual billings (with a breakdown by media), key personnel, and major accounts.

Standard Rate and Data Service, 5201 Old Orchard Road, Skokie, IL 60077; (312) 470-3100. Media directories listing all consumer magazines, trade journals, and newspapers that run advertisements.

Magazines

If you're serious about working in a business, you *must* keep up with it. And that means reading its trade journals. Here are the important ones in the advertising industry:

Ad Day/U.S.A., 400 E. 54th St., New York, NY 10022; (212) 421-3713. A newsletter reporting the latest account changes, new campaigns, promotions, new hires, and other events on Madison Avenue. Published several times a week.

Ad Forum, 18 E. 53rd St., New York, NY 10022; (212) 751-2670. A monthly magazine for marketing managers who work for large consumer corporations. Focuses on the creation and management of print and broadcast advertising campaigns aimed at mass audiences.

ADS, P.O. Box 195, Chappaqua, NY 10514. Focusing on the creative aspects of advertising, each issue of ADS presents dozens of clearly reproduced print ads and TV storyboards, along with commentary by the people who produced them. Published six times a year.

Advertising Age, 740 N. Rush St., Chicago, IL 60611; (312) 649-5000. The leading trade journal in the advertising industry. Help-wanted ads for various advertising positions appear in the back of the magazine. Published twice a week.

Adweek, 820 Second Ave., New York, NY 10017; (212) 661-8080.

This weekly trade journal is *Advertising Age*'s major competitor. *Adweek* contains a help-wanted section as well as a special section where job-seekers can advertise their services to potential employers—free!

Business Marketing, 220 E. 42nd St., New York, NY 10017; (212) 210-0100. A magazine devoted to business, industrial, and high-tech advertising. Monthly.

Direct Marketing, 224 Seventh St., Garden City, NY 11530; (516) 746-6700. Covers direct mail, mail order, and telemarketing. Monthly.

Madison Avenue, 369 Lexington Ave., New York, NY 10017; (212) 972-0600. A monthly magazine on the ad-agency business and the goings-on of Madison Avenue.

Magazine Age, 225 Park Ave., New York, NY 10017; (212) 986-7366. This monthly magazine covers all aspects of magazine publishing, including advertising. Useful for creatives and account executives who handle print advertising.

Join the Club: A Guide to Professional Societies and Trade Associations

"It's not what you know but *who* you know" goes the old saying. And in advertising, making contacts is important—both for getting things done on the job and for advancing your career.

One quick and easy way to develop a rolodex full of contacts is to join advertising clubs, societies, and associations. At the meetings, you'll meet people with similar interests as well as potential employers. The following list will get you started; just write or call for information on how to join.

Advertising Club of New York, 45 East 45th St., New York, NY 10017; (212) 697-0877.

Advertising Council, 825 Third Ave., New York, NY 10022; (212) 758-0400.

Advertising Research Foundation, 3 East 54th St., New York, NY 10022; (212) 751-5656.

Advertising Women of New York, 153 E. 57th St., New York, NY 10022; (212) 593-1950.

American Advertising Federation, 1225 Connecticut Ave. NW, Washington, D.C. 20036; (202) 659-1800.

American Association of Advertising Agencies, 666 Third Ave., New York, NY 10017; (212) 682-2500.

American Business Press, 205 E. 42nd St., New York, NY 10017; (212) 661-6360.

American Marketing Association, 250 South Wacker Dr., Chicago, IL 60606; (312) 648-0536.

The Art Directors Club, 488 Madison Ave., New York, NY 10022; (212) 838-8140.

Association of National Advertisers, 155 E. 42nd St., New York, NY 10017; (212) 697-5950.

Direct Mail/Marketing Association, 6 E. 43rd St., New York, NY 10017; (212) 689-4977.

The Direct Marketing Club of New York, 224 Seventh St., Garden City, NY 10053; (516) 746-6700.

Institute of Outdoor Advertising, 485 Lexington Ave., New York, NY 10017; (212) 986-5920.

International Advertising Association, 475 Fifth Ave., Suite 616, New York, NY 10017; (212) 684-1583.

Magazine Publishers Association, Bureau of Advertising, 575 Lexington Ave., New York, NY 10022; (212) 752-0055.

National Association of Advertising Publishers, 313 Price Pl., Madison WI 53705; (608) 233-5306.

National Retail Merchants Association, 100 West 31st St., New York, NY 10001; (212) 244-8780.

Newspaper Advertising Bureau, 1 Embarcadero Center, San Francisco, CA 94111; (415) 981-8118.

The One Club for Art and Copy, 251 E. 50th St., New York, NY 10022; (212) 935-0121.

Pharmaceutical Advertising Council, 342 Madison Ave., Suite 1915, New York, NY 10173; (212) 370-1701.

Point-of-Purchase Advertising Institute, Inc., 60 E. 42nd St., New York, NY 10165; (212) 682-7041.

Radio Advertising Bureau, 1900 Ave. of the Stars, Los Angeles, CA 90067; (213) 553-9479.

Specialty Advertising Association International, 1404 Walnut Hill La., Irving, TX 75062; (214) 258-0404.

Television Bureau of Advertising, 6380 Wilshire Blvd., Los Angeles, CA 90048; (213) 653-8890.

The Transit Advertising Association, 60 E. 42nd St., New York, NY 10165; (212) 599-2352.

Type Directors Club, 545 W. 45th St., New York, NY 10036; (212) 245-6300.

Women's Direct Response Group, P.O. Box 1561, FDR Station, New York, NY 10015.

A Glossary of Advertising Terms and Abbreviations

AD. Art director.

AE. Account executive.

BBDO. Batten, Barton, Durstine & Osborn.

Campaign. An integrated advertising program revolving around a single product and selling idea.

CD. Creative director.

Client. A company or other organization that buys the services of an advertising agency.

Concept. The central theme or idea of an ad, commercial, or campaign.

Copy/contact. A copywriter who deals with the client directly instead of through an account executive.

CPM. Cost per thousand—the amount of money it costs to reach a thousand people with an ad or commercial.

Creative. Anything related to the conception, writing, and designing of an ad.

DDB. Doyle Dane Bernbach.

Demographic. A population characteristic such as age, religion, income, education, sex, family size, or race.

Direct marketing. Type of marketing in which products are sold directly, by mail and phone, rather than through a "middle man" (distributor, sales agent, or store).

Frequency. The number of times a person is exposed to your advertising message.

JWT. J. Walter Thompson.

Layout. The design and positioning of the elements of a print advertisement (headline, body copy, illustrations, photos, logo).

Media. Refers to magazines, newspapers, radio stations, TV stations, billboards, and other communications vehicles that sell space or time to advertisers.

Psychographic. Defines the audience for an ad or commercial on the basis of psychological factors such as life-style, interests, beliefs, attitudes, or politics.

Sales promotion. An activity designed to create a temporary increase in sales rather than build a long-term image. Popular sales promotions include coupons, contests, sweepstakes, and discounts.

Shoot. To film or videotape a television commercial.

Space. Space in newspapers, magazines, and outdoor media in which advertisements appear.

Storyboard. A sequence of rough drawings that approximate the action in a commercial, with the spoken message written below each scene. Storyboards make it easier to grasp the message of a proposed commercial script at a glance.

Y&R. Young & Rubicam.

Executive Search Firms That Place Advertising Executives

Should you send your résumé to headhunters? Our answer is "Why not?" For twenty-two cents' postage, sending your résumé to an executive-search consultant gives you another shot at the advertising job of your dreams.

The good thing about search firms is that you don't pay for their services; their fee comes from the employer, not the candidate. So having a headhunter keep an eye out for a job for you won't cost you a cent. On the other hand, the recruiter is working for the ad agency— not for you. And naturally he has his client's best interests in mind. Job-seekers frequently complain of being pressured by headhunters into going on interviews and taking jobs they don't really want. Be wary of leaning on the recruiter for too much career guidance and advice. Remember, the recruiter is not a career counselor but a "headhunter." And the head he's being paid to hunt for is *yours.*

Finally, going to headhunters is merely a peripheral part of your job search—something extra to supplement letter-writing, phone-calling, interviewing, conference-attending, and other aggressive job-hunting tactics. The simple fact is that headhunters receive thousands of résumés, and unless your qualifications are one-in-a-thousand, it's unlikely that you will get special attention.

With these words of warning, here are the names, addresses, and phone numbers of executive recruiters that specialize in placing advertising and marketing professionals:

Able Personnel Agency, Inc., 475 Fifth Ave., New York, NY 10017; (212) 689-5500.

Norma Adler, Inc., 59 E. 54th St., New York, NY 10022; (212) 355-1020.

Advertising Careers Agency, 681 Market, San Francisco, CA 94105; (415) 957-9525.

The Angus Group, Inc., 2337 Victory Pkwy., Cincinnati, OH 45206; (513) 961-5575.

James Blake & Co., 1000 Woodbridge Center Dr., Woodbridge, NJ 07095; (201) 634-8400.

Marc-Paul Bloome, Ltd., 250 W. 57th St., New York, NY 10019; (212) 245-2828.

William Bolton Associates, 1700 Walnut St., Philadelphia, PA 19103; (215) 546-1330.

R. Parker Brenner, Inc., 65 E. 55th St., New York, NY 10022; (212) 935-5540.

K. Robert Brian, Inc., 2000 Market St., Philadelphia, PA 19103; (215) 561-6550.

Butterfield's, Suite 269, Plankinton Building, 161 W. Wisconsin Ave., Milwaukee, WI 53203; (414) 278-7800.

Cadillac Associates, 32 W. Randolph St., Chicago, IL 60601; (312) 346-9400.

Canter, Achenbaum Associates, 950 Third Ave., New York, NY 10022; (212) 751-9630.

The Cantor Concern, 39 W. 55th St., New York, NY 10020; (212) 481-0000.

Career Builders, Inc., 400 Madison Ave., New York, NY 10017; (212) 758-4070.

P.R. Carlier, Inc., 501 Fifth Ave., New York, NY 10017; (212) 599-0960.

Toby Clark, 655 Madison Ave., New York, NY 10021; (212) 752-5670.

Corporate Resource Group, Inc., 60 Washington St., Hartford, CT 06106; (203) 547-0900.

Crandall Associates, 501 Fifth Ave., New York, NY 10017; (212) 687-2550.

DeLalla-Fried, 950 Third Ave., New York, NY 10022; (212) 750-8860.

Dromeshauser & Graham Associates, 886 Washington St., Dedham, MA 02026.

Dunhill of Fairfield, Inc., 914 White Plains Rd., Suite 1, Trumbull, CT 06611; (203) 268-9240.

Fenner Executive Search, Box No. 9822, Advertising Age, 740 Rush St., Chicago, IL 60611.

Fenvessy & Schwab, Inc., 645 Madison Ave., New York, NY 10022; (212) 758-6800.

Jerry Fields, Inc., 555 Madison Ave., New York, NY; (212) 753-4123.

F-O-R-T-U-N-E Personnel Agency, Inc., 505 Fifth Ave., New York, NY 10017; (212) 557-1000.

Forum Personnel, Inc., 342 Madison Ave., New York, NY 10017; (212) 687-4050.

Samantha Friend Associates, Inc., 20 West Ridgewood Ave., Ridgewood, NJ 07540; (201) 445-8171.

Gardner Personnel Associates, 300 Madison Ave., New York, NY 10017; (212) 687-6616.

Karen Gillick & Associates, 221 N. LaSalle, Suite 3306, Chicago, IL 60601; (312) 236-4666.

Allan B. Hechtman, Inc., 3300 University Dr., Coral Springs, FL 33065; (305) 753-8874.

Howard-Sloan Associates, Inc., 545 Fifth Ave., New York, NY 10017; (212) 661-5250.

Judd-Falk, 124 E. 37th St., New York, NY 10016; (212) 686-1500.

Michael Latas & Associates, Box 1317, Vail, CO 81657; (303) 949-4114.

Lovewell & Associates, Inc., 100 Colony Sq., Atlanta, GA 30361; (404) 892-8930.

The McNally Group, Hamilton Lakes, 500 Park Blvd., Itasca, IL 60143; (312) 843-8700.

New England Recruiters, 900 Chapel St., New Haven, CT 06510; (203) 624-0161.

D. H. Noble & Associates, Inc., 139 E. 57th St., New York, NY 10022; (212) 355-7180.

V. A. Parr Associates, 171 Madison Ave., New York, NY 10016; (212) 889-4810.

Plaza, Inc., 55 E. Monroe St., Suite 4030, Chicago, IL 60603; (312) 263-0944.

The Pamela Reeve Agency, 409 N. Camden Dr., Beverly Hills, CA 90210; (213) 273-4950.

Sally Reich Associates, 50 Sutton Pl. So., New York, NY 10022; (212) 308-3276.

Rex Associates, 157 E. 57th St., New York, NY 10022; (212) 935-0100.

Ridenour & Associates, 230 N. Michigan Ave., Chicago, IL 60601; (312) 444-2260.

Rogers & Sands, 100 Federal St., Boston, MA 02110; (617) 426-4180.

Roth Young, 43 W. 42nd St., New York, NY 10036; (212) 869-0300.

R. V. M. Associates, Inc., 701 Westchester Ave., Suite 308 West, White Plains, NY 10604; (914) 328-7500.

Saxon Personnel, 17 E. 45th St., New York, NY 10017; (212) 557-9140.

Smith's 5th Avenue Agency, 17 E. 45th St., New York, NY 10017; (212) 682-5300.

Smith's Personnel, 1500 Broadway, New York, NY 10036; (212) 354-0100.

Special Projects Consultants, Ltd., 575 Madison Ave., Suite 1006, New York, NY 10022; (212) 225-7747.

Sussman & Morris Associates, 509 Madison Ave., New York, NY 10022; (212) 758-3411.

T. M. A., Inc., 200 W. Monroe St., Suite 505, Chicago, IL 60606; (312) 332-0444.

Victor, Paul and Associates, Inc., One Illinois Center, Suite 2824, 111 E. Wacker Dr., Chicago, IL 60601; (312) 565-1950.

Judy Wald Agency, Inc., 110 E. 59th St., New York, NY 10022; (212) 421-6750.

Walker Executive Recruitment, 350 Tyrol W., Gamble Center, Minneapolis, MN 55416; (612) 546-3700.

How to Become an Educated Ad Man (or Woman)

In the sixties, thousands of idealistic college students enrolled in journalism programs with hopes of becoming crusading reporters, rabble-rousing columnists, or muck-raking investigators. In the seventies, journalism departments began calling themselves "communications" departments. They attracted students exploring career options in a number of fields other than newspaper reporting—speech, magazine writing, public relations, graphic arts, radio broadcasting.

Now, in the 1980s, students choose their majors as much with an eye toward a job as with their general education in mind. And advertising—a glamorous, high-paying field—has now become a popular and respectable college major.

In 1983, 15,892 students were enrolled in advertising programs at eighty-six colleges and universities. A complete listing of these eighty-six degree programs can be found in the annual directory *Where Shall I Go to College to Study Advertising?,* published by Texas Tech University (phone 806-742-3385). The top ten undergraduate advertising schools (ranked by number of students enrolled) are listed below:

Michigan State University, East Lansing, MI 48824; (517) 355-8332.
Texas Tech University, Lubbock, TX 79409; (806) 742-3661.
University of Alabama, Birmingham, AL 35294; (205) 934-5268.
Louisiana State University, Shreveport, LA 71115; (318) 797-7121.

Boston University, Boston, MA 02115; (617) 353-3191.
University of Florida, Gainesville, FL 32611; (904) 392-1365.
University of Minnesota, Duluth, MN 55812; (218) 726-7171.
Northern Illinois University, DeKalb, IL 60115; (815) 753-0446.
California State University, Fullerton, CA 92634; (714) 773-2300.
University of Tennessee, Chattanooga, TN 37402; (615) 755-4157.

In case it's been a few years since you took a final or attended a
fraternity bash, here are the top *graduate* schools offering advanced
degrees in the advertising arts:

Roosevelt University, Chicago, IL 60605; (312) 341-3515.
City University of New York, New York, NY 10031; (212) 690-6977.
Northwestern University, Evanston, IL 60201; (312) 492-7271.
University of Illinois, Chicago, IL 60680; (312) 996-4388.
University of Texas at Austin, Austin, TX 78712; (512) 471-1711.

Source: Jan Foster-Penn, "Advertising 101: Learning the ABCs in College," *Adweek,* 13
February 1984, p. 36.

Ad Agencies: The Big Ten

Your best shot at working on a glamorous national advertising account
is to get a job with a big agency. Here are the ten biggest ad agencies
in the United States, ranked according to their worldwide billings:

1. Young & Rubicam, 285 Madison Ave., New York, NY 10017; (212)
210-3000.
1983 billings: $2.76 billion
Number of employees: 7,000
Key personnel: Edward N. Ney, chairman; Alexander Kroll, president;
Theresa MacDonald, administrative manager
Key accounts: Colgate-Palmolive, Dr. Pepper, Kodak, Frito-Lay, Max-
well House, Gillette, Kentucky Fried Chicken, Peter Paul, Lipton
Soup

2. Ted Bates Worldwide, 1515 Broadway, New York, NY 10036; (212)
869-3131.
1983 billings: $2.59 billion
Number of employees: not available
Key personnel: Anne Melanson, senior vice president, personnel;
Donald M. Zuckert, president

Key accounts: HBO, M&M's, Kal Kan, Panasonic, Peace Corps, Prudential, RCA, Schweppes, U.S. Navy

3. J. Walter Thompson Co., 466 Lexington Ave., New York, NY 10017; (212) 210-7000.
1983 billings: $2.52 billion
Number of employees: not available
Key personnel: Burt Manning, vice chairman, creative resources
Key accounts: Nabisco, Burger King, French's Mustard, Goodyear Tire, Close-Up toothpaste, Nestlé, Pepsi, Reynolds Wrap, Scott Paper, Toys "R" Us

4. Ogilvy & Mather, 2 E. 48th St., New York, NY 10017; (212) 907-3400.
1983 billings: $2.36 billion
Number of employees: 925 (home office only)
Key personnel: Kenneth Roman, president; Norman Berry, executive vice president, creative head; Frances Devereux, senior vice president, personnel director
Key accounts: AT&T, American Express, Avon, Campbell Soup, Q-Tips, Duracell, Hershey Foods, International Paper, Aim toothpaste, Pepperidge Farms, Polaroid

5. McCann-Erickson, 485 Lexington Ave., New York, NY 10017; (212) 697-6000.
1983 billings: $1.99 billion
Number of employees: 6,188
Key personnel: John F. Bergin, president; Ira B. Madris, executive vice president, creative director; Donald H. Noble, senior vice president, director of personnel; Francis J. Bortel, executive vice president, account strategy
Key accounts: AT&T, Beatrice Foods, Johnson & Johnson, Nabisco, Nestlé, Pabst, Sony, Texas Instruments

6. BBDO International, 383 Madison Ave., New York, NY 10017; (212) 355-5800.
1983 billings: $1.95 billion
Number of employees: 3,908
Key personnel: Bruce Crawford, president; Philip B. Dusenberry, executive creative director; Bruce Eswein II, manager, executive recruitment and development
Key accounts: Black & Decker, Dean Witter, Dow Jones, Du Pont, Firestone, General Electric, Pillsbury, Quaker Oats, Stroh Brewery, Time Inc., Tupperware

7. Saatchi & Saatchi Compton, 625 Madison Ave., New York, NY; (212) 754-1100.

1983 billings: $1.71 billion

Number of employees: not available

Key personnel: O. Milton Gossett, chief executive officer; James R. Adler, president

Key accounts: not available

8. Leo Burnett Co., Prudential Plaza, Chicago, IL 60601; (312) 565-5959.

1983 billings: $1.49 billion

Number of employees: 1,525

Key personnel: John J. Kinsella, president; Norman L. Muse, vice chairman, chief creative officer; Thomas D. Heath, vice chairman, client and marketing services

Key accounts: Allstate Insurance, General Motors, Heinz, Kellogg, Keebler, Maytag, McDonald's, Miller Brewing, Philip Morris, RCA, Star-Kist, United Airlines

9. Foote, Cone & Belding, 401 N. Michigan Ave., Chicago, IL 60611; (312) 467-9200.

1983 billings: $1.41 billion

Number of employees: 3,900

Key personnel: Norman W. Brown, president; Robert Vogel, vice president, director of human resources; Mike Rogers, executive creative director

Key accounts: Coors, Amana, Sara Lee, Kraft, Pearle Vision, Pizza Hut, Sears, Sunkist Soft Drinks, Clorox, Levi Strauss, Mazda, Citibank

10. SSC&B: Lintas Worldwide, One Dag Hammarskjold Plaza, New York, NY 10017; (212) 605-8000.

1983 billings: $1.32 billion

Number of employees: 3,603

Key personnel: Malcolm D. MacDougall, president; William S. Timm, vice president, director of personnel

Key accounts: Pall Mall, Carnation, Citicorp, Coca-Cola, Diners Club, Good Humor, Dixie Cups, Lego Systems, Lipton, Mennen, Noxzema, Sterling Drug, Heineken Beer, Amstel Light beer

Note: These agencies are ranked according to their 1983 worldwide billings as reported in *Advertising Age* (28 March 1984).

Training Programs in Advertising

Traditionally, advertising is something you learn on the job, not in the classroom. But few agencies have special training programs; at most agencies, training consists of a creative director handing you an assignment and seeing if you "sink or swim" (and that can often be an effective method).

The agencies listed here all offer more formal training programs for entry-level employees. Getting into one of these programs is a great way to learn advertising and get paid for it at the same time. But there are a limited number of openings available (less than three hundred new trainees are accepted into these programs each year). Programs are listed according to speciality—account management, creative, and media.

Account Management Training

N. W. Ayer, 1345 Sixth Ave., New York, NY 10105; (212) 708-5000. Contact: Edward J. Rogers, Personnel Director.

BBDO, 383 Madison Ave., New York, NY 10017; (212) 355-5800. Contact: Bruce Eswein, Manager of Recruitment and Development.

Ted Bates Advertising, 1515 Broadway, New York, NY 10036; (212) 869-3131. Contact: Joyce Bloom, Personnel Manager.

Benton & Bowles, 909 Third Ave., New York, NY 10022; (212) 758-6200. Contact: Ann Prescott, Personnel Manager, Creative Area.

Campbell-Ewald, 30400 Van Dyke, Warren, MI 48093; (313) 574-3400. Contact: Robert D. Ehlers, Vice President of Personnel.

Dancer Fitzgerald Sample, 405 Lexington Ave., New York, NY 10174; (212) 661-0800. Contact: Celine Schneider, Personnel Director. (*Note:* Dancer has an extensive management training program that includes account management and media. Trainees are chosen from current Dancer employees.)

Doyle Dane Bernbach, 437 Madison Ave., New York, NY 10022; (212) 415-2000. Contact: Marian Faytell, Assistant Director of Personnel.

Foote, Cone & Belding, 401 N. Michigan Ave., Chicago, IL 60611; (312) 467-9200. Contact: Dan Zigulich, Account Executive.

McCann-Erickson, 485 Lexington Ave., New York, NY 10017; (212) 697-6000. Contact: Donald Noble, Director of Personnel.

Needham, Harper & Steers/Worldwide, 303 E. Wacker Dr., Chicago, IL 60601; (312) 861-0200. Contact: Richard H. Needham, Director of Human Resources.

SSC&B, One Dag Hammarskjold Plaza, New York, NY 10017; (212) 605-8000. Contact: Margon J. McKeown, Personnel Manager.
J. Walter Thompson, 466 Lexington Ave., New York, NY 10017; (212) 210-7000. Contact: Susan Mirsky.
Young & Rubicam, 285 Madison Ave., New York, NY 10017; (212) 210-3000. Contact: Gary Villani, Manager of Employment.

Creative Training

D'Arcy MacManus & Masius, Gateway Tower, 1 Memorial Dr., St. Louis, MO 63102; (314) 342-8600. Contact: Kenneth W. Mihill, President. (*Note:* D'Arcy offers an internship for art directors that occasionally results in job offers.)
J. Walter Thompson, 466 Lexington Ave., New York, NY 10017; (212) 210-7000. Contact: Garland Goode.
Young & Rubicam, 285 Madison Ave., New York, NY 10017; (212) 210-3000. Contact: Luisa Robinson, Director of Creative Recruitment.

Media-Department Training

N. W. Ayer. Contact: Edward J. Rogers, Personnel Director.
BBDO. Contact: Mike Drake, Director of Planning.
Ted Bates Advertising. Contact: Nora Connors, Employment Representative.
Benton & Bowles. Contact: Ann Prescott, Personnel Manager.
Campbell-Ewald. Contact: Robert D. Ehlers, V.P. Personnel.
D'Arcy MacManus Masius. Contact: Jerome B. Sexton, Personnel Representative.
Foote, Cone & Belding. Contact: Dan Zigulich, Account Executive.
McCann-Erickson. Contact: Donald Noble, Director of Personnel.
Needham, Harper & Steers. Contact: Richard H. Needham, Director of Human Resources.
SSC&B. Contact: Patti Ransom, Personnel Representative.
J. Walter Thompson. Contact: Susan Mirsky.
Wells, Rich, Greene, 767 Fifth Ave., New York, NY 10153; (212) 758-4300. Contact: Michael Haggerty, Media Director.
Young & Rubicam. Contact: Barbara Ames, Senior V.P. Communication Services.

Source: John Sweeney, "Surveying entry-level training programs at agencies," *Advertising Age,* 17 May 1984, p. M-12.

Book Publishing

Is book publishing glamorous?

Many people think of publishing as the brave handmaiden to great books, an industry in which editors goad talented but wayward authors to fashion enduring art. And book publishing does have its moments—the feel of a new hardcover book, the thrill of seeing your book in a bookstore, the editorial satisfaction of unearthing a worthy manuscript, the convivial luncheons, the pungent gossip.

But don't judge a book by its cover. In a *U.S. News and World Reports* interview published shortly before his death, publisher Alfred A. Knopf said that "taste in publishing, as in all things, has declined, and that has affected the quality of what is printed. Just look at the fiction and nonfiction bestseller lists. They are full of diets, health, exercise." Knopf went on to say that most editors no longer work closely with authors, because there are just too many other things to do. "By the time they get around to publishing one book, they are already working on a new book they have just bought."

There are many other criticisms that one can level at book publishing—that the pay is paltry, that too many books are being published, that too few have any real merit, that the conglomerates have made publishing just another business—but somehow, each generation, legions of book lovers compete to become editors.

From cave walls to computer terminals, writing has been a tool for recording human knowledge, history, and our common dreams. And no matter how far the computer takes us, there will probably always be people for whom a book is something wonderful and irreplaceable.

Although our discussion of book publishing will focus on editorial work—especially the editing of adult trade* books— we acknowledge that there can be a great deal of glamour in publicity and advertising positions as well. By breaking into advertising and publicity in this field, you'll be working with books and authors, aiming toward more responsibility and good pay, and using many of the same types of interpersonal skills needed for success in editing.

Of the more than seventy thousand people in book publishing, only about 15 percent do editorial work; 25 percent work in marketing. (The others do everything else, including administration, sales, and distribution.) Here's a brief summary of some of the key positions:

- **Publicity Director** (salary range: $30,000–$50,000). A publicity director is responsible for publicizing all books on a publisher's seasonal list. According to Cynthia Kirk, director of publicity and promotion at Donald I. Fine, Inc., to do the job well, you need "a high level of energy and curiosity. You have to be interested in books and be familiar with media. You have to have the flexibility to say to yourself, 'If approach A doesn't work, I'll try approach B.'" The glamorous part of the job is working with authors, some of whom are well known. Lining up an author for "The CBS Morning News" or the "Tonight" show is "a high." Publicity directors arrange book tours, supervise the writing of promotional material, and coordinate the publisher's overall efforts at promoting their books and authors.

- **Publicist** (salary range: $14,000–$30,000). A publicist does many of the things that a publicity director does, but he or she usually works with less famous authors. Publicists usually write their own press releases and are responsible for promoting a certain number of the publisher's books. These people are instrumental in helping authors get TV and radio appearances, and, in some cases, help them plan

---

*A book that is published for the general public and sold at bookstores.

tours of different cities to promote their books. They may also help plan publication parties and events aimed at spotlighting the news angles of certain books. A *publicity assistant*, a lower-level position usually paying $10,000–$15,000, helps the publicist follow through on promotional ideas, which can involve everything from mailing review copies (books sent to the media) to distributing press releases. Generally, strong writing ability, good interpersonal skills, and a head for details are the publicist's key tools in his or her job.

- **Advertising Director** (salary range: $20,000–$50,000). This person helps create and place advertisements for the publisher's books. He or she must be familiar with the media in order to find the best "mix" of advertising—the right magazines, the right newspapers, the best TV programs—in which to advertise a particular book. Working with sales, marketing, and editorial staffs, the advertising director tries to divide attention among all the publisher's books. Realistically, though, only a handful of books get the advertising director's full attention. Before becoming an advertising director, you may start as a copywriter.

- **Copywriter** (salary range: $11,000–$25,000). Copywriters, sometimes also known as *advertising assistants*, write the advertising copy that helps sell books. This copy may be print advertising, the description of a book on its jacket (known as *flap copy*), or fliers. The job tests your abilities to put yourself into the world of a variety of books, usually about a variety of subjects. It's a delight to see an advertisement you've created appear in the *New York Times Book Review*, for instance.

- **Copy Chief** (salary range: $25,000–$35,000) supervises copywriters.

- **Marketing Director** (salary range: $40,000–$70,000) takes overall responsibility for marketing effort. He or she usually supervises ten to twenty people, including the *ad director* and the *promotion director.*

- **Book Designer** (salary range: $16,000–$25,000) designs interior and cover of each book. He or she usually has background as a mechanical artist (i.e., "doing mechanicals," artwork consisting of type proofs, positioned and mounted for photomechanical reproduction).

- **Production Aide** (salary range: $10,000–$12,000) helps assemble a book's graphics.
- **Production Supervisor** (salary range: $16,000–$22,000) oversees production work on books; helps select type and graphics; helps with the passage of a book from manuscript to finished *(bound)* books.
- **Production Manager** (salary range: $25,000–$32,000) manages production department, making key decisions on the type, photography, and other graphic elements of a publisher's books.

These positions exist at almost every publishing house and are generally considered essential. In fact, some editors complain that sales and marketing people have more influence than they do when it comes to deciding which books to buy.

It is not hard for a publicist to work his or her way up to a higher position. After publicists finish their daily chores, the ambitious souls can always volunteer to try to write a press release, to book an author on a radio show, or put together a list of TV stations that should receive a copy of an upcoming book. The road from publicity assistant to publicist to publicity director to director of publicity and advertising has been traveled many times. In this field, it is not uncommon to switch companies frequently, in search of more responsibility, more money, and a better title.

Many of the same personnel agencies, reference books, and publishing programs we mention later on will be of great help to the fledgling advertising or publicity assistant. Before a book can be published, however, it must first be edited. No wonder that many people equate the editor with the entire publishing process.

In publishing, there are many editors, but few actually edit books that are written by publishing's superstars. The glamorous side of publishing is working at one of a dozen or so top book publishers, editing the cream of the manuscripts that are submitted for publication and working with writers, agents, book reviewers, and book clubs that ease the passage of a book from conception to publication to public acceptance.

The glamour of publishing is built, in part, on its legendary figures: Bennett Cerf, the colorful founder of Random House; Alfred A. Knopf, outspoken pioneer and founder of Knopf; Max Perkins, editor to Hemingway, Fitzgerald, and Wolfe; Ken McCormick, former editor-in-chief of Doubleday; Michael Korda, flamboyant editor of Simon and Schuster.

At the moment, Korda may be publishing's most notable symbol of success and glamour. On June 3, 1984, Simon and Schuster had seven books on the *New York Times* best-seller list. Among this company's best-selling authors are Clive Cussler *(Raise The Titanic!)*, Harold Robbins *(The Carpetbaggers)*, Joan Didion *(Democracy)*, and New York City's Mayor Ed Koch *(Mayor)*.

There's nothing wrong with aspiring to that kind of heady success, but first you have to be realistic about what publishing is and what it is not.

It is not a place for writers or English majors who simply "like books." Editors edit and publish books but generally do not write them.* So don't think that publishing is the place to be while you grind out novels at night. Publishing is a business. Recently, many independent publishers have merged with or been acquired by larger companies, making them more accountable to accountants and top management than to literary ideals. Fewer and fewer commercially risky books are being published. These days, a large number of publishable books tend to be "safe bets," and one of publishing's most charming facets—the occasional risk of publishing a worthy manuscript by an unknown author—is quickly evaporating.

Publishing is also not a place for people who dream of great wealth. Salaries have always been low. Even today, St. Martin's Press starts editorial assistants at $9,000 to $11,000 a year. And even at these salaries, you're more likely to be fired for not producing in this field than you would in a similar position in the corporate world.

Samuel Vaughan, editor-in-chief of Doubleday, once listed

*With several notable exceptions, of course: Toni Morrison, Sol Stein, and Michael Korda, as well as the late Bennett Cerf and T. S. Eliot. E. L. Doctorow was also a full-time editor before beginning his career as a novelist.

some of the prerequisites he felt were necessary for success in publishing. He felt you had to be:

- passionately persuaded about print; committed to the power of the word
- in love with both the idea of books and the ideas in books
- in love with language
- capable of enduring frustration
- possessing "a taste for long odds"

When Vaughan conducts job interviews, he looks for a person with "brains, talent, judgment, energy, taste, flair, courage, and conviction—the sort of puzzling person who appreciates literature but is no snob, who can discover a new genius but can also respect books published for reasons of entertainment."

The book-publishing industry employs only about seventy thousand people (not including booksellers, book manufacturers, or other book-service employees). Only about 1 percent of those have the type of editorial positions at major publishing companies that could be considered "glamorous." There are about twenty-five hundred consistently active book publishers in the United States, but *five* companies have half of all paperback sales, and the top ten have 86 percent of the market. Roughly fifty thousand books are published each year, and only a small percentage of them ever receive any attention in the press.

According to *Publisher's Weekly,* industry leaders are bullish on publishing's growth over the next ten years. The greatest growth is occurring in trade (bookstore) books and mass-market paperbacks ("pocket"-size books distributed to supermarkets and other retail outlets in addition to bookstores). Some industry leaders have predicted that the trend toward "brand-name" authors will continue and that the computer will play an increasingly important role in the production, editing, and distribution of books.

Few would-be editors will reach the pinnacle of publishing. Few will get to edit the books of John Updike, Robert Ludlum, Erma Bombeck, Norman Mailer, or Isaac Asimov. Few will have their own tables at "21" or the Four Seasons; few will chitchat with author Tom Wolfe or publisher Bob Gottlieb or superagent Swifty Lazar. Only a handful of America's trade editors will ever know the satisfaction of seeing their authors on "The Phil Donahue show," "The Today Show," or the best-seller list. Maybe only one in five hundred editors will have tête-à-têtes with publishing superstars at the American Booksellers Convention cocktail parties or return the nods of colleagues as they stroll through the Frankfurt Book Fair, looking for European best-sellers to buy and publish in the U.S.

But being even a small part of an industry in which these things happen is enough for some: the chance to help bring books to life. Here's what editorial assistant Sue Shapiro advises would-be editors:

"I suggest that job-seekers comb LMP *[Literary Market Place]*. Large houses [e.g., Macmillan Publishing] usually have openings. Go to a house that publishes the type of book you like to read. For example, if you like serious fiction or nonfiction, try for Houghton Mifflin, Harper & Row, or Atheneum. Or try FSG [Farrar, Straus and Giroux] or Little, Brown."

Sue also talked about the negative side of editing: "It isn't a literary picnic. There are things you do that are foolish—like the incessant meetings in which nothing gets done. The joke in publishing is that if you don't find anyone to meet with, shut the door and hold a meeting with yourself."

Where can you find a comprehensive list of major American publishers—complete with addresses, telephone numbers, and the publishing house's top personnel? *Literary Market Place*, as Sue suggests, is the place to look. Known as LMP, this annual directory is used extensively by people in the book trade as well as by savvy job-seekers. It's available at most large libraries, and will show you the diversity of jobs available in the field, while providing profiles of hundreds of publishing houses.

Publisher's Weekly, publishing's major trade magazine, includes a section called "Weekly Exchange," where job-seekers and employers advertise. You won't find prestigious trade publishers advertising for senior editors in this section, because those jobs are rarities, but you will find lots of jobs that offer experience and a chance to get your feet wet.

As you study PW and LMP, you may be bewildered by the variety of managerial titles, and you may be unable to decide just whom to write and how to approach a publisher. Do you address a letter to a top editor or to the publisher of the company? Do you start by going to an employment agency? Or do you write the personnel departments of each house? Many people start by using an employment agency, but as they gain experience in publishing, they network, use contacts, and apply to decision-makers at the publishing houses themselves. When you do gain some experience, you may wish to send a letter to the publisher or president of a company. That person may route your letter to a particular department or editor, but it helps to have the letter filter down from the top.

TRAINING

While many publishing professionals agree that a strong liberal-arts background is a helpful prerequisite for editorial work, there's a debate as to the type of vocational training one should have. Many insiders believe that no training program can truly prepare you for the world of books or teach you to uncover the next *Jaws, Roots,* or *In Search of Excellence.*

Nan Talese, vice president and executive editor of Houghton Mifflin, wrote in a PW article on publishing careers, "To me, publishing inevitably is more a vocation than a profession. The greatest satisfaction is involvement in the work itself. I doubt there really are any effective training programs; the enormous number of details makes experience in the job the greatest teacher." She goes on to recommend Scott Berg's book, *Maxwell Perkins: Editor of Genius* to show young people both the "daily dross" and the "gold" of publishing.

Most publishers assume that you've had a solid college education. Usually, that means a bachelor's degree in a humanities major, with a varied diet of liberal-arts courses, business courses, and even a few courses in computer science. Great editors have emerged from a number of disciplines, but it helps to present credentials that show you're well read— literature, economics, marketing, psychology, fine arts, drama. Any courses you take in art history, graphic design, photography, or printing may also be impressive. Law courses are a big plus, too. And while publishers are not bowled over by advanced academic degrees, they may well take notice of an MBA or an advanced degree in computer science or marketing.

There are several renowned postgraduate courses in publishing, and we'll outline a few of the best. But remember that some publishing executives are skeptical that the skills necessary in the real world of publishing can be learned in a classroom. Many of the top publishers value academic courses as the best training, and may well favor a job applicant with an impressive record as an English major over a candidate who lacked the exposure to such an education. The academic courses offered today in publishing will give you a smattering of many important publishing-related skills and experiences, but the best way to "sell" these courses to your interviewer is simply to present them as a "broadening experience" rather than the equivalent of on-the-job training.

Currently, the top three academic publishing programs are offered by Radcliffe, the University of Denver, and New York University. Other excellent programs are available at several dozen colleges and universities throughout the United States.

The Publishing Procedures Course at Radcliffe (10 Garden Street, Cambridge, MA 02138; tel. 617-495-8678) is an intensive summer professional program for recent college graduates who are seriously considering a career in book publishing. Intended to convey an overall understanding of the requirements and opportunities of publishing, the Radcliffe program (tuition: $2,990) provides basic training in publishing skills and brings students into direct contact with publishers. The program has been in existence for more than thirty years.

Allen Peacock worked in the Harvard Coop textbook department while waiting to get into the Radcliffe program. Today, Peacock, twenty-nine, is an editor at Linden Press (a division of Simon and Schuster), with a growing reputation as a fine editor concerned about nurturing authors and quality literature.

The New York University Course (2 University Place, New York, NY 10003; tel. 212-598-2373), run by the School of Continuing Education, is an intensive four-week program (tuition:

$2,100) designed to provide a comprehensive overview of book publishing, from initial concept to final sale. Sessions cover acquisition of manuscripts, author-publisher contracts, editing, printing processes, proofreading, copyright, sales promotion, publicity and advertising, and subsidiary rights.

The Publishing Institute at the University of Denver is sponsored by the Graduate School of Librarianship (Denver, CO 80208; tel. 303-353-3364). The Institute offers a concentrated four-week summer program of full-time coursework devoted exclusively to book publishing.

There are also excellent courses of study in book publishing at the City University of New York, George Washington University (Washington, D.C.), Hunter College (New York City), Rice University (Houston), Arkansas State University, Hofstra University (Hempstead, N.Y.), Sarah Lawrence College (Bronxville, N.Y.), Simmons College, (Boston, Mass.), The University of California at Berkeley, and the School of Visual Arts (New York City). City University of New York boasts one of America's most distinguished publishing libraries—the William H. and Gwynn K. Crouse Library for Publishing Arts, located at 33 West Forty-second Street in New York City.

WHAT EDITORS DO

A lot of authors are not sure about exactly what editors do.

Whatever they do, New York editors rarely skip the midday meal. Lunch is as vital as paper in completing the business of publishing. Editors have lunch with authors, agents, subrights directors, book-club directors—anyone at all who can hasten the process of a book idea becoming a book. But behind an editor's leisurely lunches at New York's chic Indian restaurants, sushi spots, or even the costly Four Seasons lurks a heavy responsibility. And that responsibility varies from one editor to another, depending upon his or her position in the editorial hierarchy.

Acquisitions editors, also sometimes called *senior editors*, buy manuscripts and oversee their publication. They negotiate fees and royalties with agents and writers, attend sales conferences, meet with the publicist assigned to their books, work with authors, designers, and printers to ensure that the finished book is well-written, sound, and attractive. A senior editor with a reputation for talent and sensitivity can be a magnet, attracting top writers of all descriptions. When Ann Harris, for instance, was a senior editor at Harper & Row, she acquired and edited *The Thorn Birds*, by Colleen McCullough; *The Times of My Life*, by Betty Ford; *The Exorcist*, by William Peter Blatty; and *Altered States*, by Paddy Chayevsky.

The top editors always stretch the definition of their jobs—as when, for instance, Richard Simon and others at Pocket Books proposed to Dr. Benjamin Spock that he write a book about baby care; when Simon and Schuster's financial manager, Leon Shimkin, heard a lecture given by Dale Carnegie and suggested to Mr. Carnegie that his lectures would make a good book *(How to Win Friends and Influence People*, one of the most successful books of all time); and when Sam Vaughan suggested William Buckley Jr. try his hand at spy novels for Doubleday.

Top editors throw out the formulas; they are on the lookout for creative ways to meet the ever-changing needs of the book-buying public. And when such editors prove their worth and outgrow their surroundings, they either start their own company or, in some cases, are given their own imprint within the company—a line of books bearing their name. Richard Marek, who published the early books of Robert Ludlum, has his own imprint, as do Kurt and Helen Wolff, who were responsible for publishing *The Name of the Rose*.

Assistant and associate editors do many of the same things that senior editors do, but they generally handle fewer books and less prestigious authors. They also have less say as to what books will be acquired, and they may not be authorized to negotiate fees. In some publishing houses, however, these same titles can be misnomers, actually representing little more than euphemisms for "typist" or "clerk."

Editorial assistant has traditionally translated as glorified secretary, but this will vary from house to house. It's an apprentice position, and you'll probably do a lot of filing, typing, reading manuscripts, and writing reports on the ones you think show promise. If your judgment is keen, you'll be noticed, and usually promoted.

As the low person on the publishing totem pole, you'll probably review manuscripts from the *slush pile*—unsolicited manuscripts from unknown authors. Many editors have started here and have made a reputation by discovering a particularly promising manuscript. *Gone With the Wind* was submitted to Macmillan by an unknown author, and *Ordinary People* was submitted without an agent and became the first unsolicited manuscript Viking had published in a generation. Author William Styron once presided over McGraw-Hill's slush pile—an autobiographical detail he wove into *Sophie's Choice*—but even Styron failed to spot the potential of an adventure story he found in the pile: *Kon-Tiki*.

The senior editor is publishing's glamour-getter, a literary sleuth trying to find publishable books. The *editor-in-chief*—in some houses referred to as the *publisher*—may have a more prestigious title and earn more money, but the job is mainly administrative. As one editor-in-chief put it: "Our job is to produce fifty books out of every two thousand manuscripts we read." They plan the house's whole publishing program, balancing the season's new titles so that they fulfill the publishing house's general philosophy and marketing aims. They also control the budget and supervise staff.

No honest appraisal of the acquisitions editor's job is complete without mentioning that occasionally editors have fierce conflicts with authors. For any of a million reasons, they sometimes slip into adversarial roles as a manuscript undergoes the publishing process. Everyone, of course, wants the book to be a success, but how that success is to be accomplished can be the subject of heated debate. Writers, admittedly, can be unrealistic in their expectations. They can also be perfectionists, or they can be lazy, sloppy, irresponsible, self-centered, reclusive, and even dull. From the point of view of some writers, a senior editor often looks uncreative, conservative, stingy, unfocused, and glib—little more than an insensitive paper pusher. Writers often can't understand why it takes so long to get a decision from an editor, why advances are so low, why book schedules are so easily thrown out of whack, why editors don't return phone calls. Editors wonder why writers frequently ignore deadlines, ignore author's questionnaires, fight over every single syllable, or insist that an unrealistically large number of copies of their book be printed.

As an editor, you'll need to understand the mind-set of the agent, too. Agents get 10 to 15 percent of what their clients (the authors) receive, so they take an assertive, businesslike stance that most authors don't have the time, patience, personality, or experience to take themselves. They'll push you for a decision, tell you that the advance is too low, plead with you to keep the book in print, yell at you because the bookstores aren't stocking the book, and tease you with book ideas that may—if you act immediately—become next year's best-selling titles.

This can be irritating (or amusing), but it's part of the game of publishing, and you may as well get used to it. It can be fun to sit with Scott Meredith over lunch and hear him go on and on about Norman Mailer's new project or Arthur Clarke's latest brainchild. It can be a kick to watch an agent use powers of persuasion to turn a maybe into a yes.

Before too long, you'll know which agents, writers, and colleagues you can trust—and which you can't. Powerhouses like Scott Meredith boast about the *advances* (prepublication royalty payment) they've won for their clients (four of the top ten advances ever paid were paid to Meredith's clients: Mailer, Clarke, Carl Sagan, and Margaret Truman). Other agents are more low-key, though they may be just as likely to bring you a marketable manuscript.

Although an editor reads and edits manuscripts, those activities form a surprisingly small part of his or her day. Most of it is spent attending to correspondence, checking galleys and cover designs, talking to agents and authors, meeting with colleagues, and a million and one unglamorous tasks that eat up a workday.

After an editor uncovers a manuscript or book proposal that he or she feels has merit, the editor begins the arduous task of persuading the publisher—and perhaps a board of executives—to buy the book. This may take a few days, a few weeks, or a few months. Agents and authors chew their fingernails while the publishing house ambles toward a decision.

If the answer is no, it's usually final. But if the decision is yes, the editor starts to negotiate for the book. Usually, negotiation entails a few phone conversations with an agent. During these conversations, editor and agent come to an agreement on the specifics of the contract. Among the most important details to be discussed are the amount of the author's advance; the expected date of manuscript submission; the manuscript's anticipated length and date of publication; the ownership of reprint, book-club, serial, and foreign rights; and a number of details involving everything from dramatic rights to royalty percentages to *boilerplate language* (standard clauses) about the author's and publisher's obligations to each other.

This task is not as cumbersome as it sounds. Working your way up as an apprentice, you'll soon become familiar with how contracts are negotiated. Of the many details discussed in each contract, only a handful vary from one book to another.

If an editor signs up a famous author or a particularly promising one, or if he or she sells the reprint rights to a manuscript, the deal will usually be written up in Paul Nathan's "Rights and Permissions" column in *Publisher's Weekly* and in Herbert Mitgang's publishing column in the *New York Times*.

But the real heart of the job is in taking a manuscript and guiding it through the production process toward becoming a bound book in a store. Roughly speaking, here's what this entails, once the author has submitted an acceptable manuscript:

- Editing the manuscript
- Having the manuscript copy-edited
- Working with designers and printers to get the book and cover designed (helping to choose a typeface, jacket copy, and cover design)
- Reading and distributing book galleys (page proofs of the printed book)
- Working on last-minute changes with author
- Checking and distributing bound galleys (proofs bound for

distribution to reviewers prior to the actual publication of the finished book)
- Arranging a publicity budget and strategy with the sales force, marketing director, advertising manager, publicity director, and subsidiary-rights director
- Approving the press release
- Inspecting copies of the bound book

Other people have the responsibility of making sure that once the book is printed and bound, it finds its way to the wholesalers (companies that buy books in bulk from publishers and sell directly to bookstores and other outlets), to such large bookstore chains as B. Dalton and Waldenbooks, and to the thousands of independent bookstores across the country.

Even when the book is on the shelves, an editor will continue to be the publishing house's main conduit of information about that book. Every time an author or agent inquires about royalties, a new printing, or the possibility of the book going out of print, the editor is the person who'll be contacted.

Beyond these responsibilities, he or she will also be expected to keep abreast of the field—visiting bookstores, researching new proposals to make sure they're legitimate and won't duplicate books already in print, and reading PW to see what the competition is publishing. The editor must follow the activities of such organizations as the American Booksellers Association, the American Library Association, and the Association of American Publishers; and he or she must pay attention to lawsuits that involve publishers and details of First Amendment violations. The editor will inevitably be expected to peruse a sizable stack of trade journals, too (see pages 63-65).

One editor (who prefers to remain anonymous) shared her view of editing with us. Her story typifies both the pains and pleasures of the publishing world:

"I was an editor of my high school and college newspapers, but then I tried to break into publishing and all they wanted was typing. Even my graduate degree meant little.

"I pounded the pavements for a while and then got my first job through an employment agency. I became an assistant to several editors. But there was no movement. At most houses, there's little movement.

"So I quit and went back to the employment agency. And, after a while, I became an assistant editor at Simon and Schuster. There, they promote every six months. But that is largely because, at a chaotic house, people leave regularly. There's an expression in publishing that you choose to work either at a frenetic pace to be promoted or for a sedate, prestigious publisher where you may never get promoted. At S and S, I started at $155 a week (in the mid-1970s). Eventually, I became a senior editor at a paperback house. And, of course, there was glamour: free lunches, free movies, free plays (after all, we occasionally did business with producers and playwrights). And there's the thrill of watching your book make the best-seller list.

"Also, there are parties: authors throw themselves parties, publishers throw parties. The other day I attended an author's party given by a wealthy grandmother of the author. The house was huge, and there were Renoirs and Picassos on the walls."

We asked her what else was glamorous about being an editor, and she replied, "In all fairness, it *is* exciting to do books with celebrities—Michael Jackson, Candice Bergen, and others. And although many authors cause aggravation, many others are enjoyable to work with. If you think that being an editor at a publishing company means that you'll be working with James Joyce, forget it! But it is rewarding to make a flawed manuscript into a well-polished book."

We also asked about the publishing houses that hold allure for most editors:

"The exciting places to be right now are Simon and Schuster, Random House, Knopf, Bantam, and a few others. Viking has an intellectual glamour.

"Publishing is glamorous in general, of course. First of all, it is possible to advance—sometimes rapidly—and earn good money after a while. The expense account is nice (even the lowliest editor seems to have an unlimited expense account for lunch)."

Occasionally, editors get fired or leave their jobs to become agents, publicists, or *packagers* (people who produce books by contracting directly with authors, designers, and illustrators before offering the book to a publisher as a complete "package"). The pressure of editorial responsibilities is not for everyone. Some disreputable publishers hire only young people because they can get away with paying them practically nothing . . . and then keep only those who show unswerving devotion and who are willing to "marry" the job. One young editor, in a *Publisher's Weekly* roundup of job opportunities in the field, commented, "I'm committed to publishing, but I'm not sure that will continue when I'm thirty-five. What if I wanted to have a family? There would be no way it would be possible on this salary. It's a luxury to work in publishing as it is now, and I want to be paid for my ability."

In a *Publisher's Weekly* story announcing the retirement of Joan Manley—group vice president for books at Time-Life Books Inc. and a thirty-year publishing veteran—Manley was asked if she had any advice for women in publishing. She said that "women have always been in publishing and many have had distinguished careers. It offers more chance for equal opportunity and has a more substantial track record in that respect than, say, steel.

"The people who should stay in publishing," Manley continued, "are those who love it, despite gender. I guess my only advice is to enjoy it to the hilt, and, if you don't, get out. There's not that much money in it."

As an editor, you need to set goals for yourself or you may be thought of as someone whom time has passed by. The best editors soon develop a maturity that makes them even-tempered, reliable, and meticulous. They build solid relationships with agents and authors; they participate vigorously at editorial meetings; they take an interest in their colleagues and their colleagues' projects.

You'll work your way up by acquiring books that establish your reputation. They need not all sell fabulously well, but they should be books of quality, not just spinoffs of past ideas. Try to be well-rounded in your selections, since you don't want to get pigeon-holed as the editor who does the humor books or the how-to books. You should be known as the person who has the imagination to develop any idea well—although it's also useful to develop several particular areas of expertise.

As you work your way up the ladder, you'll learn the value of "doing your homework" (i.e., researching potential book projects so that you can tell if an author's assessment of the book's competition is accurate). You'll learn how to cut through red tape at your publishing house, how to pitch your books at editorial meetings, and how to negotiate in such a way as to keep faith with agents and editors.

Not every editor wishes to progress to the high-paying-but-administrative job of editor-in-chief, but if you do wish to get there, don't be afraid to let your superiors know that you're on a fast track. They'll respect you for it.

The glamour of book publishing is not necessarily tied, however, to working at one of the larger, more prestigious houses. The advantage of these publishers is that they tend to have worked out efficient systems for conducting business. They take a professional attitude toward employee benefits, training, and mobility. But they do not guarantee that you'll be promoted or even noticed. And a small publisher may give you a better opportunity to see how the whole publishing process works. At St. Martin's Press or at Dodd Mead, for example, it would not be unusual for an editor to wander into a publicist's office and chat informally about promotional plans for a new book.

If you're eager to get first-hand knowledge of how books are marketed, publicized, and sold, as well as edited, you may want to take a job with a publisher that has a relatively small staff, allowing entry-level assistants to share in the higher responsibilities and thus become more well rounded.

In editing, success will lead to more success. As an editor's reputation grows, he or she will draw the attention of agents and authors. Soon, that editor will be offered more and better manuscripts. For some editors, the acquisition of a "hot" manuscript from a top author is a security blanket, a failure-proof trophy of success. Book-buyers have a long memory, and when you hook up with best-selling authors, you have, in a sense, found a type of annuity: Your prestige grows with each new book the author writes.

We've tried to be realistic in this brief look at publishing. There are a number of drawbacks that are hard to accept. Publishers know the allure of publishing, and the starting salaries seem to be more like honorariums. And the publishing world, relatively speaking, is small; sometimes the industry seems petty and unfair—rewarding tasteless trash with high advances and worthy books with an uncaring shrug. In its swing toward mass-marketing, mergers, and high advances, publishing may have lost some of its earlier charm, but it has also opened up a wide range of employment opportunities and widened the circle of people for whom reading is a lifetime joy. As an editor, even though you're behind the scenes, you can relish the satisfaction of walking through a bookstore and watching people discover and enjoy what you and an author worked so hard to achieve. Every book that touches the life of another person adds another drop of immortality to the author who wrote it—and to the editor who helped shape it.

Book Publishing: Required Reading

Every Sunday, the **New York Times Book Review** discusses about fifty of the most important new works in fiction, nonfiction, children's books, and poetry, as well as carrying features on major writers. A good review in the *Times* can pave the way to best-sellerdom. The *Book Review* is sold separately at many bookstores around the country and is available by subscription independent of the Sunday *New York Times* in which it appears. For subscriptions, write to the *New York Times*, Box 5792, GPO, New York, NY 10087, or call (800) 631-2500. The cost is $22 per year.

Responsible for more book reviews than any other Washington, D.C. publication, **Book World** is the literary supplement to the *Washington Post* and has a circulation of one million. Although it reviews almost two thousand of the most significant new titles each year, it gives special attention to biographies and books on politics. In addition, it features columns on science fiction and on paperbacks. For subscriptions, write to the *Washington Post,* Washington, D.C. 20071, or call (202) 334-6000. The cost is $13 per year.

Publisher's Weekly, the major trade magazine of the publishing industry, usually gives important new books their first review about six weeks in advance of the book's publication date (most other publications review books after publication). Each capsule review not only gives an overview of the book's plot but also summarizes any special distinction it may have, such as being a Book of the Month Club selection, or having sold rights to a major magazine or film company.

The publishing world—and diligent book-buyers—look forward to two special issues each year, the spring and fall announcements, which give a glimpse of books to come. In these two thick issues, major publishers advertise their book list for the new season. Leafing through these issues, an observant book-fancier can learn exactly what the big books of the coming season will be and make book-buying plans accordingly. For subscriptions, write to R. R. Bowker & Co., 1180 Sixth Ave., New York, NY 10036, or call (212) 764-5100. The cost is $68 per year.

Examining more literary and scholarly books than other book-related publications, **The New York Review of Books** prides itself on provocative essays and interviews that address a variety of literary concerns. The twenty-year-old biweekly aims less at being timely than it does at being trenchant, and it has a flair for making odd-couple matchings of books and critics—Joan Didion on Woody Allen, for example. Gore Vidal, Susan Sontag, Tom Wicker, and Renata Adler are among its regular reviewers. For subscriptions, write to *The New York Review of Books,* 250 W. 57th St., New York, NY 10019, or call (212) 757-8070. The cost is $25 per year.

Two influential magazines of narrower scope are **Kirkus Reviews** and **Library Journal.** Founded in 1933, *Kirkus Reviews* is a thick compendium of reviews—with no advertisements—aimed at librarians. Published twenty-four times a year, each issue covers about two hundred titles, running the gamut of fiction and nonfiction, with occasional reviews of how-to books and children's titles. For subscriptions, write to *Kirkus Reviews,* 200 Park Ave. S., New York, NY 10003. The cost is $50 per year.

Library Journal, published 20 times a year, covers a wide range of fiction, non-fiction, technical, medical, and business titles. For subscriptions, write to *Library Journal,* 205 E. 42nd St., New York, NY 10017, or call (800) 257-7894. The cost is $59 per year.

Finally, two other top book-review supplements— the **Los Angeles Times Book Review** and the **Chicago Tribune Book Review**—are worth the price of a subscription to their parent publications. The L.A. *Times Book Review* has gained a national reputation in recent years, despite its occasional emphasis on California titles. For subscriptions, write to the *Los Angeles Times,* Times Mirror Square, Los Angeles, CA 90053.

The *Chicago Tribune*'s Sunday book section reviews an unusually large number of paperbacks, both trade and mass-market. The reviews are national in scope and lively in tone. For subscriptions, write to the *Chicago Tribune,* Tribune Tower, Chicago, IL 60611, or call (312) 222-4100.

A final note: Although not for the casual consumer, B. Dalton's "Hooked on Books" merchandise bulletin is perhaps the most powerful tastemaker in book retailing today. Written by Kay Sexton, Dalton's VP of Marketing, "Hooked on Books" is supplied weekly to the managers of 704 B. Dalton stores around the country, who, along with editors and salespeople in every major publishing house, read it to find out the latest publishing trends. B. Dalton's headquarters is One Corporate Center, 7505 Metro Blvd., Minneapolis, MN 55435.

Fifty Prominent Book Publishers

The following publishers are among the most prominent in the field. Some have been chosen for their quality; others for the quantity of books they publish; others for the wide scope of their lists. Many of the publishers on this list seem to garner a disproportionate amount of media and trade-press attention for their books. If book publishing holds any glamour at all—and it does—you'll find a lot of that glamour attached to these houses:

Harry N. Abrams, Inc.
110 E. 59th St.
New York, NY 10022
(212) 758-8600

Addison-Wesley
Reading, MA 01867
(617) 944-3700

Arbor House Publishing Co.
235 E. 45th St.
New York, NY 10017
(212) 599-3131

Atheneum Publishers
597 Fifth Ave.
New York, NY 10017
(212) 486-2700

Avon Books
959 Eighth Ave.
New York, NY 10019
(212) 262-5700

Ballantine Books
201 E. 50th St.
New York, NY 10022
(212) 751-2600

Bantam Books
666 Fifth Ave.
New York, NY 10103
(212) 765-6500

Berkley Press
200 Madison Ave.
New York, NY 10016
(212) 686-9820

Crown Publishers
One Park Ave.
New York, NY 10016
(212) 532-9200

Delacorte Press
One Dag Hammarskjold Plaza
New York, NY 10017
(212) 605-3000

Dell Publishing
One Dag Hammarskjold Plaza
New York, NY 10017
(212) 605-3000

Dodd Mead & Co.
79 Madison Ave.
New York, NY 10016
(212) 685-6464

Doubleday Books
245 Park Ave.
New York, NY 10167
(212) 953-4561

E. P. Dutton
2 Park Ave.
New York, NY 10016
(212) 725-1818

M. Evans & Co., Inc.
216 E. 49th St.
New York, NY 10017
(212) 688-2810

Facts on File
460 Park Ave. S.
New York, NY 10016
(212) 683-2244

Farrar, Straus & Giroux
19 Union Sq. W.
New York, NY 10003
(212) 741-6900

Franklin Watts
387 Park Ave.
New York, NY 10016
(212) 686-7070

Grolier
Sherman Tpke.
Danbury, CT 06816
(203) 797-3500

Grove Press
196 W. Houston St.
New York, NY 10014
(212) 242-4900

Harcourt Brace Jovanovich
1250 Sixth Ave.
San Diego, CA 92101
(619) 231-6616

Harper & Row
10 E. 53rd St.
New York, NY 10022
(212) 593-7000

Holt, Rinehart & Winston
521 Fifth Ave.
New York, NY 10175
(212) 599-7600

Houghton Mifflin Co.
One Beacon St.
Boston, MA 02108
(617) 725-5000

Alfred A. Knopf
201 E. 50th St.
New York, NY 10022
(212) 751-2600

The Linden Press
1230 Sixth Ave.
New York, NY 10020
(212) 245-4843

J. B. Lippincott
E. Washington Sq.
Philadelphia, PA 19705
(215) 574-4200

Little, Brown & Co.
34 Beacon St.
Boston, MA 02106
(617) 227-0730

Macmillan Publishing Co.
866 Third Ave.
New York, NY 10022
(212) 702-2000

McGraw-Hill
1221 Sixth Ave.
New York, NY 10020
(212) 997-1221

William Morrow & Co.
105 Madison Ave.
New York, NY 10016
(212) 889-3050

New American Library
1633 Broadway
New York, NY 10019
(212) 397-8000

W. W. Norton
500 Fifth Ave.
New York, NY 10110
(212) 354-5500

Oxford University Press
200 Madison Ave.
New York, NY 10016
(212) 679-7300

Pocket Books
1230 Sixth Ave.
New York, NY 10020
(212) 246-2121

Price/Stern/Sloan
410 N. La Cienega Blvd.
Los Angeles, CA 90048
(213) 657-6100

G. P. Putnam's Sons
200 Madison Ave.
New York, NY 10016
(212) 576-8900

Random House, Inc.
201 E. 50th St.
New York, NY 10022
(212) 751-2600

Reader's Digest Books
750 Third Ave.
New York, NY 10017
(212) 850-7000

Scholastic, Inc.
730 Broadway
New York, NY 10003
(212) 944-7700

Simon and Schuster
1230 Sixth Ave.
New York, NY 10020
(212) 245-6400

St. Martin's Press
175 Fifth Ave.
New York, NY 10012
(212) 674-5151

Stein & Day
Scarborough House
Briarcliff Manor, NY 10510
(914) 762-2151

Ten Speed Press
Box 7123
Berkeley, CA 94707
(415) 845-8414

Ticknor & Fields
383 Orange St.
New Haven, CT 06511
(203) 776-1878

Time-Life Books, Inc.
Alexandria, VA 22314
(703) 960-5000

Viking Press
40 W. 23rd St.
New York, NY 10010
(212) 807-7300

Warner Books
666 Fifth Ave.
New York, NY
(212) 484-8000

John Wiley & Sons
605 Third Ave.
New York, NY 10158
(212) 850-6000

Workman Publishing
One W. 39th St.
New York, NY 10018
(212) 398-9160

Selected Employment Agencies That
Specialize in Book Publishing

Able Personnel
280 Madison Ave.
New York, NY 10016
(212) 689-5550

Helen Akullian Agency
280 Madison Ave.
New York, NY 10016
(212) 532-3210

Career Blazers
500 Fifth Ave.
New York, NY 10036
(212) 732-4747

Bert Davis Associates
400 Madison Ave.
New York, NY 10017
(212) 838-4000

Mary Diehl Placement Bureau
50 E. 42nd St., #308
New York, NY 10017
(212) 687-1632

Editorial Experts Inc. Employment
  Service
5905 Pratt St.
Alexandria, VA 22310
(703) 823-3740

Gardner Personnel, Inc.
300 Madison Ave.
New York, NY 10016
(212) 687-6615

Hadle Agency
535 Fifth Ave.
New York, NY 10017
(212) 557-5000

Lynne Palmer
739 Boylston St.
Suite 400
Boston, MA 02117
(617) 536-1820

Lynne Palmer
14 E. 60th St.
New York, NY 10022
(212) 759-2942

Lyman Personnel Service
3820 Buffalo Speedway
Suite 110
Houston, TX
(713) 627-1110

Remer-Ribolow Agency, Inc.
507 Fifth Ave.
New York, NY 10036
(212) 661-9740

Roth Young of Chicago
444 N. Michigan, Suite 870
Chicago, IL 60611
(312) 368-8455

Publishing: A Brief Glossary

Advance. An amount of money advanced to the author by the publisher before publication of the book. The advance is subtracted from royalties earned from the book's future sales.

Author tour. A promotion trip, usually arranged by the publisher, to help an author generate interest in his or her book throughout the country.

Back-list. A book, often with a limited audience, published with the expectation of selling a steady number of copies over a period of years.

Breakout potential. A book with breakout potential is expected to "break out" of a particular subject or genre category to attract readers from other areas of interest, or to attract a significant number of new readers and sell much better than the author's earlier books.

First printing. The number of copies printed when a book is first published.

Front-list. All the new books presented in a selling season.

Galleys. Bound or unbound, these typeset proofs are shown to authors to help correct errors in format and content. Bound galleys are also sent to magazines, newspapers, and other reviewers for evaluation in advance of or concurrent with publication.

Hopes 'n' Dreams book. A term for a book that appeals to the hopes and dreams of readers rather than to realistic practicalities.

Impulse buy. A book placed close to the cash register at a store so that buyers may purchase it on impulse. Often displayed in a publisher-supplied countertop unit called a *prepack.*

LMP. Literary Market Place.

Mass-market paperback. A rack-size paperback book aimed at a mass audience, usually printed in quantities of 25,000 or more.

Mid-list. A fiction or nonfiction book that is neither as specialized as a back-list book nor as conspicuous as a front-list book, with an identifiable audience and a well-known author.

Multiple submissions. Submitting a book manuscript to several publishers at once, instead of one at a time.

Packager. A person who arranges the elements of a book—idea, manuscript, production—and packages all elements, either to submit them to a publisher or to produce the book himself.

PW. Publisher's Weekly, the trade magazine considered to be the Bible of publishing.

Reprint rights. The rights that a publisher buys in order to be allowed to reprint a hardcover book in a paperback format (a.k.a. paperback rights).

Royalty. Money (usually representing a certain percentage of sales) paid to an author in compensation for the continuing right to publish and sell his or her book.

Run. The number of copies printed at any one time. A trade hardcover's first run might average 5,000 to 15,000 copies, while a mass-market paperback's first printing might be 25,000 to 50,000 copies.

Serial rights. The right to serialize or run excerpts from a book, usually a new book. First serial rights give the right to excerpt part of a book *before* the book is officially published. Second serial rights give the right to excerpt a book *following* the book's publication. Only a small number of magazines buy first serial rights to books. These rights, often expensive, can generate excellent publicity for a new book while attracting new readers to the magazine running the excerpt.

Stocking stuffer. A low-priced, often whimsical book that publishers promote as a possible gift item. These books usually have wide appeal (e.g., *The Preppy Handbook, Items From Our Catalogue,* and *Dieter's Guide to Weight Loss During Sex).*

Sub rights. Subsidiary rights, including reprint, serial, translation, book-club, performance, and other rights in a book, beyond its simple presentation in its original form.

Syndication rights. The right to syndicate a portion of a new book—to edit the excerpt and distribute it to a newspaper syndicate's network of affiliated newspapers.

Trade book. A book that is published for the general public and sold at bookstores (as distinct from textbooks, which are marketed to schools).

University Presses: Not for Scholars Only

For would-be publishing professionals eager to break into the field, university presses offer opportunities that are removed from some of the competitive strife of Publisher's Row. There are a number of fine university presses, some of which have lists including the works of renowned scholars, poets, and other literati. Many such houses maintain full—albeit small—staffs of editors, publicists, and marketing professionals. For readers wanting to try out publishing before making the crucial move to New York City, there are excellent university presses in the Midwest, South, and Northwest, in addition to those up and down the East Coast. Some of the university presses listed below have even become involved in fiction as well as nonfiction. (As a matter of fact, *One Writer's Beginning,* by Eudora Welty, published by Harvard University Press, became a leading best-seller. And L.S.U. Press was the original publisher of John Kennedy O'Toole's *A Confederacy of Dunces.)*

Following are the names, addresses, and phone numbers of fifteen prominent university presses. Also, we've mentioned two of each publisher's recent titles, to give you a flavor of their offerings.

University of Arizona Press
1615 E. Speedway
Tucson, AZ 85719
(602) 626-1441

Run, River, Run: A Naturalist's Journey, by Ann Zwinger.
The Making of a Government: Political Leaders in Modern Mexico, by Roderic A. Camp.

University of California Press
2223 Fulton St.
Berkeley, CA 94720
(415) 642-4247

The Limits of Science, by Nicholas Rescher.
The Trouble With America, by Michael Crozier.

University of Chicago Press
5801 Ellis Ave.
Chicago, IL 60637
(312) 962-7700

Criticism and Social Change, by Frank Lentricchia.
Sartre and Marxist Existentialism, by Thomas R. Flynn.

Columbia University Press
562 W. 113th St.
New York, NY 10025
(212) 678-6777

The Films of George Roy Hill, by Andrew Horton.
Pensions: The Hidden Costs of Public Safety, by Robert M. Fogelson.

Harvard University Press
79 Garden St.
Cambridge, MA 02538
(617) 495-2600

The Diary of Beatrice Webb, vol. 3, edited by Norman and Jeanne MacKenzie.
One Writer's Beginnings, by Eudora Welty.

Howard University Press
2900 Van Ness NW
Washington, D.C. 20008
(202) 686-6696

The Teacher Rebellion, by David Selden.
Personal Money Management, by James F. Tucker.

University of Illinois Press
54 East Gregory Dr.
Champaign, IL 61820
(217) 333-0950

From Beowolf to Virginia Woolf, by Robert Manson Myers.
Eugene V. Debs, by Nick Salvatore.

Indiana University Press
Tenth and Morton Sts.
Bloomington, IN 47405
(812) 237-4203

Rabelais and His World, by Mikhail Bakhtin.
OPEC and the Third World, by Shireen Hunter.

Johns Hopkins University Press
Baltimore, MD 21218
(301) 338-7875

Flight in America, 1900–1983,
by Roger E. Bilstein.
The Life of Jane Austen, by John
Halperin.

Louisiana State University Press
Baton Rouge, LA 70803
(504) 388-6294

The Awakening Twenties, by
Gorham Munson.
New Orleans Jazz, by Al Rose
and Edmond Souchon.

University of Massachusetts Press
Box 429
Amherst, MA 01004
(413) 545-2217

Literary Inheritance, by Roger
Sale.
Home Remedies, by Martin
Pops.

University of Minnesota Press
2037 University Ave. SE
Minneapolis, MN 55414
(612) 373-3266

The People Named the
Chippewa, by Gerald Vizenor.
Cloning, by Robert G.
McKinnell.

The MIT Press
28 Carleton St.
Cambridge, MA 02142
(617) 253-5646

The Future of The Automobile,
by Alan Altshuler, et al.
The Copyright Book, by William
S. Strong.

University of Nebraska Press
901 N. 17th St.
Lincoln, NE 68588
(402) 472-3581

Cripple Creek Days, by Mabel
Barbee Lee.
Views of a Vanishing Frontier, by
John C. Ewers, et al.

University of Washington Press
P.O. Box 50096
Seattle, WA 98145
(206) 543-4050

The Shape and Form of Puget
Sound, by Robert E. Burns.
Medical Malpractice, by William
O. Robertson.

Books on Books: A Selected List

Berg, A. Scott. Maxwell Perkins: Editor of Genius. New York: Dutton, 1978.
Canfield, Cass. Up and Down and Around: A Publisher Recollects the Time of His Life. New York: Harper & Row, 1971.
Cerf, Bennett. At Random. New York: Random House, 1977.
Davis, Kenneth C. Two-Bit Culture: The Paperbacking of America. Boston: Houghton Mifflin, 1984.

Dessauer, John P. *Book Publishing: What It Is, What It Does.* New York: Bowker, 1981.

Mainstream Access, eds. *The Publishing Job Finder.* Englewood Cliffs, N.J.: Prentice-Hall, 1981.

Morgan, Roberta. *How to Break Into Publishing.* New York: Barnes & Noble Books, 1980.

Scherman, William H. *How to Get the Right Job in Publishing.* Chicago: Contemporary Books, 1983.

Targ, William. *Indecent Pleasures.* New York: Macmillan, 1975.

Tebbel, John. *Opportunities in Publishing Careers.* Skokie: Vocational Guidance Manuals, 1975.

U.S. Book Publishing Yearbook and Directory. White Plains: Knowledge Industry Publications, 1983.

Finance

America is a nation of job-hoppers.

A 1978 study by the College Board showed that more than a third of the work force—forty million Americans—were changing or planning to change careers that year. And the U.S. Department of Labor reports that American workers stay at each job an average of 3.6 years.

These days, more and more white-collar workers are leaving their current industry for careers in *finance*—banking, trading, financial planning, and any one of a half dozen or so other high-paying careers that involve the manipulation of other people's money.

In 1983, more than forty thousand people took the registered-representative exam, a six-hour test that aspiring brokers must pass before they can work in the profession. Training programs and courses for financial professionals are springing up everywhere, and people are willing to pay stiff tuitions to take them. Gorfrem Marketing Systems of St. Louis, for instance, offers a two-day training program in setting up a loan consulting firm. The fee: a whopping $9,900.

The financial industry is booming, and careers in finance have never been as popular as they are today. We can think of three reasons for this trend.

The first is money. College graduates are more money- and career-conscious than ever before. Career planning begins early these days; there are even career publications aimed at high-school students. And these students have material goals— a home, a car, nice clothes, vacations, entertainment, fine food, health-club memberships, hot tubs, art and other collectibles—that only a healthy income can satisfy.

If money is what you crave, few fields are more lucrative than finance. It's not unusual to earn a six-figure income as a broker, manager, or banker. And the top people in the field have annual incomes in the millions.

The second reason for this boom in finance is the deregulation of the industry itself and the diversity of investment opportunities available.

In the 1960s, most people kept their money in a passbook account at the bank, and if they had a little extra, they dabbled in the stock market. Today, the passbook savings account is rapidly becoming a thing of the past. Instead of letting their cash earn a paltry $5\frac{1}{4}$ percent interest at the neighborhood savings-and-loan, people are putting their money into treasury notes, Now and SuperNow accounts, money-market funds, mutual funds, commodities, commercial paper, cash-management accounts, IRAs, Keoghs, CDs, government securities, government-guaranteed mortgages, deferred annuities, corporate and municipal bonds, stocks, options, futures, precious metals, foreign exchanges, annuities, limited real-estate partnerships, insurance plans, unit investment trusts, tax shelters, and a host of other profitable investments.

Third, there are more people who want to take advantage of these services and more companies offering them. Investing is not just for the rich; people with average incomes are turning to mutual funds, money markets, and other investment vehicles to help them make the most of the money they've got.

Ten years ago, a brokerage firm was the only place these folks could turn to for financial assistance. Nowadays, banks, savings-and-loans, finance companies, financial planners, insurance companies, and real-estate investment firms compete with brokerage houses in offering financial services to individual investors. And this diversification has created more jobs for the people who manage and sell such services.

This chapter is written to tell you what the jobs are in finance, where to find them, and how to get them.

A WALK ON WALL STREET

Career opportunities in finance are plentiful in almost any major city in the United States, because that's where the banks and brokerage firms are. But the hub of the financial world has always been—and still is—New York City, or, to be precise, Wall Street.

Wall Street itself is a narrow street near the southern tip of Manhattan Island. But the name *Wall Street* has come to represent the small area around the street where many of the country's most influential financial operations are located. The area is bordered by Battery Park and the Hudson River on the west, South Street Seaport and the East River on the east; and Wall Street is surrounded by colorful neighborhoods—Chinatown, Little Italy, Soho, Tribeca. The Statue of Liberty can be seen from some of the westernmost streets in the area. But the twin towers of the World Trade Center dominate the Wall Street skies.

The financial industry as we know it began when the New York Stock Exchange was formed, in 1792, for the trading of stocks and bonds. Thanks to the computerization of the financial industry, the NYSE is now able to handle tens of millions of transactions daily. But it is no longer a monopoly; there are many other exchanges for the trading of securities, with the American Stock Exchange being the New York Exchange's largest competitor. And there are thousands of stocks traded *over the counter* (outside of the exchanges).

Competition for jobs on Wall Street or in any other major financial center is fierce. But part of the problem is that most job-seekers set their sights on a career as a stockbroker without realizing that there are many other exciting, lucrative career opportunities in finance.

These careers fall into two basic categories: *front office* and *back office*. The front office, also known as *production*, involves everything that makes money for the firm, including sales (the job of the brokers), trading, underwriting, corporate and public finance, investment banking, investment advising, mergers and acquisitions, and arbitrage. (If these terms are unfamiliar to you, don't worry. They're explained later in the chapter and in the glossary at the end.)

The back office provides the support services that keep the front office going. These services include operations (general management), data processing, telecommunications, personnel, training, compliance, legal services, and securities analysis.

Phil Caso, an account executive at a Wall Street investment firm and a former operations manager for Citicorp, explains the difference between back and front office this way: "Support spends money. Production makes money."

Front-office people contribute to the company by selling services and bringing in income. Back-office people contribute by running the operation in the most efficient, cost-effective way possible. If a telecommunications manager cuts a $10 million phone bill by 20 percent, he can save the company $2 million. Few brokers bring in that much in commissions.

Front-office people receive compensation as a commission based on their sales, so there's no limit to what a broker or financial planner can earn. Back-office people are paid a straight salary, but these salaries reflect the wealth of their employers, and it's not unusual for a manager in operations, telecommunications, or data processing to earn $50,000 to $100,000, or even more.

Before you leap into a career as a broker or investment banker, take a close look at your personality and decide what profession you are best suited for. Some people enjoy the excitement of sales. Others prefer a more structured work life, and they make better managers. Pinpoint your ambition and go after it. But don't worry: No matter what career goal you set, you'll be pursuing a well-paid position.

Knowing where to look is a big help when you go after these profitable positions. There are basically three types of organizations that employ financial people:

- Brokerage houses (such as E. F. Hutton and Merrill Lynch).
- Commercial banks (such as Citibank, Chemical Bank, Bank of America).
- Insurance companies and other financial-service organizations (such as Shearson/American Express, John Hancock, and Prudential-Bache).

With deregulation of the financial industry, the lines between these three categories are becoming blurred. Banks, brokerage houses, and insurance companies are all offering a

wide assortment of investment alternatives under the um-
brella label *financial services.* We'll discuss some of the pros
and cons of working at one place or the other later in the
chapter when we cover specific jobs in the industry.

Employers in the financial industry range in size from one-
office brokers to multinational banks and corporations, with
the larger organizations offering the most diverse opportunities. Citicorp, for example, the world's largest commercial
bank, is divided into three groups: an institutional-banking
group that serves corporate customers, a private-banking
group that caters to individual investors, and a capital-
markets group that trades securities.

Before you contact a potential employer, send for their
annual report, corporate-capabilities brochure, and other literature on their company and services. This research pays off
in two ways: It uncovers career opportunities in the organization so you can focus your own job-hunting efforts, while
impressing interviewers that you're a candidate who is thorough enough to find out more about their firm.

JOB-HUNTING TACTICS FOR FINANCIAL FOLKS

A recent seminar held in New York City in "Career Opportunities on Wall Street" stressed the importance of having a sharp,
professional résumé. The instructor, financial planner Janice
Remer, offered these five tips on résumé-writing:

1. **State your objective.** If you know what position you want,
   write a specific objective at the top of the résumé. If you
   are applying for several different positions, use several
   different résumés, each with a different career objective. If
   you don't know the type of job you want, omit the objective. (It's better to leave it out than make some vague
   general statement.)
2. **Use reverse chronological order.** Start with your current
   position and work backward. For each position, include
   the name of the company, your title, a job description, and
   the years you were there.

3. **Outline your accomplishments.** Listings for each job should be more than mere description; they should highlight your responsibilities and your accomplishments.

Avoid overuse of the cliché phrase "was responsible for." Substitute such action verbs as: accomplished, achieved, audited, improved, increased, sold, set up, created, designed, developed, established, expanded, introduced, invented, launched, marketed, operated, organized, planned, prepared, researched, started.

Also, be specific. Instead of "made cold calls to prospects," say, "made 100 cold calls per day and brought in 60 new customers in 4 months."

4. **Other background.** Include relevant education, training courses or seminars, publications, speaking engagements, professional affiliations, skills, foreign languages, civic activities.

5. **Make it letter-perfect.** Have at least two people proofread your résumé for content and flow, while looking for misspellings and typos. Remer says that half the résumés in circulation have at least one typo. So if yours is perfect, you're already ahead of 50 percent of the crowd.

A professional résumé serves a dual purpose. It presents the employer with reasons to hire you, and it shows off your communications skills—an area of increasing importance to companies that must explain complex financial services to lay customers. "In the wake of the deregulation of the banking industry, consumers and bank personnel are faced with a confusing, shifting array of options they have never faced before," explains an article in the newsletter *Simply Stated* (November 1983). "More and more banks are learning that plain English writing and effective forms design can help clarify the picture for everyone."

Assuming you do have the communications skills to persuade a bank or brokerage firm to give you an interview, you want to go in as well prepared as possible. Do some research, both about the company in particular and about the industry and type of job in general.

You don't have to be able to debate economics with Milton

Friedman, but you should have a basic understanding of the
nature of the job you're applying for and the jargon of the
business. If you don't know your Ginnie Mae's from your
Fannie Mae's, do some reading before you go on the interview.
(A bibliography, as well as a list of schools offering courses,
appears at the end of this chapter.)

You'll also feel more prepared if you rehearse for the interview. Have someone drill you with a list of questions you're
likely to be asked by the interviewer. The most frequently
asked questions include:

- Why should I hire you?
- What are your strongest abilities?
- How do your skills relate to our needs?
- What are you looking for?
- What would you like to know about us?
- Tell us something about yourself.
- Why are you looking for a job now?
- What are your strengths and weaknesses?
- Where do you want to be five years from now?
- Why do you want to work for us?
- What are your three major accomplishments?
- What have you disliked in jobs you've had?
- What kinds of people do you like to work with? What kinds
  frustrate you?
- How long before you can contribute?
- What has dissatisfied you about your performance in the
  past year?
- How long a commitment will you give us?
- What would be your ideal job?
- When are you available?
- What is your present salary?
- May we call your boss?
- What other positions have you interviewed for?

Not all interviews are for specific jobs. In a special type of
interview called the "information interview," job-seekers ask
to see important people in the business not for a job but merely
for advice and information.

Surprisingly, many busy people will gladly give you ten to

fifteen minutes of their time to chat about their business, their company, and their personal achievements; perhaps it's because being asked to give an expert opinion is a powerful form of flattery that few people can resist.

The primary goal of the information interview, then, is to learn something useful that will help you in your job search. You can also use the information interview to get referrals. And if the person you speak to is really impressed with you, the information interview may quickly turn into a job interview. (But that happens at the interviewer's discretion, not yours.)

To someone without an "uncle in the business" or other contacts on Wall Street, information interviews are a great way to get started. Here's an eight-step process for making the interview go as smoothly and productively as possible:

1. Begin with an "ice breaker." Mention the mutual friend who gave you the executive's name, talk about baseball or the weather, compliment the executive on his impressive offices. Spend about a minute on idle chatter so you two can get acquainted.
2. Next, tell the executive why you wanted the meeting. Say that you appreciate his taking time to talk to you, and let him know what you want to accomplish in the ten to fifteen minutes you will be spending together.
3. Give a brief description of your background, so he knows who and where you are right now.
4. Ask the questions you came to ask. They may be questions about the company, the industry, a specific job function, or even the executive himself (what he does, how he got his job, how he got started in the business).

   You can also try to uncover, discreetly, the executive's needs—his company's hiring policies, current positions open, openings that may come up in the next six months, and the type of candidates they're looking for. If the executive hints that you might be considered for one of these jobs, find out what you can do to improve your chances of being hired and when you should contact the executive to set up another meeting.
5. If it seems appropriate, ask for referrals. Get names, titles,

addresses, companies, and phone numbers. Ask if you can use the executive's name when you contact these referrals.
6. Don't take up more of the person's time than was originally scheduled for, unless he invites you to stay longer. If you see him looking at his watch, end the meeting sooner. Thank him for his time, and ask if you can keep in touch through an occasional phone call, letter, or business lunch.
7. Always send a thank-you note after every meeting. This is common courtesy, but it's done so rarely that it will make you stand out from the crowd.
8. Keep a file of contact sheets, one for each person you've talked with. The contact sheet should indicate the name, title, company, phone, address, date of meeting, comments on the meeting, and a record of follow-up conversations and contacts.

One of the questions most frequently asked at information interviews is "Do I need an MBA to work in the financial field?" The answer will vary, depending on the company and the job, but in most cases it's "no." Most entry-level positions do not require MBAs. And you can become the most successful broker or financial planner in the world without an advanced degree.

One career-changer who made the move to finance without having an MBA is Lucinda Reinold. Reinold, who has a Ph.D. in art history and wrote her dissertation on seventeenth-century Dutch painting, taught art history for a number of years at Carleton College and the University of the Pacific.

Frustrated by the low pay and predictability of her work, Reinold took courses in accounting, computer programming, precalculus mathematics, and economics to give herself a background for business. She did fund-raising work to make contacts. She also attended career seminars, and followed up by arranging personal meetings with some of the speakers—many of whom were women in the banking industry.

One of these women led Reinold to a job interview with Crocker Bank, where she was hired as a loan examiner. As part of the job, she spent three weeks in the Far East doing credit reviews for corporate and international loans.

After a year and a half at Crocker, Reinold was hired by Bank of America as a financial-services officer in the commercial-lending unit. When Reinold made the transition from art history to banking, she was thirty-five years old.[1]

When you are offered that first job, be aware of what the going rate is for a similar position in competitive firms. This knowledge can be your bargaining chip to a higher starting salary. As a beginner, you don't have the track record that would earn you high pay, so your only argument for a higher salary is "But this is the standard entry-level salary for financial-services reps!"

Another point to keep in mind: Surveys show that 80 percent of the people who turn down the first salary offer get a second offer . . . even if it's only a few hundred dollars higher.

FINANCIAL CAREERS: AN OVERVIEW

Here, in alphabetical order, are some of the best career opportunities in finance. Each area is described in brief; two of the hottest, best-paying careers—stockbroker and financial planner—are discussed in more detail later on.

- **Analyst.** The analyst is a *researcher* who studies companies in an attempt to predict their future prosperity. If accurate, such predictions can greatly benefit those who are advised to purchase a promising stock.

  There are two types of analysts: *sell-side* and *buy-side*. Sell-side analysts work for brokerage firms. They analyze stocks and tell traders and brokers which to sell.

  Buy-side analysts work for major corporate buyers of stocks, such as investment funds or pension plans. The buy-side analyst advises his or her company on which stocks will pay off so that they can get the most return on their investments.

  You usually need an MBA to become an analyst. The exception is if you've got strong *experience* in a specific industry that would be helpful in analyzing the financial soundness of companies and stocks in a particular field.

Many analysts specialize in one area—such as oil, retail, food, high-tech products. A starting salary for an analyst is generally $30,000 or so.

Succeeding in this job requires strong research skills. You have to know how to go beyond a company's annual report and publicity releases to understand their true financial position. And that sometimes takes investigative skills rivaling those of a private detective or newspaper reporter.

For instance, one analyst couldn't get into a briefing session on a particular company's new computer. So she hung out at a bar where the factory workers gathered after work. By eavesdropping, she learned that the company was having serious problems in the manufacture of the new computer. Based on this information, she told her superiors to sell off all their stock in the computer firm. They did, and her recommendation saved them a lot of money when the computer bombed—and the stock price fell—a few months later.

Analysts need good communications skills. It's not enough to uncover facts and make recommendations; analysts also have to prepare reports on the stocks they investigate. If the reports are boring or hard to read, the brokers and investors will ignore the analyst's reports— and hence the advice they contain.

The Financial Analysts Federation sponsors a program that trains students for a Certified Financial Analyst (CFA) degree. They are located at 1633 Broadway, New York, NY 10019; tel. (212) 957-2860.

- **Broker.** A career as a stockbroker is the "dream job" of the financial field. Brokers are salespeople who, for a commission, buy and sell stocks and bonds for their clients— corporations and individuals.

Income potential in this field is virtually unlimited, and the top brokers have annual incomes in the millions of dollars. Best of all, becoming a broker gives you a chance to work independently and does not require an MBA. Although more and more people are entering the field, there's always room at a brokerage house for a broker who can produce results. To become a "registered representative" (the industry term for a stockbroker), you must pass the Series 7 exam sponsored by the National Association of Securities Dealers (NASD). (For information on the test, contact NASD at 2 World Trade Center, 98th Floor, New York, NY 10048; tel. (212) 839-6200.)

- **Financial writer.** Money is a mystery to most people. So, if you understand the intricacies of economics and can explain them to people in a lively, interesting fashion, you probably qualify for a job as a financial writer.

The best preparation for this career is an MBA combined with experience in journalism. As a financial writer, you'll earn more than most mainstream writers and journalists, but less than the brokers, bankers, and investment advisors you write about.

There are three basic types of jobs for financial writers. The first is working as a financial journalist. There are dozens of financial publications, and all have staff writers who cover the financial aspects of various industries. Some of the top money magazines and papers are the *Wall Street Journal, Money, Barron's, Financial World, Institutional Investor, Forbes, Fortune,* and *Business Week.*

The second type of job is working as a staff writer for a financial firm. Banks, brokerage houses, insurance companies, and financial-services organizations publish a tremendous amount of literature on their products—everything from annual reports and feature articles, to letters to shareholders and news releases for the press, to newspaper advertisements and in-house newsletters. These publications are written not by brokers or managers but by professional writers with a feel for finance. Staff writers do not need an MBA.

The third job is publishing a financial newsletter. As the financial world becomes more confusing, these newsletters proliferate to fill the information gap. Although it's a crowded field and many newsletters fold after just a few issues, those that make it can generate a healthy income for their publishers. For financial writers who crave independence and a chance to earn more money, publishing a newsletter may be the answer.

Finally, if you tire of a writer's salary and want to earn

really big bucks, financial writing is an excellent entry to other, more lucrative jobs in finance. As you interview brokers, bankers, and corporate chiefs, you make contacts that may lead to a future position.

For example, a friend of ours started out as a financial reporter for *Variety*, covering the business side of the movie business. Bored with reporting, he went back to school at Harvard University, earned his MBA, and was hired by Warner Communications to do business planning for entertainment-related ventures. After a year at Warner, he was lured away at a higher salary to be the chief financial officer of a high-tech manufacturing firm in Silicon Valley.

- **Financial planner.** Financial planning is a relatively new career area. A financial planner is someone who helps his or her clients—usually individuals, sometimes businesses—plan their entire investment strategy. The financial planner helps his or her clients develop a financial goal, then advises them on what investments can best achieve that goal.

  Financial planners advise us about investments in much the same way that doctors advise us about our health and lawyers counsel us in legal matters. Many financial planners are also accountants, insurance agents, and lawyers. But anyone can become a financial planner by getting a degree or certificate in the field.

- **Lending officer.** A lending officer is a bank employee whose job is to evaluate whether the bank should give loans to the people and businesses that apply for them. Making loans is a major source of bank revenue, so there are many lending officers in every bank.

  This is one of the best entry-level opportunities in commercial banking. Many banks have training programs for lending officers, and you don't need previous financial experience to qualify. Some banks require an MBA, but many others do not.

- **Marketing or product manager.** Marketing is a relatively new field in the financial industry. It has grown in importance because of the diversity of financial services and the increasing competition among banks, brokerage houses, and insurance companies.

Financial marketing is divided into several areas: advertising, sales promotion, market research, new-product development, direct mail. But the field of marketing has always been open to beginners, and financial marketing is no exception.

Some banks and brokerage houses have entry-level marketing positions for college graduates. Others prefer to hire experienced marketing people with backgrounds in other industries—especially packaged goods, where marketing has always played a major role in the success or failure of such consumer products as soap, soda, detergent, and toothpaste.

There are many job opportunities in financial marketing. The *product manager* has overall responsibility for marketing a single "product" or "product line," such as options, direct investments, tax shelters, ERISA annuities, life insurance, mutual funds, municipals, money markets, income investments, or any one of a host of other investment vehicles.

The *marketing manager* provides marketing services to the various product managers. These services can include everything from market research and technical documentation to the design and creation of trade-show displays, sales literature, print advertisements, and slide shows.

Technology is playing an important role in financial-service marketing. Many of the larger banks have departments that specialize in the production and marketing of electronic-banking services, such as automated teller machines and banking-by-computer. Some of the larger brokerage houses are also exploring this technology.

- **Money manager.** The money manager, also known as a portfolio manager, handles the assets and investments of banks, pension funds, insurance companies, and other corporate funds. Some money managers are staff employees; many others are independents.

  Unlike the financial planner, who is limited to giving advice and taking orders, the money manager has much more control over the fund he manages. He can buy or trade stocks, bonds, and other investment vehicles without getting approval from his client or employer on every transaction. Some money managers may have to report to a vice president when they make major trades or buys; others make decisions at their own discretion.

As a money manager, your success depends on your performance. You will continue to manage your client's fund as long as you generate an acceptable return on your investment. In exchange, you'll be paid a fee based on a percentage of the amount of money you manage. This fee can range from 0.5 to 2 percent. On the other hand, if the fund does not prosper under your management, the client will quickly find someone else to do the job.

The best training for money management is to work as a broker. Money management is an excellent field for people who have an entrepreneurial streak and who like responsibility and independence.

- **Operations manager.** Operations is the best entry-level field in the financial industry. You don't need experience or an MBA. Yet an operations manager with a few years of experience can earn a six-figure annual salary, plus a bonus based on performance.

Operations involves managing the flow of work in a brokerage house or bank. The key to success in operations, according to Phil Caso, a former operations manager for Citicorp, is finding "faster and better ways to process work, manage people, and save money."

When you go after a job in operations, brush up on the jargon first. Know that *R & D* is not research and development but *receipt and delivery* of securities. *P & S* is not postscript; it's *purchase and sale.*

Most brokerage houses and banks are computerized. So a working knowledge of computers is a big plus to the entry-level operations candidate.

Some people use operations as a stepping stone to a job as a broker or trader. But many others find operations financially and personally rewarding in its own right and prefer this managerial type position to the more high-pressure world of selling and trading.

- **Salesperson.** There are many positions besides broker or trader in which one can make a lot of money selling financial products. *Wholesalers* are sales representatives who specialize in one type of investment, such as real-estate tax shelters. They generally cover a certain territory, so the job may entail a lot of travel. They also have to work with brokers and dealers at banks and brokerage houses.

Cash management is another sales opportunity, this one on the banking side. A *cash-management service* is any service that helps a customer manage his or her money more profitably or efficiently, and banks employ sales representatives whose job it is to sell these services to the bank's corporate customers.

Getting into financial sales requires an aggressive personality and some previous sales experience in another industry, such as industrial equipment or retailing. An MBA is not required.

- **Trader.** The secret of trading is simple: You buy low and you sell high.

What is being traded? Stocks, bonds, commodities, currency; anything with a value that frequently fluctuates. By buying a stock or commodity when it is worth $10 and selling when the price goes up to $13, you can make $3. Multiply that by tens of millions of transactions a day and you can quickly see how trading generates profit.

Of course, trading is a risky business. The stock you buy at $10 a share might go down to $1—and stay there. You can make $10,000 one day and lose twice as much the next.

Unlike stockbrokers, who earn a fixed commission regardless of whether the stock they recommend to their client does well or poorly, traders earn or lose money only according to how the trade goes. That's a major difference between the two.

Another big difference is that traders buy and sell according to their instincts, and they call their own shots. Brokers are really only advisers; their clients are ultimately the ones who make the decision to buy, sell, or pass.

A job as an order clerk can sometimes lead to a position as a trader. Order clerks are the ones who stand on the floor of the stock or commodities exchange and shout out buy and sell orders—a scene made famous by such films as *Trading Places.*

- **Underwriter.** Also called *investment banking,* underwriting is the process of helping a corporation create and sell financial products (usually a stock or bond; sometimes a commercial paper or other product) to raise money for growth and expansion.

  Corporate finance is hard to get into. You need an MBA unless you have strong experience in a particular industry. Once you're in, you'll work long and hard—seventy to eighty hours a week is not uncommon. In a recent interview with the *New York Times Magazine,* investment banker Felix Rohatyn was quoted as saying: "The day I don't put my business first is the day I'll be out of business." (Rohatyn is one of the top investment bankers in the country and earns more than two million dollars a year.)

  Investment-banking firms make their money in two ways. They get a fee for putting together a stock or bond deal. And they get a commission based on a percentage of the amount of stocks or bonds sold. They are makers of big deals and are very well paid for their services.

- **Venture capitalist.** This is a specialized job for which there is a limited number of entry positions.

  One way corporations raise money is through the sale of a stock or bond, as described above. But a second way is to raise money from private investors who are called venture capitalists. In exchange for investing their money in your company, the venture-capital firm becomes a part-owner of your business.

  It follows that they get a good return on their investment if your business flourishes; they lose their money if you fold. For this reason, venture-capital firms must carefully analyze the resources, assets, skills, talents, products, and sales potential of the companies seeking their money. A high degree of business knowledge and financial expertise is needed to make such assessments.

BROKERS: THE SALESPEOPLE

Becoming a stockbroker (known in the industry as a *registered representative)* is the most popular career path in finance. There are 130,000 stockbrokers in the United States, with 40,000 or more taking the qualifying exam every year.

The stockbroker used to be called "the customer's man" because he or she dealt with the customer's investments and executed stock and bond trades according to the customer's instructions. Today many stockbrokers call themselves "financial advisers" or "consultants" because they are advice-givers rather than mere order-takers, and because they handle a broader range of financial services.

You don't need an MBA or even a college degree to become a broker. The key qualification employers look for is an aptitude for sales. As a registered representative, you are a salesperson, and you must be able to work unsupervised, organize your own selling efforts, uncover and follow up leads, present products, work with customers, satisfy their needs, make cold calls, and deal with rejection. If you sell well, you'll be rewarded, because brokers are paid a commission based on sales.

Entry-level brokers work on salary until they've been trained on the job. For recent college graduates, the salary is minimal; it can be as little as $200 a week. If you are changing careers and can't afford a tremendous pay cut to make the move, some brokerage houses may pay you 75 percent of your present salary.

Once you've been trained—and that takes six months to a year—you go on straight commission. Usually you can draw a weekly paycheck against your commission. This draw can range from $200 to $1,000 a week, depending on your sales and your employer.

A rule of thumb is that a broker must bring in $100,000 a year in commissions before his firm begins to break even on the cost of hiring him and providing him with support services such as office space, telephones, research reports, and administrative staff. As a result, many brokerage houses will fire brokers who fail to meet the $100,000 mark. And some of the larger firms set $250,000 as the broker's minimum quota.

As you can see, stockbrokers can earn enviable incomes. If a person makes $80,000 a year, he or she is in the top 2 percent salary bracket in the country. But as a broker, earning $80,000 a year (gross) is considered a poor showing.

The percentage of commission the broker gets to keep increases in proportion to sales. If he brings in $150,000 a year or less in commissions, he gets to keep one-third, but if he brings in $1 million a year or more, he might keep 40 to 45 percent.

Only 1 percent of stockbrokers in this country bring in commissions of $1 million or more per year. Among these "superbrokers" are Mary Ellen Kay, of Becker Paribas, who generated $1.2 million in commissions in 1983, and Richard Greene, of Merrill Lynch, who brought in $4.2 million that same year. Overall, 1983 was a good year for brokers, with commissions hitting a record total of $3.7 billion.

There's an unfortunate "catch-22" involved in breaking into this business, however. You can't work as a stockbroker until you've passed a test called the NASD Series 7 General Securities Examination, but you won't be allowed to take the test unless you're sponsored by a brokerage firm!

The way around this paradox is to get hired by a firm that will train you in related areas until you've taken the test and can sell stocks and bonds. There are basically four types of companies you can work for: national wirehouses, regional brokers, small brokers, and discounters.

National wirehouses are the large brokerage houses, such as Merrill Lynch and Paine Webber. All the large firms have formal training programs for entry-level brokers.

Merrill Lynch, the nation's largest brokerage house, has four management-training programs for new college graduates: one in general assignment, one in securities analysis, one in operations management, and one in computer systems. In 1983, two thousand people applied to the general-assignment program, which can lead to, among other things, a position as a broker.

Unfortunately, Merrill Lynch had a limited number of openings and hired only forty of the two thousand applicants. And that's the problem with training; too many people applying for a limited number of spots makes it tough to break in.

A typical training program lasts anywhere from six to twelve months. Trainees spend one or two months in each of a number of different areas: sales, securities research, capital markets, operations. At the end of training, they choose an area, and, of course, many choose to be brokers.

The second type of brokerage firm is the regional firm, whose operation is restricted to one state or other geographic region (unlike national wirehouses, which have offices nationwide). These medium-size firms offer a mix of formal training and on-the-job experience.

The third option is to work for a small firm, which typically has one office. These firms can't afford year-long formal training programs; they need you to be productive right away. So if you go to work for a small brokerage house, you'll be given a lot of responsibility quickly and will have to learn on the job. This can, however, be the best education, provided there's someone at the firm willing to teach you as you go. You will probably start as an assistant to a broker, and if your broker is a friend and mentor, you can get ahead rather rapidly.

The fourth employment option is to work for a "discounter," such as Charles Schwab. Unlike regular brokerage firms, discounters do not offer advice but simply execute trades according to the customer's instructions. Because they do not spend time consulting with customers, discounters offer trading services at reduced commissions. Thrift institutions and banks also offer discount brokerage services. A discounter is not the best place to work if you want to develop the selling and consulting skills that are the core of being a successful broker.

Stockbrokers serve two basic markets: retail and institutional. The retail market consists of individual investors—people like us, you, and your Uncle Joe.

Most brokers serve the retail market for the simple reason that there are more people out there than corporations. Retail brokers generally have a large number of clients—anywhere from fifty to five hundred—with accounts ranging from $1,000 to $1 million or more.

The institutional market consists of banks, insurance companies, pension funds, and other large institutional investors. Brokers who serve this market may have only a handful of customers. But these accounts can range from $1 million to $50 million and more. Of the two markets, retail is easier to get into; institutional accounts are not all that plentiful.

In addition to choosing a market, you might also choose a specialty, such as blue-chip stocks, high-tech stocks, municipal bonds, options, or futures. Or, you might remain a generalist, offering your customers advice on a broad range of financial products.

But, in a sense, all brokers are specialists to some degree. There are more than six thousand stocks being traded in the United States today, and no broker can keep an eye on more than a small percentage of them. Mary Ellen Kay watches only twenty to thirty stocks at a time. Some brokers may track several hundred, but never more than that.

Keeping up with the market can be a taxing task. Here's how Ray Wax, a Wall Street stockbroker, described it to interviewer Studs Terkel:

> We're all hooked in. I'm watching every transaction. Everything that happens in the market I see instantaneously. I have a machine in front of me that records and memorizes every transaction that takes place in the entire day. . . .
> I watch eighteen million, twenty million shares pass the tape. I look at every symbol, every transaction. I would go out of my mind, but my eye has been conditioned to screen maybe two hundred stocks and ignore the others. I pick up with my eyes Goodrich, but I don't see ITT. I don't follow International Tel, I'm not interested in that. I don't see ITT, but I do see IBM. There are over thirty-two hundred symbols. I drop the other three thousand. Otherwise, I'd go mad. I really put in an enormously exhausting day.
> I'm up at six thirty. I read the *New York Times* and the *Wall Street Journal* before eight. I read the Dow Jones ticker tape between eight and ten. At three thirty, when the market closes, I work until four thirty or five. I put in a great deal of technical work. I listen to news reports avidly. I try to determine what's happening. I'm totally immersed in what I'm doing.[2]

Brokers do more than just watch tapes or computer screens, however. Most of a broker's time is spent calling customers and prospects on the telephone. One-on-one personal selling is the way in which brokers do business with old clients and find new ones. And the telephone is the most efficient tool for contacting the greatest number of people in a given day.

A top broker earned a million dollars in commissions in his first eighteen months on the job. His secret? He worked from 7:00 A.M. to 8:00 P.M. and made *four hundred* calls every day.

A college senior with no business experience was having trouble breaking into the brokerage business. He approached four firms and told the branch manager of each, "I will work in your office making cold calls, for free. If you are pleased with the results, hire me."

For each firm, the student made two hundred to three hundred calls over the course of several weeks. Each set of calls yielded fifty to sixty sales leads, which turned into two to three new customers for each brokerage firm. The student got job offers from all four companies—two in training, two as a beginning broker.

Marilyn Neckes, an entry-level broker with Broadchild Securities, started by making fifty to one hundred cold calls a day. Within a few months, she had eighty clients.

One of the central purposes of financial advertising and direct mail is to generate sales leads for brokers. The brokerage firms who advertise know they're more likely to sell to someone who has indicated interest by clipping a coupon or mailing a reply card than someone they call cold out of the phone book.

Zip magazine reports that stockbrokers typically call four of every ten sales leads generated by direct mail. Of the four leads, they sell two.

The most successful brokers don't rigidly stick to any single method of selling. They try different approaches to see what works and what doesn't. Everyone has his or her own style. Mary Ellen Kay of Becker Paribas wants total control of her clients' funds, while Merrill's Richard Greene prefers to make suggestions, explain his strategy, and let the client approve it before he acts.

Mary Kay won't take on a client who has less than $100,000 to spend. Greene sets no minimum.

Greene and Kay work out of major "money center" cities—

Kay from New York, Greene from Boston. But Francis Traynor, who is a million-dollar broker himself, prefers to work from lovely Pensacola Florida, where he can be close to the beaches and palm trees.[3]

Unlike the manager, whose success is measured by his title, salary, and his climb up the corporate ladder, the salesperson's success is measured by *sales*. Once you're a broker, you can build your career simply by being better and more successful at it. As one broker told us, "Sure, being a broker is a good entry for trading, management, or corporate finance. But most of us prefer to stick with being brokers, because the job has unlimited income potential."

FINANCIAL PLANNERS: THE ADVISORS

With today's deregulation and explosive growth in the financial industry, the services of an adviser who can guide you in managing your money are needed more than ever before. And that's where the financial planner comes in.

The financial planner is a personal investment adviser. Working one-on-one with ordinary people like you and us, the financial planner helps his or her clients set financial goals, assess their willingness to take risks, and make the investments that will help them achieve the goals they've set.

The demand for qualified financial planners is on the rise. "Ten years ago only the very rich used them," writes Nancy Dunnan in an article for *Living Anew*. "But due to today's complicated economy, more Americans are turning to this type of pro for guidance."

Janice Remer, a financial planner with Corpro, says the planner must be a combination of counselor, salesperson, and technician. Financial planners counsel clients on planning investment strategy. They then sell to their clients the financial services they've recommended. And the financial planner must have a technical understanding of how these services work and what the risks are.

Unlike a trader, whose only contact with the world may be

over a phone or computer terminal, financial planners work closely with a variety of people. They have to inspire trust and confidence in their clients. And they must consult other financial experts—bankers, actuaries, accountants, attorneys, trust officers, property and casualty advisers—to uncover the best investment opportunities.

The most important aspect of financial planning, according to Remer, is assessing the client's financial and psychological needs, then creating an investment strategy that meets those needs. "Sit down with the client and get a feel for his philosophy," Remer advises aspiring planners. "Don't just push one product. Get to know the person. Is he a risk-taker? Does he need income? Is he conservative?"

The financial planner must realize that every client is unique. A married couple in their sixties who are looking forward to a secure retirement have different financial goals than, say, a young, single person just starting his or her career. In the same way, a corporate executive's financial situation may be quite different than that of a free-lance writer or artist.

Good financial planners create investment strategies tailored to their clients' income, assets, emotions, and personality. Most strategies encompass six basic areas:

1. **Risk management.** Risk management is financial protection against disaster, accident, and disability. The basic investment vehicle is insurance.
2. **Retirement planning.** The goal of retirement planning is to allow a client to retire when he wants in the style he wants. The investment tools planners work with here are IRAs, Keoghs, and pension funds.
3. **Tax planning.** Tax planning helps clients "pay less to the IRS." If a client is in the 50-percent bracket, for example, one of every two dollars he or she earns goes to paying taxes. Even the average U.S. wage-earner spends two hours and forty-nine minutes of every eight-hour workday earning the money to pay federal, state, and local taxes. The financial planner must know how to use tax-free bonds, IRAs, and various tax shelters to lower the client's yearly tax payments.

4. **Business planning.** If a client owns his own business, or if his compensation is tied to his firm's success, he'll have special financial considerations that the planner can help him with.
5. **Estate planning.** The goal of estate planning is to lower the taxes paid on a client's estate when he or she passes away, so that the heirs get the most money possible.
6. **Investment planning.** Investment planning involves helping the client make the investments that will achieve his or her financial goals. These goals and investment strategies vary, depending on the client.

For a retired person, the best investment may be a conservative portfolio of blue-chip stocks, which yield a modest but regular income. On the other hand, a person who doesn't live off the dividends from his or her stocks and has extra money to invest might be better off investing a portion in high-risk stocks, where there's a chance of doubling or tripling the money quickly.

A self-employed person, burdened with large quarterly tax payments, will probably want Keoghs, tax-free bonds, real estate, and other tax shelters that reduce his or her tax payments.

It is the financial planner who advises the investor on how much money should be invested in each of these six areas. If the planner's advice is sound, the investor becomes prosperous.

As for the planner, he or she is compensated in any of a number of different ways. Financial planners that offer advice only but do not actually sell products usually charge an hourly rate ($100 per hour is average), a commission based on a percentage of the client's net worth or annual income, a flat fee (ranging anywhere from $500 to $5,000), or a combination of flat fee and commission.

Planners that act as brokers and sell stocks, bonds, and other products often charge both a flat fee ($300 to $3,000) plus a commission on every transaction (typically 8 to 8½ percent on mutual funds and 10 to 30 percent on tax shelters).

The best way to prepare for a career in financial planning is to go back to school and get a degree or certificate in the field.

A number of degree and certificate programs are listed at the end of this chapter. With most, you can keep your present job and take the courses at night. Some are even correspondence courses.

One of the most popular programs is the Certified Financial Planner (CFP) certificate offered by the College for Financial Planning in Denver, Colorado. Since it was launched in 1972, six thousand people have completed this program; nineteen thousand are now enrolled. Topics covered include life and health insurance, annuities, mutual funds, income-tax planning, retirement planning, options, convertible securities, futures, real estate, and tax shelters.

Before you enroll for the next semester, be aware that financial planning is a highly competitive area. Says Janice Remer, "Whenever there's a job opening, the company gets bombarded by résumés." To stand out from the crowd, make sure your résumé is crisp and professional in appearance and style, and that the content reflects your abilities and major accomplishments.

Networking also helps here. Go to meetings of professional societies, such as the International Association of Financial Planners. Make contacts. And follow up by phone and mail. A business card exchanged over a drink can often lead to a job three months down the road. Tailor your networking to making contacts at companies that hire financial planners. Three basic types of organizations do so: banks, brokerage houses, and insurance companies.

Many major banks (including Chemical Bank, Citibank, and Bank of America) offer financial-planning services to banking customers. In some banks, the financial-planning department is called the *private banking division* or the *trust department*.

Banks prefer to hire candidates with MBAs. Starting salaries range from the high twenties to the low thirties—less if you have no more than a bachelor's degree. In addition to salary, you might also receive a bonus based on performance.

Financial planners in banks don't have to go out and find customers, because the bank already has a built-in customer base. So if you are a financial planner who doesn't like attending sales meetings and making cold calls, a bank might be the best place for you.

A number of large brokerage houses also offer financial planning services. These firms often have formal training programs for entry-level planners.

In a bank, the focus is on consulting with the customer and helping him manage all aspects of his finances. In a brokerage firm, the emphasis is on selling products. So, in addition to his salary, the financial planner at a brokerage house receives a commission based on sales.

Insurance companies do things a bit differently. Their products are sold through branch offices run by insurance agents or brokers. Years ago, these insurance agents sold insurance only. But today many of them offer a broader range of services, including mutual funds and total financial planning.

Agents operate autonomously from their parent companies and act more like entrepreneurs than salaried employees. The agents develop their own sales leads and handle their own clientele. They are paid a straight commission based on sales.

By building your agency and taking on as much new financial-planning business as you can handle, your income can match those of the nation's top stockbrokers. And joining the million-dollar club isn't a bad way to live.

Required Reading for Wall Street Wizards

Books

Hirsch Organization. *The Directory of Exceptional Stockbrokers.* Write to the Hirsch Organization, 6 Deer Park Trail, Old Tappan, NJ 07675. The directory is published annually and costs $39.95; it profiles the country's 125 top stockbrokers.

Mayo, Herbert B. *Investments.* Hinsdale, Ill.: Dryden Press, 1983.

Porter, Sylvia. *Sylvia Porter's New Money Book for the Eighties.* New York: Avon, 1979. A comprehensive, 1,300-page layman's guide to personal money management by one of the most widely read financial writers in the world.

Sobel, Robert. *Inside Wall Street.* New York: W. W. Norton, 1977. Describes the Wall Street financial district and how it operates. Has chapters on the American Stock Exchange, the New York Stock Exchange, and investment banking.

Turner, Dennis. *When Your Bank Fails.* Princeton, N.J.: Amwell, 1983. The author predicts a collapse of our banking system and states his case convincingly. Although the book isn't easy to read, it will teach beginners in the field a lot about the basics of banking.

Victor, G., and Jerry S. Rosenbloom. *Personal Financial Planning.* New York: McGraw-Hill, 1983.

Periodicals

ABA Banking Journal, 345 Hudson St., New York, NY 10014; (212) 620-7200. Monthly magazine for the banking community.

American Banker, 1 State Plaza, New York, NY 10004; (212) 943-0400. Daily news tabloid covering banking and finance for the top management of banks and other financial institutions.

Barrons National Business and Financial Weekly, 22 Cortlandt St., New York, NY 10007; (212) 285-5243. Articles on industries and companies written with an investor's point of view.

Business Week, 1221 Sixth Ave., New York, NY 10020; (212) 512-2000. Weekly business magazine. Published by McGraw-Hill.

Commodities Magazine, 219 Parkade, Cedar Falls, IA 50613; (319) 677-6341. Monthly magazine for people who trade commodities.

Commodity Journal, American Association of Commodity Traders, 10 Park St., Concord, NH 03301; (603) 224-2376. Bimonthly tabloid for investors interested in commodity trading.

Finance: The Magazine of Money and Business, 25 W. 39th St., 15th Floor, New York, NY 10018; (212) 221-7900. Magazine for senior executives and decision-makers in the business and financial communities.

The Financial Security Digest, Robert White, Inc., P.O. Box 1928, Cocoa, FL 32923; (305) 632-8652. Billed as "the official journal of the American Association of Financial Professionals."

Financial World, 1450 Broadway, New York, NY 10018; (212) 869-1616. A news magazine for investors.

Forbes, 60 Fifth Ave., New York, NY 10011; (212) 620-2200. Weekly business magazine.

Fortune, 1271 Sixth Ave., New York, NY 10020; (212) 586-1212. Monthly business magazine.

Investor's Daily, 150 Broadway, Suite 811, New York, NY 10038; (212) 964-7380. Daily newspaper for investors.

Money, Time-Life Building, Rockefeller Center, New York, NY 10020; (212) 582-1212. Monthly magazine offering financial advice for upper-income readers.

The *New York Times,* Business Section, 229 W. 43rd St., New York, NY 10036; (212) 556-1234. Concise reports on the day's important business events.

Registered Representative, Plaza Publishing Co., Inc., 4300 Campus, Newport Beach, CA 92660; (714) 979-3666. Monthly magazine covering the securities industry for retail stockbrokers.

The *Wall Street Journal,* 22 Cortlandt St., New York, NY 10007; (212) 285-5000. The Bible of the financial community. A daily paper of business events.

Other resources

Borg-Warner. A toll-free hotline giving news updates of financial information. (800) 621-5445.

DowPhone. For a $25 annual subscription fee, DowPhone lets you use your push-button telephone to get instant information on the stock prices of over 6,500 companies, plus business news, market reports, industry reports, and government and economic news. Call (800) 257-0437 for details.

Standard & Poors. Stock reports on 3,500 companies. 25 Broadway, New York, NY 10004; (212) 208-8000.

Value Line Investment Survey. Detailed coverage and ratings of 1,700 stocks. 711 Third Avenue, New York, NY 10017; (212) 687-3965.

Wall Street Transcript. Weekly publications containing scores of brokerage house reports on individual companies. 120 Wall St., New York, NY 10005; (212) 747-9500.

Organizations of Interest to Financial Folks

American Association of Financial Professionals, Box 1928, Cocoa, FL 32923; (305) 632-8654. Trade association for financial professionals.

Financial Analysts Federation, 1633 Broadway, New York, NY 10019; (212) 957-2860.

International Association of Financial Planners, 5775 Peachtree Dunwoody Rd., Atlanta, GA 30342; (404) 252-9600 or 951-8410.

New York Futures Exchange, 20 Broadway, New York, NY 10004; (212) 623-4949.

New York Institute of Finance, 70 Pine St., New York, NY 10270; (212) 344-2900.

Where the Jobs Are

Wall Street hopefuls have many potential employers to choose from—
insurance companies, banks, brokerage houses, financial-service
firms. Listed below are some of the best places to work.

Ashwell & Company, 208 S. LaSalle, Suite 290, Chicago, IL 60604;
(312) 372-0070.

Bank of America, P.O. Box 37026, San Francisco, CA 94137; (415)
622-8277.

Bank of Boston, P.O. Box 1976, Boston, MA 02105; (617) 742-4000.

Bank of New York, 48 Wall St., New York, NY 10015; (212) 530-1784.

Bankers Trust, 16 Wall St., New York, NY 10015; (212) 775-2500.

Barclays Bank of New York, N.A., P.O. Box 200, Great Neck, NY
11022; (800) 632-4455.

Bevill, Bresler & Schulman Incorporated, Investment Bankers, 301
South Livingston Ave., Livingston, NJ 07039; (201) 994-4700.

Ehrlich Bober Advisors, Inc., Investment Management Services, 80
Pine St., New York, NY 10005; (212) 607-5700.

Brown & Company, 20 Winthrop Sq., Boston, MA 02110; (617) 742-
2600.

W. T. Cabe & Co., Inc., Rockefeller Center, 1270 Sixth Ave., New York,
NY 10020; (212) 541-6690.

Chase Manhattan, 1 Chase Manhattan Plaza, New York, NY 10081;
(212) 552-2222.

Chemical Bank, 277 Park Ave., New York, NY 10172; (212) 310-
6161.

Citibank, 399 Park Ave., New York, NY 10022; (212) 559-1000.

Davis/Zweig, 150 S. Wacker Dr., Suite 1920, Chicago, IL 60606;
(312) 388-8737.

Dewey Square Investors, One Financial Center, Boston, MA 02111;
(617) 654-6219.

Drexel Burnham, 55 Broad St., 6th Floor, New York, NY 10004; (212)
480-5188.

Dreyfus, P.O. Box 600, Middlesex, NJ 08846; (800) 872-5466.

European American Bank (EAB), 10 Hanover Sq., New York, NY
10015; (212) 437-4300.

The Equitable, Financial Services, 3490 Lawson Blvd., Oceanside, NY
11572; (800) 345-8540 (in Pennsylvania, 800-662-5180).

Fidelity Investments, 82 Devonshire St., Boston, MA 02109; (800)
225-6190.

First Albany Corporation, 90 John St., New York, NY 10038; (212) 619-5500.

First National Monetary Corporation, 4000 Town Center, 15th Floor, Southfield, MI 48075; (800) 221-2900 or 654-6110.

First National Trading Corporation, First Center Office Plaza, 26913 . Northwestern Hwy., 6th Floor, Southfield, MI 48034; (800) 551-5200.

Fleet Financial Group, 55 Kennedy Plaza, Providence, RI 02903; (401) 278-5800.

GIT Investment Services, Inc., 1655 N. Ft. Myer Dr., Arlington, VA 22209; (703) 528-6500.

Gruntal & Company, 14 Wall St., New York, NY 10005; (212) 267-8800.

Hertzfeld & Stern, 30 Broadway, New York, NY 10004; (212) 480-1800.

HHG, 29 Broadway, New York, NY 10004; (212) 962-0300.

E. F. Hutton, 1 Battery Park Pl., New York, NY 10004; (212) 742-5000.

IDS/American Express, Inc., Personal Financial Planners, IDS Tower, Box 9464, Minneapolis, MN 55440; (800) 437-4332.

Janney Montgomery Scott, 26 Broadway, New York, NY 10004; (212) 248-1500.

Josephthal & Company, 120 Broadway, New York, NY 10271; (212) 577-3000.

Kemper Financial Services, Inc., 120 South LaSalle St., Chicago, IL 60603; (312) 332-6472.

Kenneth Kass & Co., Inc., 147 Columbia Tpke., Florham Park, NJ 07932; (201) 966-1595.

Kidder Peabody, 10 Hanover Sq., New York, NY 10004; (212) 747-2000.

Lehman Brothers, 55 Water St., New York, NY 10041; (212) 558-1500.

Leventhal & Co., Inc., 25 Broadway, New York, NY 10004; (212) 425-6116.

Lind-Waldock, 30 South Wacker Dr., Chicago, IL 60606; (312) 648-1400.

Manufacturers Hanover Trust, 270 Park Ave., New York, NY 10017; (212) 286-6000.

Marsh Block & Co., Inc., 50 Broad St., New York, NY 10004; (212) 514-6400.

Merrill Lynch, 1 Liberty Pl., New York, NY 10080; (212) 637-7455.

Morgan Stanley, 1251 Sixth Ave., New York, NY 10020; (212) 974-4000.

Moseley, Hallgarten, 1 New York Plaza, New York, NY 10004; (212) 363-6900.

Neuberger & Berman Management, P.O. Box 4299, Boston, MA 02211; (800) 451-2507.

John Nuveen & Co., Inc., 61 Broadway, New York, NY 10006; (212) 668-9500.

Ovest Financial Services, Inc., 90 Broad St., New York, NY 10004; (212) 668-0600.

Pace Securities, Inc., 225 Park Ave., New York, NY 10017; (212) 490-6363.

Paine Webber, Inc., 140 Broadway, New York, NY 10005; (212) 437-2121.

Prescott Ball, 1 World Trade Center, New York, NY 10048; (212) 938-7000.

T. Rowe Price Associates, Inc., 100 East Pratt St., Baltimore, MD 21202; (301) 547-2000.

Prudential Bache, 100 Gold St., New York, NY 10292; (212) 791-1000.

RMJ, Government Securities, 130 John St., New York, NY 10038; (212) 668-5250.

Rose & Company Investment Brokers, Inc., 30 Rockefeller Plaza, New York, NY 10112; (800) 435-4000.

L. F. Rothschild, 55 Water St., New York, NY 10041; (212) 425-3300.

Salomon Brothers, 1 New York Plaza, New York, NY 10004; (212) 747-7000.

Charles Schwab Discount Brokerage, 120 Broadway, New York, NY 10272; (800) 542-4300.

Scudder, 345 Park Ave., New York, NY 10154; (212) 350-8370.

Shearson/American Express, 2 World Trade Center, New York, NY 10048, (212) 321-6000.

Donald Sheldon & Co., Inc., One Wall St., New York, NY 10005; (212) 747-9215.

Muriel Siebert & Co., Inc., 77 Water St., New York, NY 10005; (212) 743-2378.

Smith Barney, 1345 Sixth Ave., New York, NY 10105; (212) 399-6000.

The Vanguard Group of Investment Companies, 8 Penn Center, Suite 1025, JFK Blvd. and 27th St., Philadelphia, PA; (800) 523-7025 (in Pennsylvania, 800-362-0530).

Waterhouse Securities, Inc., 44 Wall St., New York, NY 10005; (212) 344-7500.

York Securities, 44 Wall St., New York, NY 10005; (212) 425-6400.

A Glossary of Financial Terms

American Stock Exchange. The second-largest securities exchange in the country. Located in New York City.

Arbitrage. In arbitrage, you buy an item in one market and sell it, at a profit, in another market. Items traded this way include stocks, bonds, foreign currency, gold, silver, and other commodities.

Bear market. A market that is declining because investors believe that stock prices are going to fall.

Beta. A measure of how a stock performs relative to the market as a whole.

Blue chip. A company with sound management, good resources, and growth potential.

Bond. A certificate that pays interest once or twice a year and is redeemable on a specific date—usually five years or more after the date of issue.

Broker. A person who buys and sells securities and commodities for a commission.

Bull market. A market that is advancing because investors believe that stock prices are going to go up.

Capital gains. Money made through the sale or exchange of capital assets, such as securities or real estate.

CD. An interest-bearing receipt payable to the depositor for funds deposited with a bank.

Commercial paper. Unsecured short-term promissory notes issued by corporations and sold to corporate and individual investors.

Commodity. A product that people trade for investment purposes, such as coffee, sugar, or cotton.

Corporate bond. Bond representing a debt of a corporation. They come in denominations of $1,000 and mature in ten to forty years.

Deferred annuity. An annuity contract in which the annuity doesn't start until after a specified period.

Discretionary account. An account in which a stockbroker can buy and sell stocks for a client without consulting him or her.

Dividend. Portion of corporate profits paid for each share of stock.

Equity. The current value of an investor's property or securities.

Fannie Mae. Nickname for the Federal National Mortgage Association, an independent agency that purchases mortgages from banks, insurance companies, and other financial institutions to sell them as investments.

Ginnie Mae. A security backed by mortgages insured or guaranteed by the federal government.

Government securities. Securities issued by U.S. government agencies but not guaranteed by the federal government.

Growth stock. A "hot" stock whose value is expected to increase continuously over an extended period of time.

IRA. Individual retirement account, an individual pension account for which contributions are tax deductible.

KEOGH. A tax-qualified retirement plan established for self-employed individuals and nonincorporated businesses. Contributions to the KEOGH are tax-deferred until the account begins paying benefits at retirement.

Leverage. The power to earn or lose large sums on an investment.

Liquid. A liquid investment is one in which an investor can easily get his or her money back.

Money market. An investment vehicle that makes high-interest securities available to the average investor who wants immediate income and a relatively safe investment.

Municipal bond. Bond issued by a state, county, city, town, or village. Interest paid on these bonds is tax-exempt.

Mutual fund. A professionally managed portfolio of stocks.

New York Stock Exchange. The largest and most prestigious securities exchange in the world.

Option. An agreement to buy or sell a security or commodity within a set time and according to specified guidelines.

Over the counter (OTC). Security not listed or traded through one of the regular stock exchanges.

P/E ratio. The ratio of a stock's price to the company's earnings per share.

Penny stock. Stocks that sell at less than $1 a share.

Quotron. A machine stockbrokers use to get timely, accurate information on stock prices.

Savings account. A bank account from which money can be withdrawn by passbook but not by check.

Savings bond. U.S. savings bonds are available in face-value denominations ranging from $50 up to $10,000, and are sold for one-half their face value. They mature in ten years.

SEC. Securities and Exchange Commission. An agency established by Congress to protect investors.

Security. Stocks and bonds.

Security exchange. An organization that provides a market for the trading of bonds and stocks.

Stock. A share of a corporation.

Stock market. The buying and selling of stocks for profit.

Tax shelter. An investment vehicle that allows the investor to legally avoid paying a portion of income tax by taking advantage of current tax regulations and IRS rulings.

10-K. Detailed financial statement that companies must file each year with the Securities and Exchange Commission.

Thrift institutions. Mutual savings banks, savings-and-loan associations, and credit unions.

Utility. A publicly owned facility, such as a gas company or power plant.

Zero coupon bond. A bond sold at a big discount from its face value and redeemed at full value at maturity.

Executive Recruiters Who Hunt Heads on Wall Street

Al-Dor Personnel Agency, 150 Broadway, Suite 605, New York, NY 10038; (212) 349-5440.

Argyle Personnel Agency, 170 Broadway, Room 409, New York, NY 10038; (212) 233-3555.

Bankers Search Inc., P.O. Box 15203, Stamford, CT 06901; (203) 348-4935.

William H. Brawley Associates, P.O. Box 486, New Canaan, CT 06840; (203) 966-5697.

Chas Associates, 170 Broadway, New York, NY 10038; (212) 227-7804.

Cornwall Personnel Agency, Inc., 180 Broadway, 3rd Floor, New York, NY 10038; (212) 349-2520.

Creative Search Affiliates, 1385 York Ave., New York, NY 10021; (212) 734-5323.

Cross Personnel Agency, 150 Broadway, 9th Floor, New York, NY 10038; (212) 227-6505.

Drum Personnel, 150 Broadway, New York, NY 10038; (212) 233-7550.

Jacquelyn Finn & Susan Schneider Associates, Inc., 1625 Eye St. NW, Suite 822, Washington, D.C. 20006; (202) 822-8400.

Gilda Gray Personnel Agency, 150 Broadway, Suite 1701, New York, NY 10038; (212) 964-9100.

Richard Gregory Personnel Agency, 160 Broadway, Suite 1105, New
York, NY 10038; (212) 349-1300.

Interlangue International, Inc., 41 E. 42nd St., New York, NY 10017;
(212) 949-0170.

Kling Personnel Agency, 180 Broadway, New York, NY 10038; (212)
964-3640.

Michael P. Maloney and Associates, 56 Pine St., 13th Floor, New
York, NY 10005; (212) 425-7311.

R. J. Mastro, 150 Broadway, Suite 1014, New York, NY 10038; (212)
267-5200.

Metcalf, Milazzo Personnel Agency, Inc., 150 Broadway, Suite 1102,
New York, NY 10038; (212) 962-5300.

MVP Personnel & Associates, 150 Broadway, Suite 1005, New York,
NY 10038; (212) 571-1830.

Prescott and James Personnel Agency, 170 Broadway, Suite 910, New
York, NY 10038; (212) 227-9300.

J. Anthony, Randolph Associates, Inc., Suite 1801, 50 Broad St., New
York, NY 10004; (212) 943-2060.

Scott Personnel Agency, Inc., 181 Broadway, New York, NY 10007;
(212) 227-5150.

Rita De Silvio Associates, Inc., 150 Broadway, Suite 1502, New York,
NY 10038; (212) 349-6585.

Staam Personnel Agency, Inc., 150 Broadway, Suite 501, New York,
NY 10038; (212) 732-6500.

Staat Personnel Agency, 15 Maiden La., Suite 801, New York, NY
10038; (212) 964-2733.

Steadfast, 160 Broadway, Suite 603, New York, NY 10038; (212) 374-
1292.

Winston Agency, 535 Fifth Ave., New York, NY 10017; (212) 557-
5000.

Educational Programs in Financial Planning

Following are some educational institutions that offer a mix of degree
and nondegree (certificate) programs in financial planning and related
subjects:

Adelphi University, Garden City, NY 11530; (516) 294-8700. Certificate: Certificate in Financial Planning. Degrees: B.S. in Management and Communications (with four courses in financial planning).

The American College, 270 Bryn Mawr Ave., Bryn Mawr, PA 19010; (215) 896-4500. Certificates: Chartered Life Underwriter (C.L.U.), Chartered Financial Consultant (C.F.C.).

Boston University/Metropolitan College, 755 Commonwealth Ave., Boston, MA 02215; (617) 353-4496. Certificate: Certificate in Investment Planning.

Brigham Young University, 395 JKB, Provo, UT 84601; (801) 378-1211. Degrees: B.S. Business Management with concentration in finance, B.S. in Family Science with concentration in Family Financial Planning and Counseling.

California State University at Long Beach, School of Business, Dept. of Finance, Long Beach, CA 90840; (213) 498-4569. Proposed courses and major in Personal Financial Planning.

University of California, Berkeley Extension, 2223 Fulton St., Berkeley, CA 94720; (415) 642-4111. Certificate: professional designation in Personal Financial Planning.

University of California, Davis Extension, Davis, CA 95616; (916) 752-0880. Certification: professional designation in Personal Financial Planning.

University of California, Los Angeles Extension, Dept. of Management and Business, P.O. Box 24901, Los Angeles, CA 90024; (213) 825-7031. Certificate: professional designation in Personal Financial Planning.

The College for Financial Planning, 9725 Hampden Ave., Suite 200, Denver, CO 80231; (303) 755-7101. Certificate: Certified Financial Planner (C.F.P.).

Drake University, Cole Hall, Room 204, Des Moines, IA 50311; (515) 271-3921. Degree. B.S.B.A. in Finance with concentration in Personal Financial Planning.

Georgia State University, College of Business, Dept. of Insurance, University Plaza, Atlanta, GA 30303; (404) 658-3840. Degrees: M.B.A. and Ph.D. with major in Insurance and concentration in Financial Planning.

Golden Gate University, 536 Mission St., San Francisco, CA 94105; (415) 442-7272. Certificates: Certified Financial Planner. Degrees: B.S. and M.S. in Financial Planning, M.B.A. in Finance or Management with a specialization in Financial Planning. Also located at 818 West 7th St., Suite 1001, Los Angeles, CA 90017; (213) 623-6000.

Kirkwood Community College, 6301 Kirkwood Blvd. SW, P.O. Box 2068, Cedar Rapids, IA 52406; (319) 398-5411. Certificate: Money Management Adviser.

New York University, School of Continuing Education, 50 W. 4th St.,
Shimkin Hall, New York, NY 10003; (212) 598-3052. Degree
program in financial planning.

San Diego State University, 3092 Lloyd St., San Diego, CA 92119;
(714) 265-5200. Degrees: B.B.A. with major in Finance and
concentration in Financial Services, M.S. in Business Administration with concentration in Financial Services.

University of Sarasota, 2080 Ringling Blvd., Sarasota, FL 33577; (813)
955-4228. Degrees: B.B.A. and M.B.A. with Financial Planning
major.

Source: J. William Mize, "How CPA's Can Enter Financial Planning and Expand Their Roles as Financial Professionals," *The Financial Professional,* March–April 1984, pp. 54–55.

Gourmet Food

You're the wrong Paul
You're from Gaul, Paul
Cooked your goose, Bocuse?
Try gumbo stew, Paul!
Like at K-Paul
It's Cajun's day, Paul
And *nouvelle* is *outré*.
So fry some red fish,
A dirty rice dish—
Welcome down home, *mon ami!**

Even if your name isn't Paul—like Paul Bocuse of France, or Paul Prudhomme of K-Paul's Kitchen in New Orleans—you can still be a part of America's love affair with gourmet food.

America is in the midst of its latest food craze—celebrating its roots. Suddenly, everything is Carolina ribs, Tex-Mex barbecue, and Boston clam chowder. Sushi? Chocolate-chip cookies? Croissants? Fondue? Is there any end to our infatuation with gourmet food?

The image of the indomitable, hard-to-please chef who cares about perfection as much as he does about food is fast becoming American legend. Specialty food shops offering take-out gourmet fare bring smiles to the faces of busy professionals in New York, San Francisco, Dallas, and Detroit. Wholesalers such as Mrs. Fields and her colleague-in-cookies David (David's Cookies) Liederman have shown their brilliance at putting all their eggs (and flour, milk, and chocolate) in one

*With apologies to the lyricist of "It's All Right With Me" basket and then watching the basket. Caterers have become culture heros, competing with each other in a type of gastronomic *Chariots of Fire*.

Where can you fit in? Many places. But the most glamorous jobs—and those that are the most competitive—are working with the owners of the top restaurants, the top caterers, the top wholesalers. By carefully studying how a restaurant with the consistent quality of an Oyster Bar (New York) or an Ernie's (San Francisco) does business, you can start preparing for the day when you'll open your own restaurant. By seeing the planning, preparation, and follow-up of an efficient catering operation, you'll learn that great catering involves more than just turning out dandy hors d'oeuvres. You may want to pursue your interest in a career in the restaurant or catering business by enrolling in an intensive program like the Culinary Institute of America, or in a less intense course at a local school. This chapter tells you what preparation is needed.

The first thing you have to do is develop your sensitivity to food—its appeal, its taste, its combinations, its history, its cost. You'll find that America has always had good food and grand restaurants. The image of Mama stirring the pot all day or spending a whole morning rolling out the dough for cookies or making cake frosting without help from a mix is emblematic of turn-of-the-century America. The quality of American food began to decline around the time of World War I, and by World War II had reached an all-time low. The postwar generation didn't see any sense in spending all day cooking and all night eating.

TV dinners were born. Sara Lee started. At the same time, we discovered Cantonese food, teriyaki, tacos. We moved from Fannie Farmer to James Beard, Julia Child, and Craig Claiborne. The restaurant review became a standard item in many American newspapers.

The early 1970s brought us *nouvelle cuisine,* and suddenly everyone was lightening the sauces, preparing vegetables el dente, and avoiding red meat. Nouvelle cuisine, the American Bicentennial, the rediscovery of our own roots all led us to the New American Cuisine—a celebration of native American foods like crab cakes, pumpkin soup, or Virginia ham.

An appreciation of good food—like a sensitivity to great

drama, literature, or photography—is a prerequisite for would-be cooks as well as for the managers of food operations. Food people will tell you that such sensitivity is born within you, but it is probably also molded by one's eating experiences, cooking experiences, and what one reads in restaurant reviews and gourmet-food magazines. Do you care if your salad dressing caresses each leaf of Romaine or sits, soggily, at the bottom of your salad bowl? Do you bristle when a waiter is so untrained and inexperienced that he inevitably asks, "Now, who gets the red snapper?" Do you care about the ritual of brewing a fine cup of coffee? Or do you call chocolate mousse "chocolate pudding"? Food people craft fine meals the way an author crafts fine sentences. If this type of meticulousness seems ridiculous to you, you won't be very happy in the world of gourmet food.

CATERING

Catering, unlike wholesaling, involves dealing directly with a client. This business is more than food; it is a service. A personable manner, a good head for details, and an enterprising personality are as valuable to a caterer—more valuable—than a certificate from the Cordon Bleu or any other fine cooking school.

Caterers do more than cook. They may handle a wide variety of services for various functions, including weddings, bar mitzvahs, office parties, fund-raising events, banquets, museum openings, theater openings, and private parties. In fact, caterers who work in a city can build a business in just one office building—handling everything from baby showers to client lunches to Christmas parties. You can lock up a whole neighborhood, including arts organizations, religious groups, and any other community activities at which people congregate.

Now, exactly what type of person gets into the catering business? Basically, there are three types of people. The first are people already in the food business—food-service people, dieticians, nutritionists, home economists, deli owners, restaurateurs. These people, active either in food preparation or in sales, may see catering as glamorous and more specialized than running a restaurant or managing a cafeteria.

The second type of person who goes into catering is the retiree or the housewife. These people may find catering stimulating, or may want to see if they can make money with a skill they enjoy.

The third category is simply anyone who leaves a regular job because he or she feels that there must be a better way than working for a boss nine to five. These entrepreneurs look around them and see a world full of caterers who seem to be doing well—going to parties, meeting people, and cooking exotic cuisines.

But before you sign up for the twenty-one-month chef-training course at The Culinary Institute of America in Hyde Park, New York, or send a résumé to your neighborhood caterer, take a look at some of the realities of the catering business.

As a caterer, you spend 90 percent of your time selling, planning menus, and meeting customers, and only a small percentage of your time cooking. It's fun to be asked for your expert opinion about which foods may be appropriate for a wedding or what flowers are right for a wine tasting (unscented), but don't lose sight of the fact that people will pick your brains before signing you up. Caterers soon learn to charge for their planning as well as their cooking. After all, they're experts. It's their job to know, for example, that flowers cut below eye level are appropriate for an intimate dinner party; to know who stands where on a receiving line.

If you prefer to start a catering business rather than be an apprentice to a caterer, you'll have to investigate the types of permits you need. In New York City, for example, you must have a license from the health department. Also, the catering space must be commercially zoned (i.e., you can't work out of your home kitchen). You'll need worker's compensation, disability, and unemployment insurance.

With eagerness, a willingness to learn, experience in cooking, and an ability to deal with all types of people, you can land a first catering job. You can consult local newspapers to see which caterers advertise, stop in to apply to the ones you are interested in, and check the phone book under "caterers" to see if there are others that sound interesting. You'll find that the more successful the caterer is, the less he or she will be involved in actually cooking the food. When a caterer becomes successful, he or she generally handles more and more nonfood items. The caterer may be assigned to get the invitations printed or the flowers arranged or the utensils rented. The caterer may also be called upon to provide everything from matchbooks to menus, from magicians to girls who pop out of cakes and shout, "Happy Birthday!"

As you move up in the field, your range of contacts will expand. You'll plan parties on yachts . . . at museums . . . in movie theaters . . . at town houses. Unfortunately, on New Year's Eve, when everyone is running around kissing everyone, you probably won't be kissed. After all, who kisses the *help*?

So catering is a glamorous but very mixed bag. You may want to start in the business by joining a small caterer and learning the trade firsthand. That way, you can practice your cooking and your selling skills while apprenticing.

Top caterers—such as New York's Glorious Foods—are in constant demand. If your food is great and you know how to sell, you can name your own price. And by marking up (everything except liquor; it's illegal to mark up liquor), you can earn $20,000 to $50,000 a year—even more.

As an additional source of experience, you may want to find a mentor among the owners of gourmet stores in your area (see pages 140-141.). A great gourmet store helps acquaint you with the finest provisions and food vendors. By asking good questions, you can pick up tips on which foods are most popular, how people shop for food, what type of catering business is most common in your area.

CHECKLIST: QUESTIONS TO ASK YOURSELF BEFORE YOU START YOUR CATERING BUSINESS

Imagine yourself in this scenario: You want to start a catering business. You've had experience in planning luncheons at your local social club. Everyone adores your Caesar salad, coq au vin, and chicken in chutney sauce or chile. You find that you are already giving lots of free advice to people who are planning dinner parties, office parties, and Christmas parties.

You have begun thinking about how you could set up shop as a caterer, but you're unsure as to how your skills will transfer to the *business* of catering. Also, you're afraid that you may not be thinking of all the things you should be thinking about as you begin to construct a plan for your business.

Here, then, is a helpful list of some of the major questions you should be considering. In some cases, we've even tried to help you "think aloud" about who you'd ask for help or how you'd solve a particular problem.

Where should my catering business be located? Although many caterers begin their professional lives by using their own kitchens, in some states this practice is illegal. You'll probably need a place of business zoned for a food operation. Before signing a lease on a store, have a feasibility study done. Check important details such as nearby foot traffic, population density of the area, local competition, and the rent you'll have to pay.

Will I have the skills to succeed? Only you know the answer to this, but don't underestimate yourself. Your skill at managing your own kitchen, budgeting, cooking, and planning are a good starting point. You'll have to become familiar with the ways in which you can promote your business, and learn to do the kind of hard thinking that businesspeople do.

Start thinking about different kinds of promotion. You have personal friends and acquaintances, plus those of your family. You may be able to produce inexpensive fliers for distribution throughout the neighborhood. Perhaps the local newspaper will run a press release about an interesting aspect of your operation. Or you could send a brief newsletter about your business to potential clients. Word of mouth will provide you with lots of free publicity if you take the initiative. Let people know that you're in business. In the beginning, give free demonstrations of your culinary skill just to give people a taste of your talent.

Thinking like a businessperson comes with practice. Will you feel comfortable asking for half of your fee in advance? You'd better! Because a last-minute cancellation could literally leave you holding the bag. In fact, if you are laying out money to rent utensils and other equipment for a party, you may need to ask for *more* than half of your fee in advance. (The other half should be collected on the day of the catering function itself.)

How much capital will I need before I begin? Again, the answer will vary widely. Most caterers agree that it's wise to raise more capital than you think you'll need, because there are endless possibilities for emergency expenses. Talk to an experienced accountant or business planner to estimate how much money you would need to have on hand if you didn't show a profit during your first six months or year in business. Being undercapitalized is a great mistake.

The U.S. Small Business Administration can help you figure out how much capital your operation will require. Call the SBA office nearest you and request a copy of "Starting and Managing a Small Business of Your Own." The SBA will give you guidelines for a loan, a schedule of prebusiness workshops held in your region, and advice about developing a workable business plan.

The SBA also sponsors two organizations that offer help from people who have been successful in your business field: SCORE (the Service Corps of Retired Executives) and ACE (the Active Corps of Executives).

What hidden costs will there be when I move into my location? Rent, as you probably know, is just the beginning. You'll need utilities: telephone and electricity, at the very least. You will probably need to post a security payment as well as rent (the amount of security needed varies widely). And there may well be remodeling costs. Remodeling is necessary to accommodate a space to the particular needs of your business, but it may also be required to meet health-department regulations governing such matters as kitchen specifications, floors, ventilation, and cleanliness.

Remodeling costs can be saved if you are willing and able to do some of the work yourself. But even if you do, you'll still need to buy paint, brushes, lighting fixtures, and plumbing supplies.

Will there be fees for licenses? Yes. You'll need to check with local authorities to find out the licenses and permits you'll need. Don't forget that such utilities as telephone and electricity may require deposits before they become operational.

How will I know what equipment I'll need? Start by making a comprehensive list of all of the equipment you'll need. Then ask for the advice of people who have had experience in your field to see what you've left out. You should try to think of everything—from napkins to baking pans to the van you may need to deliver the food. Make a second list of those items that you'd prefer to rent. It often makes good sense to rent some of the more expensive equipment, at least when you are starting out.

How do I price my services? Only experience will teach you what things *really* cost and how much you need to charge to make a profit. Your fee will depend, of course, on the menu, the services you are providing, the number of people attending, and the fees of local competitors. Many caterers find it easy for their clients to focus on a per-person price, which includes the miscellaneous expenses and food expenses within it. So, for example, if you charge $15 per person for a cocktail party, the more people who attend, the higher your profit should be. The fewer people there are at a function, the higher the per-person costs will be.

If you are expected to bring glassware or utensils, or to provide bartenders, you must figure in those costs as well as a mark-up on each service you provide. Preparation time and planning time are also real costs that must be figured into your per-person rates.

How will I find employees to help out during busy times? Most caterers build a network of helpers who can work on an as-needed basis. In New York City, actors are one source of part-time help. For suburbanites and rural caterers, college students provide a pool of people. You can also use local bulletin boards, newspapers, and word of mouth to find help with cooking, serving, and clerical duties.

What if I (gasp!) poison someone? Then you've definitely lost a customer. Shop around for insurance that offers you full coverage for such mishaps at low rates. Start your search by speaking with your current insurance person as well as by asking other caterers how they handle insurance.

I'm still concerned that there are costs we're leaving out. Are

there? Yes. Food, supplies (everything from paper towels to brooms), financial advice, legal advice. You'll probably be paying estimated taxes on a quarterly basis, so you'll want to ask your accountant how to set up those payments. Advertising and publicity costs can be substantial at the beginning. Let's run through the types of costs that initial publicity and advertising might entail:

- A flier—very simple, one page, black ink on white paper—could cost from $100 to $300 to produce (assuming you write it yourself and need fewer than five thousand copies).
- A press release will cost you the stamps it takes to reach the media. But compiling a list of suitable radio stations, TV stations, and magazines could take some time and research.
- Advertising costs depend upon the media you have in mind for the ads. Small display ads can be produced for under $200, but the cost of ad space in a magazine will vary widely. Local "shopper" newspapers are relatively inexpensive advertising vehicles. The best advertising, of course, is word of mouth from satisfied customers who have attended a function you've catered.

What other things should I keep in mind? You'll need to keep abreast of food and drug laws regarding additives, preservatives, and other food products, such as saccharin.

Sample Catering/Food Store Promotions

The following three promotional materials are good examples of how a food operation can present its best face to the public. The press release (first page reproduced on page 121), letter to potential catering clients, and flier appeal to different audiences.

The press release was sent to newspapers, magazines, radio shows, and TV talk shows; the catering letter was sent to food-service people and office managers at large companies; the flier was distributed on street corners one day when the streets were particularly crowded due to an event in Central Park.

These promotions, although written for a New York City food operation, may spark ideas for your own promotion, however different

Abbondanza

1647 Second Avenue, New York 10028, (212)879-6060

Contact:
          THE COMMUNICATION WORKSHOP,   East 85th Street, New York 10028

For immediate release:

          ABBONDANZA, MANHATTAN'S FIRST ROSTICCERIA, OPENS ON UPPER

          EAST SIDE--ABUNDANT DELICACIES WITH AN ITALIAN ACCENT

NEW YORK, NY, May 18th--In Italian, Abbondanza means abundance. And
Abbondanza is the perfect word to describe Manhattan's first
"rosticceria," which officially opens on May 18, 1981.

A rosticceria is a store which features cooked foods prepared on the
premises, along with a variety of other entrees which may be purchased
for eating at home.

Abbondanza offers--for the first time--truly authentic Italian dishes
prepared in an open kitchen for all to see. Owner Lou Galterio explains
his concept this way: "People think of Italian food as just pizza,
pasta and provolone. I want them to see that Italian food is just as
sophisticated as French food--if not more."

To ensure that Abbondanza's offerings would be Italian--and not
Italian-American--Lou Galterio imported a chef who spent more than 30
years heading up the kitchens of Italy's finest hotels.

                              (MORE)

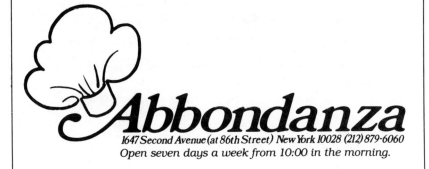

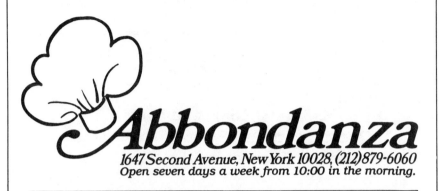

Abbondanza
1647 Second Avenue, New York 10028, (212) 879-6060
Open seven days a week from 10:00 in the morning.

The Abbondanza recipe for a perfect time in Central Park:
fair weather, a fine event and festive picnic pleasures from Abbondanza.

Menu Suggestions

Sliced Prosciutto and
  Mozzerella Roll

*

Insalata de Mare   (Seafood Salad)
Caponata   (Eggplant, Onion
                    and Spices)
Fugiolini   (String Beans
                    with Bermuda
                    Onion in
                    Vinaigrette)

*

Walnut Bread
Fruits in Brandy
Italian Butter Cookies
Thermos of Espresso
  (You provide the thermos.)

Events in Central Park

New York Philharmonic
July 29, August 5 & 12
The Great Lawn (81st St.), 8:00 pm

Grand Opera
July 2, 9, 16, 23, & 30
The Bandshell, 8:30 pm

Shakespeare-in-the-Park
The Tempest: June 26-July 26
Henry IV, Part I: July 29-August 30
Delacorte Theater (81st St.)
8:00 pm, Tuesday-Sunday
6:15 ticket distribution

Dance Festival
September 3-13
Delacorte Theater, 8:00 pm

If you're planning a get-away weekend, remember that Abbondanza
will make up a package of delights including cheeses, appetizers,
entrees and desserts for you to enjoy—or as the perfect house gift.

your location and potential customers may be. For example, a flier can be created to capitalize on a local cultural event; a press release can be written to focus on a new service you offer customers; a letter to potential catering customers can be timed to the Christmas season.

Caterers' Commandments:
Questions to Ask Prospective Clients Before Deciding on the Menu . . .

Comment

1. "When is the party?"

A lot of people are shoppers. They may be thinking that one day they'll need a caterer for their son's bar mitzvah or their daughter's wedding. By asking this question, you'll start to separate the shoppers from the buyers. Be courteous to both shoppers *and* buyers.

2. "How many people are you expecting?"

Before you start talking price, menu, and so forth, find out whether you'll be serving four or four hundred. It will give you a guideline as to what is physically, financially, and gastronomically possible.

3. "Where will the party be held?"

In a home? A hall? Yankee Stadium? The physical surroundings will suggest not only the mode of service but also what you'll need besides food. Caterers make a lot of money by providing waiters, glassware, floral arrangements, entertainment, tables, liquor, and many other party accessories.

4. "What's the occasion for the party?"

A crucial question. The answer will set the tone for the whole affair.

5. "What kind of party will it be?"

What style? Buffet? Cocktail party? Sit-down dinner? If someone is planning a five-hour cocktail party, it's up to the caterer to pipe up, "Don't you think we should feed the people?" Cocktail parties last two hours, not six.

6. "What time of day will the party be held?"

Naturally, the time will suggest food possibilities and what type of meal is appropriate.

7. "What else can we provide?"

Since most caterers break even on the food, they try to provide other services. Of course, everything is marked up: A fork that you rent for 25¢ can be provided for 30¢. You can provide waiters, hat-check attendants, glassware—almost anything. As mentioned before, though, you can't mark up liquor. Most municipalities strictly prohibit caterers from selling liquor at a profit.

8. "What kind of kitchen facilities will be available?"

This consideration can also affect your choice of menu. Not all occasions will allow you to prepare 100 percent of the food ahead of time; you can't concoct a five-course dinner for thirty people without use of a roomy, well-equipped kitchen. So before you start planning for chocolate soufflé, be sure there's a good oven at hand.

9. "Do you have any particular foods in mind?"

Clients just love to keep you guessing. Most people know what they'd like, but they first want to hear your ideas. Still, this question helps them focus on specifics.

10. "Do you have particular food favorites . . . or foods you hate? Do you have any dietary restrictions?"

If question number 9 draws a blank, you may wish to probe about the client's own favorite foods. It's also important that you get a list of food he or she hates. People are funny about food ("Oh my God! Is that a *caper* in the salad? Throw the whole thing out! I can't abide capers!") As for restrictions, unless you're catering a party for overweight kosher diabetics, you may not have to worry about making each dish salt-free, fat-free, and sugar-free. But it's still a good idea to offer a choice to people who are perhaps avoiding meat or sugar ("I'll need a wedding cake . . . but it can't have any sugar, okay?").

Hot Caterers

Catering has become big business in many cities across the country. The following list mentions a few of the more prominent American caterers. You might want to speak with them to find out how they got started and how they run their business:

Bennie Ferrell Catering Co.
4141 Hollister
Houston, TX 77080
(713) 460-0480

Columbia Catering
1776 E. Jefferson Rd.
Rockville, MD 20852
(301) 231-8200

DeGustibus
2020 Massachusetts Ave.
Cambridge, MA 02140
(617) 354-3836

Donald Bruce White Caterers, Inc.
159 E. 64th St.
New York, NY 10021
(212) 988-8410

Gaper's
30 West Washington
Chicago, IL 60602
(312) 332-4935

Glorious Food
172 E. 75th St.
New York, NY 10028
(212) 628-2320

Gourmet Parties
1057 NW 119th St.
Miami, FL 33116
(305) 688-8661

Kay Kahle
2520½ West Creek
Houston, TX 77027
(713) 623-8495

Ridgewell's
5525 Dorsey La.
Bethesda, MD 20816
(301) 652-1515

Van Wyk Associates
3548 Sacramento St.
San Francisco, CA 94118
(415) 921-6363

Word of Mouth
1012 Lexington Ave.
New York, NY 10021
(212) 734-9483

Becoming a Chef

Although it doesn't take elaborate training to sling hash in a local greasy spoon, it takes considerable time, effort, and training to become a chef. The procedure to become a chef can be as grueling as that of earning a Ph.D. or M.D. Briefly, we'll give you a rundown of the type of training and experience it would take to work your way up to the rank of Certified Master Chef.

The American Culinary Federation in St. Augustine, Florida, sets specific standards for the achievement of various titles among chefs. The standards provide minimum requirements in education, plus experience in other types of service.

The ranks leading up to that of Master Chef are Certified Cook, Certified Working Chef, and Certified Executive Chef. Two other grades, if desired, are Certified Pastry Chef and Certified Culinary Educator.

A certified cook needs 20 education points, 20 experience points, and 4 association points. Roughly, this translates into a college education and several years experience as a cook in a restaurant or other type of food institution. Association points are gained by membership involvement in local chapters of the American Culinary Federation.

A candidate for the rank of certified working chef (CWC) must accumulate 20 education points, 26 experience points, 5 association points, and 14 additional points derived from additional education, experience, or association activities.

A certified executive chef must have earned 55 experience points (for example, one year of hotel experience earns 6 points). In a way, you could think of these points as being similar to college credits and additional "credits" given for life experiences.

The master chef (Certified Master Chef) is a person whose point requirements might take fifteen to twenty years' experience. In addition, candidates must take a grueling ten-day practical examination at the Culinary Institute of America. The examination is only given at the Culinary Institute of America because it is the only educational facility in the United States with the kitchen space needed to offer such a comprehensive test. The skills tested by the examination include everything from costing and marketing to food preparation and meat fabrication (the delicate art of reducing meat—a leg of lamb or a side of beef, for example—to a state in which it can be cooked).

In our listing of culinary institutions, we list a number of schools that offer formal and often lengthy programs. We recognize that although not all readers aspire to this level of training or accomplishment, it may be interesting to get a taste of what type of hard work awaits you if you do pursue the culinary arts in a serious manner.

At the Culinary Institute of America, for example, every student takes a core curriculum. The courses are given in twenty fourteen-day blocks. There are also courses in food science and meat fabrication. And all students are required to take several French courses.

A course in store-room operations teaches students everything from receiving to storing food, as well as delivering it to kitchens. The food-preparation courses are enticingly specific; for example, everyone takes a course in Oriental cooking. There's a charcuterie course, aimed at teaching students about the glories of French charcuterie specialties, such as terrines, pâtés, and gallatines. Along the same line, there are courses in garde-manger (cold food), seafood, and classical baking and pastry. Courses in wines, appetizers, beverages, and cost control are also mandatory, as is a course in designing one's own restaurant.

So following is a list of America's best schools for the dedicated culinary student. These schools are noted for their high-quality instruction, and some offer expensive, lengthy programs. They are divided into three types: culinary institutes, restaurant schools (where the emphasis is on the restaurant industry), and hotel-management schools (where courses in cooking and hotel management are emphasized). For more information, you may contact the International Association of Cooking Schools at 1001 Connecticut Ave. NW, Washington, D.C. 20036; tel. (202) 293-7716.

Culinary Institutes

Culinary Institute of America (C.I.A.), P.O. Box 53, Hyde Park, NY 12538; (914) 452-9600. Considered one of America's top cooking schools, the Culinary Institute of America offers a twenty-one-month program leading to an Associate in Occupations Studies degree. The $14,000 tuition covers room and board, books, uniforms, laundry, insurance, and a knife kit. About eighteen hundred students study on this seventy-five-acre campus near Franklin Delano Roosevelt's boyhood home. Admission requirements include six months' experience in some aspect of the food industry (preferably cooking in a varied kitchen), two letters of reference from professionals in the industry, and official transcripts from high school or college. Graduates can expect to receive about five job offers and earn an average starting salary of $16,800. Distinguished graduates include Mike Muzyk and Bruce Egdahl, chefs at New York's La Côte Basque. Scholarships are available.

New England Culinary Institute, R.R. #1, Box 1255, Montpelier, VT 05602; (802) 223-6324. Tuition: $9,500 per year for a two-year program. Financial aid is available.

New York Restaurant School, The New York Cooking Center, 27 W. 34th St., New York, NY; (202) 947-7097. Tuition: $5,175 (not including knives and uniforms). The New York Restaurant School offers an intensive twenty-week program divided into two stages: fifteen weeks of daily instruction that includes five-and-a-half hours a day in culinary and restaurant-management skills, and five weeks of on-the-job training in the school's restaurant. Interview required before acceptance. $2,500 guaranteed student loan.

Newbury Junior College, 129 Fisher Ave., Brookline, MA 02146; (617) 739-0510. Tuition: $5,625 per year for a two-year program that leads to an Associate Degree in Applied Science in Culinary Arts. Scholarships and financial aid available.

California Culinary Academy, 215 Fremont St., San Francisco, CA 94105; (415) 543-2765. Tuition: $2,500 per semester. Entire course is given in four semesters for a total sixteen-month program. Financial aid is available after acceptance.

Baltimore's International Culinary Arts Institute, 1921 South Gay St., Baltimore, MD 21202; (301) 752-1446. Tuition: $7,977 for a one-year course. The school offers two one-year programs, one in baking and pastry, the other in restaurant skills. Classes are given from 8:00 until 3:15 five days a week.

L'Académie de Cuisine, 5021 Wilson La., Bethesda, MD 20814; (301) 986-9490. Tuition: $11,500 for two thirty-six-week programs that last from October through June. The first year is spent in classes at the school; the second year, students are sent to restaurants to serve apprenticeships. No financial aid available.

Restaurant Management Schools

School of Hotel Administration, Cornell University, Statler Hall, Ithaca, NY 14853; (607) 256-4990. Tuition: $9,600 per year; room and board, $3,600 per year. This four-year program leads to an undergraduate B.S. degree. Graduate program also available.

School of Hospitality Management, Florida International University, Tamiami Campus, Miami, FL 33199; (305) 554-2591. Tuition:

approximately $1,320 per trimester (school is structured on a two-year trimester program) for nonresidents. Financial aid and scholarships are available.

School of Consumer and Family Science, Department of Restaurant and Hotel Institutional Management, Purdue University, 106 Stone Hall, West Lafayette, IN 47907; (317) 494-4643. Four-year program.

Hotel-Management Schools

School of Hotel Administration, Cornell University, Statler Hall, Ithaca, NY 14853; (607) 256-4990. See above for details.

College of Hotel Administration, University of Nevada, Las Vegas, 4505 Maryland Pkwy., Las Vegas, NV 89154; (702) 739-3230. Tuition: $1,100 per semester plus $36 a credit. For this four-year program, you need 128 credits to graduate with a B.S. degree in hotel administration. Scholarships and financial aid are available.

School of Hotel, Restaurant and Institutional Management, Michigan State University, 425 Eppley Center, East Lansing, MI 48824; (517) 355-1855. Tuition: $90.50 a credit for the first two years for out-of-state residents; $93.50 a credit for last two years. Full-time students take twelve credits a term. Financial aid and scholarships are available.

THE RESTAURANT IN YOUR HEAD

The best production of a play is the one staged in the reader's mind. Only our imagination can idealize the values of what a fine theatrical production or a great restaurant should have. This section concerns itself with ideals. Whether you wish to one day own or manage a restaurant, you probably have begun to form an image in your mind of how it would look, what you would serve, how you would run it. Along with our fantasizing, we'll tell you where you can start your quest toward being a manager or manager/owner.

Most managers start out by working in entry-level positions in the food industry. Many have been waiters, bartenders, cashiers, dishwashers, or busboys. Relatively few restaurant managers have gone to school specifically to specialize in restaurant management. But if you aspire to managing a hotel restaurant or a first-class restaurant of any sort, you might want to check out restaurant-management courses at local colleges or inquire about apprenticeship possibilities at nearby hotels.

Managers provide hands-on guidance of all aspects of a restaurant, and in our "Considerations for Fledgling Restaurateurs," we cover just a few items that owner/managers must consider in their day-to-day business.

It goes without saying that managers must have the same mind for details that caterers need; they should be astute bookkeepers, easygoing with the public, talented at finding business systems that make a restaurant work efficiently. But let's dwell on the part of the job that is a prime prerequisite: a profound interest in and feeling for good food and the overall experience of dining.

In this regard, reading restaurant reviews can be a great education for anyone interested in restaurant management. Since serving food is a type of show business, a restaurant review can be an eye-opening experience, zeroing in on problems that people involved in a restaurant might never be able to see for themselves. A shrewd reviewer will comment not only on food, service, ambience, and prices, but also on such issues as the consistency of the cooking, the staff's experience, the noise level, the lighting, the proximity of the tables to one another, the wine list, and whether the flowers on the table are fresh or wilted.

The democratization of gourmet food has made the average person sensitive to how food should be served as well as to what foods are in vogue. Therefore, a fledgling manager may want to subscribe to such popular food magazines as *Gourmet, Food & Wine, Bon Appétit,* and *The Cook's Magazine.*

Each year, thousands of people open new restaurants. Many have put several years into learning their trade. In New York City, about twelve thousand applications for new restaurants are filed every year. About 60 percent of these new restaurants close within their first year, according to Fred G. Sampson, president of the New York Restaurant Association. The major reason for failure is that they are undercapitalized. Restaurateurs often do not understand the extent of the investment they must make before this type of business shows a profit. The other common reason for failure is simply a lack of know-how. That know-how includes a talent for promotion; an ability to find, hire, and keep competent employees; and the discipline to serve food that is consistently good.

Too often, potential owner-managers think about the wrong things when they plan that ideal restaurant. They may imagine their restaurant as a great place to socialize, meet with friends, hobnob with important people, and receive compliments on the wonderful food. But nothing can prepare a first-time owner for the shock of meeting the bills.

One owner who had worked in half a dozen restaurants decided she wanted her own place. Starting as a waitress, she had worked her way up to manager. But when she opened her own restaurant, troubles started immediately. On the day she became the official owner, city inspectors told her that her kitchen's exhaust system was no good. Cost: $5,500. On another occasion, she closed the restaurant for renovations that were expected to take ten days; the work ended up taking a month. And the costs for maintaining the restaurant were astonishing—insurance, salaries, government agencies, music, repairs, and food. Sometimes she barely had enough money in the cash register to stock her kitchen with meat for the lunch business. Then, in the afternoon, she'd take the money she earned and buy meat for dinner.

Another restaurant owner, George Martin, learned the hard way that restaurant management takes both discipline and experience. The restaurant, according to a feature article on this East Side pub, ran virtually without management. There was no cost-control system, no employee-conduct code, no regular bookkeeping. Stealing was commonplace. Some people believe that bartenders were pocketing more than $300 per shift by simply not ringing up drinks. Smart waiters made more than a hundred dollars extra each week. Within two years, the restaurant was out of business.

One way to avoid some of the pitfalls is to talk with experienced restaurateurs. There are numerous college extension courses on restaurant management. There are, of course, four-year programs in restaurant management available at such schools as Cornell University, the University of Nevada at Las Vegas, and Michigan State University, among others.

Apprenticeships in restaurant management are available for serious students, and you can find out about some of these apprenticeships by writing to the National Institute of Food Service Industries, 20 N. Wacker Dr., Chicago, IL 60606; telephone (312) 782-1703. They'll be happy to send you a package of materials on apprenticeship programs as well as on the food-service industry itself. One interesting fact about the food-service business as a whole: There are more than 250,000 jobs in the field that are *unfilled*, and it is estimated that this vacancy will not change before 1990.

Among the other places to contact for specific information about restaurant-management careers are the American Hotel and Motel Association (888 Seventh Ave., New York, NY 10019; 212-265-4506) and the American Hotel and Motel Association's Education Center (1407 S. Harrison Rd., East Lansing, MI 48823; 517-353-5500). The Education Center is an especially good source of information about correspondence courses in restaurant management.

To gain a knowledge of the culinary side of your field, write to the American Culinary Federation, P.O. Box 3466, St. Augustine, FL 23084; telephone (904) 824-4336. They can send you information about culinary institutes, apprenticeship programs for cooks, and community-college programs that offer theory-related cooking instruction. They'll also send you information about their certification program that cooking students go through as they climb the ladder of cooking skill and experience.

As a manager-owner, the more you know about how your cook does his or her job, the better chance you have of making your restaurant successful. Better yet, just try to cope with the rigors of being a chef in your own restaurant for a single hour—you'll see how difficult the job can be.

The real test comes when the orders fly in hot and heavy and you must have everything ready at the right moment and at the right temperature. By being a waiter, waitress, busboy, assistant chef, or assistant manager in a restaurant, you can watch other people make mistakes—and you can learn from them. Doctors, lawyers, and other high-rollers may be interested in the glamour of owning a restaurant, but they should be more interested in the track record of the people who will actually run it.

When you are ready to go on your own, you may still need help in the form of partners. The reason? Because restaurants eat money. Not just for the food and the rent and the help, but also for the equipment, the heat, the refrigeration, the insurance, the licenses, the thousands of unexpected, out-of-the-blue bills that cross your desk all year long. To open even a modest one-hundred-seat restaurant in the downtown area of a major city, $350,000 is not considered an unreasonable investment. And you'd better make sure that your initial bankroll includes at least six months' worth of operating expenses.

Salaries for the help will, of course, vary widely. A restaurant manager may make anywhere from $15,000 to $50,000 a year. Chefs average $20,000 to $25,000 a year (White House chefs earn about $50,000 a year). The owner's profit is simply what's left over after everyone (and everything) has been paid.

Traditionally, people who have worked their way up in restaurant management get to a stage where they want to start earning for themselves. But most people won't pay $50 for an adequate dinner for two; they'd rather go out fewer times and pay more when they do go out. Yet restaurant owners have to raise their prices to make a profit. According to Joseph Baum, the restaurant consultant who helped create New York's Four Seasons and Windows on the World, the price of food alone represents from 34 to 42 percent of the total check. And there's a lot more to running a restaurant than just buying food. Simply dressing up a restaurant can cost a bundle. The annual budget for flowers at New York's La Grenouille is $75,000.

As a restaurant owner, you'll spend your time aiming at impossible perfection, even if you run a hamburger joint. Ray Kroc, the late owner of McDonald's, was every bit as exacting in his restaurants as the fussiest chef. Kroc demanded that french fries be thrown out if they were seven minutes old; hamburgers after ten minutes, and coffee after thirty minutes. He insisted that servers deliver a hamburger, french fries, and shake within fifty seconds. Kroc also established the weight and contents of each hamburger, as well as cooking time, roll size, and amount of onions per burger. By doing this, he was able to gain consistent quality and little waste.

He also did what all smart entrepreneurs do: He plowed the profits back into the company. Just as a filmmaker sometimes envisions every frame of a film before he actually shoots it, a restaurateur dreams about affording lots of flowers, crystal wineglasses, and gleaming silverware.

The restaurateurs at the top of their profession can afford to "polish" their restaurant's performance every evening. They know that, for instance, it's rude to remove any plates from a table before the last person in the party has finished eating that course. The inexperienced waiter or restaurateur may think that speedy removal of dishes is always a good idea, but the first-rate manager would rather leave the dishes alone than rush the remaining diners.

A great restaurant does not present the bill until the diner requests it. When a waiter slaps a bill down with dessert, he's effectively saying, "Finish eating, pay the bill, and leave."

Another example of the thoughtfulness that comes with experience and an eagerness to please: Ask your waiters to name prices when they list the specials of the day. Don't put diners in the embarrassing position of having to ask.

Top restaurateurs realize that courtesy is always good business. At one restaurant, a couple who had made a reservation for 8:00 P.M. were told, "We'll have your table for you shortly. Have a seat at the bar." At first, this sounded like the usual invitation to a long wait and expensive drinks. But the maître d' added, "The drinks are on us." Before the couple was half-finished with their drinks, the table was ready. It was 8:08 P.M. "We don't like to keep our people waiting," said the maître d', "and we like them to come back."

Running a restaurant, as you can see, is a full-time job. And excuses aren't tolerated. When a diner asks for espresso and you tell him that the machine is broken, you can kiss that customer good-bye. If there is any glamour amidst the headaches and stress of the restaurant business, it is the glow that comes over you when a customer looks you in the eye, smiles, and says sincerely, "Everything was excellent. I'm going to tell my friends. . . ."

Considerations for Fledgling Restaurateurs

Why is it that three out of every four new restaurants go out of business the first year? There can be many reasons other than poor food, such as undercapitalization, an undisciplined staff, a bad partnership, or the failure to secure a sufficiently long lease. Here are a few of the considerations that every restaurateur must heed as he plans his restaurant. The commentary on each represents an amalgam of opinions garnered from experienced restaurateurs:

Theme. A restaurant's theme determines its location. A quick-food operation needs a busy area. And although a deli or a coffee shop is a known quantity, you have to establish a theme for a restaurant called Bob's. A comfortable identity helps give people the impetus to try you out. Sardi's theme is Broadway; the Cattleman's theme is the old West.

Design/Decor. Design is important, but do you know what really makes a restaurant lovely? People. There can be sawdust on the floor, rude waiters, and cramped seating, but lots of people make you put up with it all.

Size. You must know the number of customers needed to generate enough income to stay afloat. This will involve some fancy calculation of just how much you make per head and what your percentage of profit is. A forty-seat restaurant sounds cozy, but can you serve enough dinners at the right price to stay alive? How fast can you turn over each table? Will people sit all night? There go your profits! A forty-seater can work—but only with a high profit margin on each meal.

Seating. There are two types: leisurely and quick. How long you can expect people to sit is keyed to your price structure. Remember: If your restaurant is empty, no seat will be good enough for the customer, but if the place is full, you could sit him down next to a neutron bomb and he might feel lucky to be there at all.

Hours of operation. Stick to them. If you say you're open until 11:00 P.M., then stay open that late every time. Give yourself a certain amount of time to build the clientele. Don't let your restaurant's hours of operation be determined by a staff itching to get home. Are you staying open for lunch? For dinner? Some restaurants only attract lunch crowds; others, only dinner.

Price structure. Cheap food doesn't assure success, and expensive dishes don't assure failure. It's the value that will determine success. Whatever your price structure, make sure people think it's worth the money.

Personnel and hiring. You don't need fancy help if you're running a steak house, but you do if you're running a French restaurant; the more professional the staff, the more you pay them. You can mark up pasta by a much higher percent than you can mark up steak, because steak is already expensive. Fortunately, you don't need as highly talented a kitchen staff to serve steak as to create more complex dishes.

Equipment. Do you have the broiler space you need? Freezers? Make sure you can handle a crowd. Do you have the room to prepare salads? The grill space to do fifty hamburgers at a time? People expect you to be able to cope with the busy times; they don't want excuses like "The espresso machine broke down" or "I forgot to order your appetizer" or "The kitchen is too busy to make garlic bread."

Menu. The look of a menu is important. The menu must fit in with your restaurant's theme and help the customer relax without his realizing that he's being made to relax. An imaginative, well-designed, well-balanced menu suggests that the food is prepared with similar care and concern.

Service. The first rule: Make sure someone acknowledges the customer. Even if it's just to say, "I'll be with you in a second." Nothing is more disconcerting than to be plunked down at a table and then ignored by waiters and busboys.

Presentation. People expect polite service, pleasant atmosphere, and food that looks better than food they can prepare at home. It's show business; you have to perform. When you get a call from a customer who's bringing a client to lunch, you perform. The same is true if you're helping a customer romance a new sweetheart.

Controls. When you make rules and regulations, stick to them. Your waiters should know how to dress, when to show up, what to say. If you don't run a tight ship, they'll show up in yellow, not white . . . or they may not show at all.

Income projections. You must project income based on an expected volume. No restaurant is packed all of the time. Tables never turn over as fast as you want them to.

Advertising and promotion. The trick here, as in any business, is to have your advertising and promotion bring in more money than they cost. This is where most fledgling restaurateurs lose their shirt. Very few restaurant people know anything about promotion. A great review in a major newspaper is worth more than any paid advertisement for your restaurant.

Partnerships. When you do enter into a partnership, make sure that you divide your duties clearly. Perhaps one can handle the "front of the house" while the other handles the back. Maybe one will manage during the day, the other at night. Whatever you decide, agree on policy before you open the doors.

Five Stars in Stormville: A Behind-the-Scenes Look at Harralds

At first, it was just curiosity. A friend had mentioned that one of America's most comprehensive travel guides awarded five stars to only thirteen restaurants in the entire country. Since I follow restaurants the way some people follow soccer or the stock market, I immediately tried to name all thirteen restaurants.

"Let's see; Lutèce . . . Ernie's . . . The Maisonette in Cincinnati . . .," I began, but soon my guesses veered off-track. When I saw the list, however, my nodding head greeted each name as if it were an old friend, because all the restaurants either had large reputations or were predictably ensconced in well-populated or well-to-do areas. Except one.

In the Northeast, the only other restaurant besides Lutèce to be awarded five stars was called Harralds, located in the township of East Fishkill, in Dutchess County, New York.

Most maps of New York don't even show Fishkill (or Stormville, the restaurant's mailing address), and yet, if the guide book was to be believed, somewhere in that village about sixty-seven miles north of New York City was to be found a gourmet's paradise.

Like Alice in Wonderland, I became "curiouser and curiouser." Having adjusted to the notion that gastronomic nirvana could be found in a town with fewer inhabitants than any one street in Manhattan, I soon learned that the restaurant was further distinguished by its chef, Ava Durrschmidt—the only female five-star chef in the United States—who achieved her incredible success in less than a decade.

Since other wonders of the world, such as the Taj Mahal, Versailles, and Yosemite, are also a bit off the beaten path, I decided that I'd hop in my car to see if there really was such a place as Harralds.

Almost two hours later, after a pleasant drive through the rolling hills and stately elms of Westchester and Dutchess counties, I pulled into the parking lot of Harralds.

More surprises were in store as Harrald Boerger, maître d' and co-owner, came out to greet me. I was prepared for the cozy, wood-beamed dining rooms awaiting me inside the restaurant—a converted farmhouse that dates back to Revolutionary days—but the breathtaking view of the grounds forced me to stare and keep staring.

Matching the Tudor-style restaurant was a cottage serving as a wine cellar. There, more than six thousand bottles of wine aged in fifty-nine-degree comfort. The patio, used for summer dining, was dappled with the shade from Norwegian firs and maples. To one side of the patio was a trout tank, assuring the freshness of Ava's *truite au bleu*. From the patio, one could gaze at seventeen acres of backyard and forest while enjoying the sweet scent of freshly mowed grass.

Harrald Boerger, who reigns over the dining room as his wife reigns over the kitchen, is a paradoxical man, part *boulevardier*, part perfectionist. He is charming, warm, and has a radiant smile reminiscent of Maurice Chevalier's. He loves to sip coffee with his guests while talking about the artists and writers who have influenced his life— Voltaire, Wilde, van Gogh, Mozart. But just beneath this dilettantish exterior is a man who dreams of running the finest restaurant in the world and who has already committed extraordinarily large chunks of money and time to making that dream a reality.

Ava credits her five stars to what she calls "the Five D's": drive, determination, discipline, devotion, and dedication. A native of the resort city of Wiesbaden, West Germany, Ava grew up with an innate sense of good taste as well as the kind of fortitude that would have assured her success in practically any field she chose. She was not a chef but a textile engineer when she married Harrald in 1964. They brought to the United States a desire to establish a country restaurant which would be equivalent to the fine provincial restaurants of Europe. Unfortunately, they could not tolerate the temperaments of the fine chefs whom they interviewed, and eventually Harrald suggested that Ava could do the job herself.

Ava took private courses with several of the finest chefs at the Culinary Institute of America in nearby Hyde Park, among them Albert Kumin (who was pastry chef at the White House during the Carter Administration). Harralds opened in 1972, and achieved its first four-star rating two years later. The fifth star was added in 1978.

When asked why there aren't more female chefs, Ava answers, "Cooking doesn't leave much time for an active social life. You sacrifice a lot. When others go to the beach or to the beautician, you're in a hot kitchen. Your freedom is very limited if you want to succeed." Here is one woman who has never needed anyone to liberate her; her ambition, zeal, and self-confidence come at you like bullets.

I suddenly had the feeling that dinner might never be able to live up to my expectation—or theirs.

Yet dinner—three hours long, six courses wide—was sublime.

—Gary Blake

Great Gourmet Food Stores and Markets

Imagine yourself surrounded by food—chocolate, caviar, Smithfield hams, pasta, cookies, smoked salmon. That's what it's like working at a great gourmet store or food market. The aroma of freshly ground coffee beans, the delicate carving of French roast duck, the buttery smell of fresh croissants—would you like these things to enhance your working conditions? If so, you may want to contact one or more of the following food palaces, and inquire about entry-level positions in the kitchen or behind the counter.

Balducci's
424 6th Ave.
New York, NY 10014
(212) 673-2600

Bremen House
220 East 86th St.
New York, NY 10028
(212) 288-5500

Corti Brothers
5770 Freeport Blvd.
Sacramento, CA 95820
(916) 391-0300

Dean & DeLuca
121 Prince St.
New York, NY 10013
(212) 254-7774

Epicure Market
1656 Alton Rd.
Miami Beach, FL 33139
(305) 672-1861

Farmer's Market
Third & Fairfax
Los Angeles, CA 90036
(213) 933-9211

Fraser-Morris
931 Madison Ave.
New York, NY 10021
(212) 988-6700

French Market
1632 Wisconsin Ave. NW
Washington, D.C. 20007
(202) 338-4828

Hamlin's
89 Kercheval
Grosse Point Farms, MI 48236
(313) 885-8400

Horn of Plenty
442 S. Woodward
Birmingham, MI
(313) 645-2750

Lexington Market
400 W. Lexington St.
Baltimore, MD 21201
(301) 685-6169

Macy's
Herald Square
New York, NY 10001
(212) 695-4400

Petak's
1244 Madison Ave.
New York, NY 10128
(212) 722-7711

Pike Street Market
85 Pike St.
Seattle, WA 91801
(206) 625-4764

William Poll
1051 Lexington Ave.
New York, NY 10021
(212) 288-0501

Quincy Market
Faneuil Hall
Boston, MA 02118
(617) 269-6330

Simon David
7117 Inwood Rd.
Dallas, TX 75209
(214) 352-1781

Swiss Colony
Fayette Mall
Lexington, KY
(606) 272-6012

Truffles
3701 NE 45th St.
Seattle, WA 91081
(206) 532-3016

Zabar's
2245 Broadway
New York, NY 10024
(212) 787-2000

Movies

The movie industry. The words alone evoke a thousand images of glamour. One imagines the stars; the giant studios; the motion-picture conglomerates; the famous—and in some cases infamous—directors; the producers; the turn-of-the-century moguls who started the business; and scores of luminaries and publications related to the industry. Indeed, there is scarcely another business that projects the aura of glamour as convincingly as the film industry.

Is there a way in? Of course. But bear this in mind: It isn't all gilt and flash. In fact, breaking into this business entails a lot of hard work for a lengthy period of time. Sure, you can wind up an idol if you become the next Clint Eastwood, Jane Fonda, or Steven Spielberg. You can also spend a lot of time as a production assistant laying linoleum on the floor of a movie set in a tiny town you've never heard of (and never want to see again).

So unless you have an uncle in the business, don't buy an expensive pair of dark sunglasses yet. The path to stardom—in almost any specialty in this field—can be arduous. It can also be one of the most rewarding roads you'll ever travel.

Let's get one thing straight right from the start: There are dream jobs in the film industry, and then there are positions that can help you make your way up the ladder to one of those coveted dream jobs. As you've already surmised, there are more stepping-stone jobs than star spots. But that's okay, because if you have the determination (the same determination you'll undoubtedly need to get ahead in any of the areas described in this book) you can land a wonderfully fulfilling and lucrative position in the motion-picture business.

While you're working your way up, always remember this indisputable point: "Nothing good comes easily." It's a real fact of live.

"VICTORY HAS A THOUSAND FRIENDS, AND FAILURE IS AN ORPHAN."

Think about that quote. If it inspires you to succeed, make a copy of it in letters two feet tall and hang it up in a prominent place in your living room. Once you begin in the film business, you're going to need regular inspiration to survive. So any device, regardless of how silly it may seem, should be used to help you achieve your long-range goals.

But, for the present, you should concentrate, first and foremost, on landing a job—almost any job—that makes you a bona-fide part of the business. Soon after you've learned how to do your job well, decide on *exactly* what area of the industry you'd like to work in.

One of the things you'll learn fairly early in your career is that in the feature-film business, success means eating, breathing, and sleeping films. Succeeding involves more than simply moving from one job to another. You must adopt an ambitious life-style.

If there is one business in which there is no room for the half-hearted, it's the motion-picture industry. A director and camera crew, for example, may spend six or more months filming a feature-length film in Indonesia. Are you ready to pack up and take control of a camera on an assignment such as this? How will your wife or husband feel about your being away for lengthy periods of time? Would you be able to cope with an equatorial climate for 180 days straight? Can you stand the pressure of doing a job well for, say, twelve or more hours a day, six or seven days a week?

These questions aren't meant to frighten you away from the business. They're designed to stimulate an enthusiastic attitude. One of the key factors that will determine your success in this industry is your ability to structure your life-style around the demands of your career. If you can't or simply don't want to do this, don't get involved. You'll be wasting time that you could have devoted to pursuing a career more in line with your personality, skills, long-range objectives, and needs.

Rich Patterson, editor of *American Cinematographer*, describes this commitment in an editorial published in his magazine's August–September 1984 issue:

> The commitment required of a crew member makes working on a film a very intense, and often very satisfying, experience. The sense of dedication and the sheer energy level on a production can promote camaraderie and emotional involvement among the crew. As a steady diet, however, working twelve hours a day, six days a week, a thousand miles from home can wreak havoc on an individual's psyche, not to mention his relationships with his family.

If you truly believe that you can meet the rigors posed by filmmaking, read on; there's a lot more you'll want to know.

Let's assume that you have the requisite interest and desire to break into films. Let's also assume that you recently graduated from college with a degree in almost anything (related or unrelated to film) or that you're switching careers and have no experience in the motion-picture business. How do you land your first job?

Although getting a degree in filmmaking or any other related area can be an initial step in the right direction (and this is becoming increasingly true), the motion-picture industry absolutely demands hands-on experience. Unless you are a budding George Lucas or Woody Allen and you've made a really big splash with a reel you put together while you were still in film school, you probably won't start out as a Hollywood director. More than likely, you'll begin as a *production assistant* (generally called a *PA*), receptionist, secretary, or in a similar entry-level position.

Don't let this discourage you. In films, as in few other industries, you can move up the proverbial ladder of success in any number of unpredictable ways, even switching from one specialty to another. Unpredictable, that is, until the opportunity arises—and you seize it.

Consider the career path of Constantine Makris, who, with a

dozen years in the business, is a successful camera operator. Constantine filmed *The Ultimate Solution of Grace Quigley*, starring Katherine Hepburn and Nick Nolte. Makris also worked as a camera operator on director Louis Malle's film *Almo Bay* as well as on other feature-length films.

Says Makris, "While I was still in college, I was selling Christmas trees as a part-time holiday job. One day a customer asked me to tie to his car the tree he had just purchased. While I was doing so, he asked, just to kill a few minutes, what I'd like to be doing when I graduated.

"Because I was vaguely thinking about some aspect of the film industry—I wasn't even sure which—and since I had taken some communications-arts courses, I responded, 'Films, maybe.' Believe it or not, he gave me the name and number of someone he knew who was in a position to hire entry-level people as production assistants to work on filming commercials for various products.

"Instead of calling the person whose name he had given me, I did little more than call the man who bought the Christmas tree. In fact, I called him regularly for months. Finally, to get me off his back, he made the call that I should have made. I was hired—at no pay, I might add—to be a PA during the filming of a Benjamin Moore paint commercial.

"At the end of the shooting, which lasted three days, I was, fortunately, the recipient of three days' wages at whatever the nonunion minimum wage was in the early 1970s. Let's call that amount peanuts. Those three days of PA work defined the extent of my film-industry career for the next year or so.

"About twelve months after I worked on the paint commercial, the head PA on that shoot remembered me, I was astonished to learn, and called me to ask whether or not I was available to 'strike sets'—that is, tear apart sets that were no longer needed. It was, as is common in the industry, per-diem work at nonunion wages. But I was interested, so I accepted the job.

"Once at work again, I began to familiarize myself with as many technical aspects of the business as I could. I also made as many contacts as possible; this is an industry that hinges largely on personal and professional contacts. Eventually, I became a head PA—but not before working my tail off.

"Two years after I began regular per-diem PA work, I was sponsored for membership in the union, NABET, the National Association for Broadcast Employees and Technicians, the smaller of the major unions. IATSE [International Alliance of Theatrical Stage Employees and Moving Picture Machine Operators] is the larger one, and the Directors Guild of America is another.

"Once in the union, I became a grip, a position I held for six years. Grips do a seemingly endless variety of chores: They construct parts of sets, perform carpentry services, and are responsible for the overall safety of the set. They rig lights; build grids from which lights and anything else can be hung; hook up cameras to dollies or other conveyances; 'set flags' (that is, darken areas on a set); and handle countless other tasks, many of which require the grips to work closely with people in several other job areas.

"Once I became a grip and began working somewhat regularly in this new capacity, I took an interest in cameras, which is where I felt the action was. I decided that being a cameraman was a desirable and realizable goal.

"I began to absorb everything that I could about cameras and their operation by observing the better cameramen on the sets. I soon discovered that there are scores of different cameras used in making a feature-length film. When I felt knowledgeable enough to take the union's 'loader' test (a loader is a second assistant cameraman) I did. By passing both the practical and written parts of the exam, I moved into a new position, leaving behind my many years as a grip.

"Eventually, after I practiced using a number of cameras as a loader, I moved up once again into the position of camera operator, one of the people who works directly with a director of photography. As of autumn 1984, I've been performing in this function for two-and-a-half years.

"It's satisfying and rewarding in several ways. But it can be tough, too, and there's still a lot to learn, a lot more ground to cover for a young guy in this business.

"I'm glad that I stuck it out. Had I not been aggressive, persistent, and resolute—and had I not made the film industry a way of life—I never could have gotten this far."

Although there seems to be some degree of logic in the progress of Constantine Makris's career, his opportunities might never have materialized. Instead of staying on what is known as the "technical" side of the business, he could have wandered over to the production side, where the ultimate job is that of director.

You've read that at one point Constantine entered a union. If you intend to earn a good salary over a long period of time—that is, if you intend to forge a viable career in the movie business—getting into a union is imperative.

There are tests—written, and in many cases practical—and you will need a sponsor: someone already in the union that you want to join. But none of this is impossible, especially at NABET, where the various job-classification tests are given more frequently than they are in IATSE. Union pay scales are, as you might have guessed, considerably higher than nonunion rates.

We've assembled a brief rundown of several film-industry jobs and the annual salary you might expect to earn in each category. The range within any given category varies widely for very good reasons; for one thing, the number of days you'll work per year as well as the amount of overtime you'll put in (if any) may fluctuate considerably from year to year. This is largely a function of how many films are being made in any given year, where they are being shot, where you live, what union you're in, and other related factors.

Again, if you are good at your job and if you've made the right contacts and have proceeded enthusiastically as you move from assignment to assignment and boss to boss, you should expect to work more each year and reap the greater financial rewards of doing so.

Naturally, the figures listed on page 148 are approximations.

Points refer to a percentage of the motion picture's profits. In theory, almost anyone working on a feature-length film can earn points. In reality, points are generally offered only to major stars, producers, directors, writers, and executive producers. On smaller-scale productions, a director of photography may be given points. In some cases, film-laboratory owners working on minor films may earn points.

On the Technical Side

Position	Annual low	Annual high
Third grip	$ 15,000	$ 40,000
Key (head) grip	15,000	65,000
Electrician	15,000	40,000
Camera operator	20,000	65,000
Prop person	15,000	45,000
Technician	15,000	45,000
Director of photography	100,000	1,000,000 (plus points)
Assistant cameraman	15,000	65,000
Cameraman	150,000	250,000
Wardrobe	15,000	60,000+
Make-up	15,000	250,000
Hairdresser	15,000	250,000
Sound man	15,000	60,000
Gaffer	15,000	65,000
Editor/script supervisor	15,000	65,000

On the Production Side

Position	Annual low	Annual high
Production assistant	$ 12,000	$ 25,000
Second assistant director	15,000	100,000
First assistant director	20,000	100,000
Production office coordinator	15,000	50,000
Unit manager	15,000	60,000
Production manager	15,000	100,000
Location manager	15,000	60,000
Producer	No limits (plus points)	
Line producer	25,000	200,000+
Director	No limits (plus points)	
Writer	No limits (plus points)	
Secretary	10,000	50,000

Usually, the offering of a percentage of a film's profits depends upon how the production is financed. If the people financing the film don't have a lot of up-front money, they may tend to offer more points to more people in order to attract the required talent—creative and technical—to the project.

CAREER OPPORTUNITIES IN FILM

Before elaborating further on the nature of the industry, let's take a look at a number of job opportunities in feature-film production:

- **Director.** A film's director is in charge of and makes final artistic judgments during the three basic phases of filmmaking: preproduction, production, and postproduction.

  In the preproduction phase, the director makes all the decisions—hundreds, sometimes thousands—on the final script, casting, sets, costumes, props, effects, locations, budgets, and schedules.

  In production, the director not only directs the actors but also places the cameras, chooses the lenses, and otherwise composes scenes and people to tell a story. The director exercises full responsibility over the production company.

  In postproduction, the director oversees the editing, dubbing, scoring, and other finishing processes that bring a film up to preview.

- **Assistant director.** The assistant director is to a director what the staff sergeant is to a captain. This person helps the director with all facets of directorial responsibility.

  Before filming, the assistant director prepares the elements of production for the director, including a script breakdown to establish the shooting sequence and schedule.

  When filming begins, the assistant director assures on a day-by-day basis that all needed personnel, equipment, and supplies are ordered and made ready for the director.

  The assistant director is on the set at all times except when assigned by the director to direct a second unit or handle some other special duty. The assistant director handles hundreds of details in servicing a director and may make creative suggestions. Regardless of the circumstances, his total allegiance must be to the director.

- **Associate director.** Among other responsibilities, the associate director prepares a production breakdown when requested by the director. He or she lays out floor plans, presets the director's cues, checks studio facilities, performs timing functions, and assists the director in maintaining communication with all personnel involved in the production of the film.

- **Film editor.** Most of the footage shot for a movie never makes it into the picture you see on the screen. The film editor is the person who cuts, splices, and connects miles of celluloid into a coherent, entertaining film.

  Unlike videotape images, which can be manipulated electronically, film is edited by physically cutting and splicing reels at an editing table. And the skill with which the film is edited has a major effect on the quality of the finished product—which is why good film editors are in great demand.

  During editing, the editor works closely with the film's director. Together, they determine which scenes will be included and which will be cut, the length of each scene, and the order, timing, and pace of the transitions from one scene to another. "The most interesting thing about film editing is the fact that it's always different, always challenging," said film editor John Carter in an interview for *Millimeter* magazine. "There's not one picture that you work on that is like the next."

- **Production assistant (PA).** This entry-level job entails assisting the director, associate director, and others who are in charge of a production. Responsibilities range widely, from getting coffee for the cast to safeguarding equipment and loading trucks.

- **Unit publicist.** The publicist's job is to gain media attention for the film. Responsibilities include preparing press kits and biographies on key cast and crew members; feeding stories to the press; coordinating media interviews with the film's stars and director; preparing regular news releases on the progress being made; ghostwriting feature articles and gossip pieces; and making still photos and film clips available to editors and reviewers.

Today's film publicist has a degree in journalism, communications, or English and some previous work experience with a newspaper or TV or radio station. The Publicists Guild (Local 818 of the International Alliance of Theatrical and Stage Employees) has 556 members in the United States and Canada.

- **Marketing.** If you want to work for a major motion picture studio, marketing is a good place to start. To get into this area of the movie business, you need prior marketing or sales experience—not necessarily in a related industry.

  The job of marketing is to get people to go see the movie. Marketing is responsible for distributing the film to theaters, scheduling its release date, licensing products related to the film (toys, dolls, clothing), and special promotions. Says Frank Mancuso, head of marketing and distribution at Paramount, "My challenge is to squeeze every last dollar out of every movie we do."

- **Unit production manager (UPM).** The unit production manager's chief concern is the business side of production. The UPM prepares the budget for approval and controls payroll and other production expenses. But the UPM's functions are not restricted to fiscal matters. For on-location shoots, the unit production manager is responsible for arranging transportation and accommodations and is accountable for the general care of the film company.

- **Grip.** There are various types of grips in the film industry, and they each do different things. A *construction grip*, for example, works with the set builder to perform such tasks as erecting walls and executing carpentry assignments.

  A *key grip* is the lead person under whom all other grips work. Among other things, a key grip rigs the lights needed on a set. He will also, along with other grips, build ceiling grids from which various lights and objects needed in the production can be hung.

  A *dolly grip* is responsible for hooking up cameras to

dollies and other conveyances. In many cases, several grips are needed to mount the cameras.

Grips also *set flags*, which means that they darken areas on the set to create shadow effects. And grips are involved in stagehand work, including the construction of scaffolding. In general, they interact with many different types of motion-picture industry workers—much more so than, say, set builders, script people, or editors. In this respect, a grip is often in an opportune position to learn a great deal about how a film is made. Because of this interaction, the grip may also be in a good position to determine where he or she would most like to work next.

- **Camera operator.** Quite simply, this person operates a sophisticated motion-picture camera. The operator must be able to quickly and efficiently execute camera movements requested by the director and the director of photography. A *cameraman* needs to be skilled in both camera operation and lighting. A *director of photography* must be capable of lighting any scene that will appear in the film on which he or she is working.

- **Producer.** A good producer is a good organizer. The producer hires the entire crew, including the director.

  A producer may also raise money to shoot the film and even develop the concept and story idea for the movie. Some producers also assume the role of assistant director. In general, the scope of a movie defines, to a large extent, the nature of the producer's position.

- **Continuity person.** This job involves taking careful notes on the physical aspects of each shot during the film. The continuity person makes certain that everything remains in its proper position from the shooting of one scene to the next. In this way, he or she ensures *continuity*, or visual consistency, throughout the film.

- **Gaffer.** A gaffer is responsible for the lights on the set. He or she is the head electrician who works with the director of photography on anything related to lighting. Determining the size of the lighting crew and the size of the generators needed to produce power for the lights are among the gaffer's many responsibilities.

- **Location manager.** A location manager is responsible for obtaining permission to use appropriate locations at which a film will be shot. These locations can range from Mount Everest and the Dead Sea to the bathtub in an old Victorian mansion or a telephone booth on a busy city streetcorner.

- **Location scout.** A location scout assists the location manager in finding ideal filming spots. Scouting is so important and difficult that today there exist private agencies whose sole function is to provide locations for filmmakers.
- **Production-office coordinator.** People in this position work in production offices and handle a wide variety of problems. Their responsibilities range from such basic tasks as typing to larger dilemmas such as finding out why a mobile home that was supposed to be used on location has mysteriously disappeared.
- **Sound man.** The sound man records and coordinates all the elements of a movie's soundtrack from the actors' voices to background noises. High-quality tape decks are used for this purpose, as are boom microphones. A sound man must be well-versed in the use of recording equipment. Some sound men even purchase their own equipment.
- **Prop master.** The prop master is in charge of all the props used on the set. He or she must make sure that the props arrive on time, look good, and are properly positioned before the film is shot.
- **Screenwriter.** Let's say your dream is to write a screenplay and have it made into a movie. How do you go about it?

  First, you need to learn the craft. College courses and how-to books in screenwriting can get you started. And the Writer's Guild (555 West 57th St., New York, NY 10019; 212-245-6180) has some handy publications on screenplay format and screenwriters' fees.

  Second, you need to know how to sell your screenplay. Screenplays are bought or contracted for by producers and motion-picture studios. But these people won't read your material unless you're represented by an agent. A complete listing of script agents can be found in *Literary Market Place,* an annual directory published by R. R. Bowker.

How far you want to develop your screenplay before approaching an agent is up to you. A script starts as a *premise*—a one- or two-sentence description that sums up what the film is all about. The premise can be developed into a *treatment,* a 15- to 20-page prose description of the plot of the story. A finished *feature-length film script* will run anywhere from 90 to 120 typewritten pages. If you have contacts in the business, you may be able to sell them the bare bones of an idea over lunch or cocktails. If you're new at the game, write the whole script and sell the complete package.

Outside of college courses and how-to books, there's no formal training available for aspiring screenwriters. The best way to learn is to hunt down some published scripts (many film scripts are published in book form and available at bookstores) and study them. And, of course, you should write and rewrite your own screenplays until you feel they're good enough to sell. Screenwriter Rosemarie Santini says journalism is good training for screenwriting because it teaches you to condense a lot of facts into a tight story.

Most people who dream of selling their scripts never do. But if you succeed at screenwriting, you can earn considerable sums: A large studio will pay upward of $250,000 for a single feature-film script. Be aware, though, that just because you sell a script it doesn't guarantee it will be made into a film; many studios buy hundreds of scripts a year but produce only a dozen or so. "Most Hollywood writers make money writing stuff that never goes to camera," Santini laments.

HOW TO SUCCEED IN THE MOVIE BUSINESS

Christopher Misiano, a key grip, has been in the movie business for eight years. He has worked on such diverse projects as the feature film *Atlantic City* (starring Burt Lancaster and

Susan Sarandon), Bruce Springsteen's 1984 rock videotape "Dancing in the Dark" (directed by Brian DePalma), Billy Joel's 1984 rock videotape "The Longest Time" (directed by Jay Dublin), and Miller Lite commercials (produced by Bob Giraldi). Chris is also a director of photography at JPC Visuals, a New York City-based production and editing company.

Chris's advice on how to succeed: "Set your goals early. Don't simply say, 'I want to be a director.' Decide whether you'd like to be an industrial film director, an advertising/ commercial director, or a feature-film director. Develop your interests quickly and keenly, and hone your skills accordingly. If you want to work on documentaries, begin doing so as soon as the opportunity arises. Same goes for feature-length pieces and commercials.

"Circles within the film business are very tightly circumscribed, and switching from one area to a completely different area, although possible, isn't an easy task. Word-of-mouth information about, for instance, a grip, prop man, or cameraman is usually confined to these tight, individual industry circles.

"Remain aware of the fact that each business area defines a different life-style. Filming commercials for a consumer-products company, for example, will present a somewhat less stressful life-style than working on feature films. It takes less time to shoot commercials, whereas a feature film can send you out of town for lengthy periods.

"On a feature shoot, the home life you once enjoyed may become a peripheral aspect of your existence. So think carefully before you choose. But don't wait too long to make that important decision.

"I strongly recommend reading the book *Name Above the Title*, by director Frank Capra. Capra directed *It's a Wonderful Life, Mr. Smith Goes to Washington, Meet John Doe, Mr. Deeds Goes to Town*, and *Lost Horizon*, among other movies. The book discusses a director's life-style and can be invaluable to someone considering a career in this demanding but potentially very lucrative area of motion pictures."

IS THERE MOVIE LIFE OUTSIDE HOLLYWOOD?

Here's a question asked by many people thinking about careers in film: Is it necessary to be based in Hollywood or New York to make a go of it in the business?

Hollywood, with its studio conglomerates, ideal weather, and large, diverse talent base, is deliberately set up for efficient filmmaking. But as a result of partial studio breakdowns, location filming is increasingly popular nowadays.

Many cities and states have established film commissions to entice filmmakers to work in specific locales. Atlanta and Texas have been aggressive in this respect. And they are rapidly becoming filmmaking centers; thirty feature-length motion pictures, including *Tender Mercies* and *Silkwood*, were shot in Texas in 1983 alone.

New York City also has a film commission, and location films are continually being shot in Manhattan and the metropolitan area. The Old Astoria Studios in Queens—the largest studio on the East Coast—has been reactivated at a cost of $50 million. The Silvercup Bread facility, also located in Astoria, is being converted to accommodate the filming of feature-length productions and will soon become one of the country's major film studios. A third Astoria studio, the Broadway Studio, was once an old Greek movie theater.

Texas is a "right-to-work" state, which means you don't have to be a union member to work on a film made there. New York, on the other hand, is unionized.

So while Hollywood is still the core of the industry, opportunities abound elsewhere, more so today than ever before.

YOUR NAME IN LIGHTS

No matter where you go—Hollywood or New York, Atlanta or Texas—acting is considered the most glamorous aspect of the film business. After all, stars can make the movie sizzle or sink.

Maybe you are more interested in pursuing a career as an actor than in getting involved with technical or production areas. And the sky's the limit if you become a well-known performer. But if you choose this career path, you'll need talent, looks, drive, and a healthy dose of good luck to make it to the top.

We asked actress Paula E. Sheppard to tell us about her movie career. Paula starred in *Alice, Sweet Alice* (costarring Brooke Shields), *Liquid Sky,* and *Tam Lin.* She has also appeared in a number of soap operas, including NBC's *Another World.*

Says Paula, "There are two major areas in which you must succeed if you're going to act. First, you have to perfect your craft by continually performing and taking direction well. Second, you must market yourself effectively; you have to learn how to find acting jobs, because only by working at your craft will you generate future assignments.

"Talk to knowledgeable people—those who know how to secure appointments with casting agents, for example. Have a good-quality, eight-by-ten glossy photograph made of yourself (smiling). Write a top-notch résumé: one that looks and sounds highly professional.

"Then buy a copy of *The Ross Report,* which lists agents, producers, and casting agents. Send your photo, résumé, and a well-written cover letter to the agents you select. And purchase or rent a telephone-answering machine so that an agent can contact you while you're not at home. You'll be amazed at how many people call while you're not in.

"There's no doubt about it: Breaking into acting with no previous experience is very difficult. But if you're tenacious, you should be able to get an agent to at least meet with you, at which time he may just discuss matters . . . or, if you're fortunate and persistent, he may ask you to read part of a script.

"A good way to attempt breaking into performing—assuming you've been studying acting and know how to do it—is to land parts in commercials. Doing so enables you to get a Screen Actors Guild [SAG] card. With this document it becomes somewhat easier to obtain work.

"At the start, most actors perform as free-lancers. When you free-lance, only one agent at a time is permitted to submit your name for an acting job. Your photo is forwarded from your agent to a casting director. A phone call from the casting director to your agent means that the director is interested in seeing you. When this is the case, your agent will promptly call you, hopefully to discuss the role. The next step is the audition, then *call-backs* [being called back for a second reading of the script] and, if all goes well, your being hired.

"Anyone who has had no formal training whatsoever would be wise to investigate several of the acting studios in major metropolitan areas. They tend to train people primarily for the stage, but anyone worth his salt learns how to adapt a particular set of techniques for screen acting.

"Although there are many pitfalls to avoid, two of the most perilous are insecurity and indecisiveness. Unfortunately, much of the road to success is strewn with situations that instill considerable insecurity and indecisiveness: auditions, for example. But it is because auditions can be frightening that you *must* learn to excel at them. Auditioning is a technique that has to be mastered if you expect to win parts and earn a living as an actor.

"Don't feel worthless if you aren't asked to come back. If you're sure that you have the talent—not to mention a universe full of drive and the spunkiest attitude this side of Saturn— keep working at your craft, keep honing your skills. Eventually, you should succeed; the heights you'll achieve are, of course, unpredictable. But when you consider how lean so many big stars were before they became big—Lucille Ball, Joan Crawford, Marilyn Monroe, Ava Gardner, and Jackie Gleason, to name just a few—you realize that anything can, and sometimes does, happen in this business.

"Don't be discouraged because you're told that you're too thin, too fat, too old, short, young, tall, or in any way not the right type for a role. A person who is too short for one part may be just perfect for the leading role in another film.

"Right from the start, try to get a good handle on what parts you're best at playing. Stay away from the part of a high-school cheerleader if you know that you're much more convincing when you portray a psychotic murderess.

"When you feel comfortable with a part, *land that audition.* If it still feels good during the audition, you've probably done a satisfactory job, whether or not you end up with the part. But if you feel as if you're faking it, forget it. Faking it rarely works.

"Always use honest self-criticism. Confront your weak spots straightforwardly so that you don't delude yourself into the false belief that you're good at something when you actually may not be.

"Your sense of worth should never be invested in your brilliance as an actor before it's invested in your abilities as a meaningful person. Only when your acting becomes a function of your *self* will you really see—and be able to effectively correct—your weaknesses. And only after you really get in touch with yourself as a person can you contribute the essential element of richness that is so critical to your playing a role superbly.

"When you land an acting job, you must learn to put yourself in the hands of the film's director. Don't argue with the director; instead, listen to him and learn to take direction well. And always roll with the punches, even when you feel that a director's decision is poor and your acting will suffer because of his judgment. It's all part of the game, and you might as well learn how to play it as soon as possible.

"One other thing you'll have to master is *patience.* Being patient is extremely important. Make-up artists, for instance, may take several hours making you up for a role. If you can't deal with this, you'll have a problem in the acting business. If you disregard the concept of continuity and get a tan on Saturday (when you didn't have one during Friday's filming), you'll be in trouble on Monday morning, because you'll look quite different than you did at the last shooting.

"You will also be asked, as every actor is, to repeat your performance of a scene many, many times. After a few repetitions, your movements in front of the camera may not feel comfortable or spontaneous. Fight this discomfort at all costs and learn to do each take as perfectly as possible—as if it was your very first take of the day. This, too, is another key to success.

"Last, remember that a good actor must constantly keep his character 'available.' He must be able to summon the character's personality the moment he walks on-camera. If you don't master this, you will be working at a serious disadvantage—one that will hinder your chances of getting acting jobs.

"And don't worry about your ability to memorize lengthy passages in a script. In the movie business, more than a few minutes' worth of lines is considered to be a lot."

Required Reading for Future Filmmakers

Periodicals

Action, 1516 Westwood Blvd., Suite 102, Los Angeles, CA 90024. Bimonthly. Covers film news.

The Alpha Viewfinder, Alpha Cine Laboratory, 1001 Lenora St., Seattle, WA 98121; (206) 682-8230. Quarterly. Contains classified help-wanted ads for jobs in the film industry.

American Cinematographer, ASC Holding Corp., 1782 N. Orange Dr., Hollywood, CA 90028; (213) 876-5080. Monthly magazine on film production.

American Cinemeditor, 422 South Western Ave., Los Angeles, CA 90020; (213) 660-4425. Quarterly. Articles on film editing.

American Film, American Film Institute, John F. Kennedy Center for the Performing Arts, Washington, D.C. 20566; (202) 828-4060. Monthly magazine for film professionals, teachers, and enthusiasts.

American Premiere, 183 N. Martel, Suite 1, Los Angeles, CA 90036; (213) 852-0434. Monthly magazine for and about people in the film industry—executives, producers, directors, actors, and others.

Back Stage, 165 W. 46th St., New York, NY 10023; (212) 581-1080. Career-related articles and help-wanted ads in film and other entertainment industries. Weekly.

Boxoffice Magazine, RLD Publishing Corp., 1800 N. Highland Ave., Suite 316, Hollywood, CA 90028; (213) 465-1186. Monthly magazine about the motion-picture industry. Aimed at theater owners, film producers, directors, and financiers.

Cineaste Magazine, 200 Park Ave. S., New York, NY 10003; (212) 982-1241. A magazine on the art and politics of the cinema. For students, enthusiasts, and people who make or distribute films. Quarterly.

Daily Variety, 1400 N. Cahuenga Blvd., Hollywood, CA 90028; (213) 469-1141. Daily newspaper covering the motion-picture and entertainment industry in Hollywood.

Film Comment, Film Society of Lincoln Center, 140 W. 65th St., New York, NY 10023; (212) 877-1800. Bimonthly magazine for film buffs.

Filmmakers Monthly, P.O. Box 115, Ward Hill, MA 08130. Covers feature-film and independent-video production.

Film Quarterly, University of California Press, Berkeley, CA 94720; (415) 642-6333. Quarterly. In-depth analytical articles on the style and structure of films.

The Hollywood Reporter, 6715 Sunset Blvd., Hollywood, CA 90028; (213) 464-7411. Complete coverage of the entertainment industry, with special focus on the financial aspects of show business. Daily.

The Independent, 625 Broadway, New York, NY 10012. Newsletter for independent filmmakers.

Millimeter, 826 Broadway, New York, NY 10003; (212) 477-4700. Feature articles on the film industry. Monthly.

Moving Image, Sheptow Publishing Co., 609 Mission St., San Francisco, CA 94105; (415) 989-4360. How-to, informational, and technical articles on filmmaking. Published eight times a year.

On Location Magazine, 6777 Hollywood Blvd., Suite 501, Hollywood, CA 90028; (213) 467-1268. Bimonthly. Covers film and tape production; articles are technically oriented.

Photo Screen, Sterling's Magazines, 355 Lexington Ave., New York, NY 10017; (212) 391-1400. Articles on movie and TV stars. Bimonthly.

ScriptWriter Magazine for Entertainment Writers, 250 W. 57th St., Suite 1432, New York, NY 10019; (212) 582-1321. Monthly magazine for scriptwriters.

Shooting Commericals Magazine, Knowledge Industry Publications, Inc., 701 Westchester, White Plains, NY 10604; (914) 328-9157. Emphasizes commercial production for production companies, ad agencies, equipment houses, and actors.

Show Business, 134 W. 44th St., New York, NY 10036; (212) 586-6900. Weekly. For performers, producers, technicians, directors.

SMPTE Journal, Society of Motion Picture and Television Engineers, 862 Scarsdale Ave., Scarsdale, NY 10583; (914) 472-6606. Monthly technical journal on motion-picture and TV production.

Weekly Variety, 154 W. 46th St., New York, NY 10036; (212) 582-2700. For entertainment professionals.

Directories

Audiovisual Market Place, R. R. Bowker Company, New York, NY 10036; (212) 916-1600. Annual directory listing audiovisual producers, distributors, production companies, and related associations.

Film Daily Year Books, Film Daily, New York, NY. Directory of motion picture companies, services, and personnel.

Guide to Film and Video Resources, University Film Study Center, Cambridge, MA; (617) 253-7612. Lists film-production companies.

International Motion Picture Almanac, Quigley Publishing Company, 159 W. 53rd St., New York, NY 10022; (212) 247-3100. Annual directory of the film industry. Lists producers, distributors, services, agents, organizations, and unions.

On Location: The National Film and Videotape Production Directory, 6777 Hollywood Blvd., Suite 501, Hollywood, CA 90028; (213) 467-1268. Annual directory of film and videotape production–related services—production facilities, film processing, insurance, lighting, hotels, truck rentals, casting, etc.

Pacific Coast Studio Directory, Hollywood, CA 90028; (213) 467-2920. Quarterly directory. Lists production companies, representatives, agents, unions, guilds, organizations, and associations.

Books

Behlmer, Rudy, ed. *Memo from David O. Selznick.* New York: Viking, 1972. A behind-the-scenes look at the making of *Gone With the Wind* and other Selznick classics, as chronicled in Selznick's personal correspondence.

Brownlow, Kevin. *Hollywood: The Pioneers.* New York: Knopf, 1979. Film history illustrated with three hundred rare photographs of early Hollywood.

Capra, Frank. *The Name Above the Title.* New York: Macmillan, 1971. Capra's autobiography.

Kael, Pauline. *Deeper Into Movies.* Boston: Little, Brown, 1973. A collection of movie reviews from one of the best-respected movie critics in the country. Useful for its insight into the role movies play in American culture.

Kanin, Garson. *Hollywood.* New York: Viking, 1974. Autobiographical account of Hollywood in the 1930s and '40s by one of its most celebrated writer-directors.

Mast, Gerald. *A Short History of the Movies.* New York: Bobbs-

Merrill, 1971. Traces the evolution of the motion-picture industry
from 1895 to 1970.
Pechter, William S. *Twenty-four Times a Second: Film and Film-
Makers.* New York: Harper & Row, 1971. A collection of critical
essays on film, filmmakers, and the theory of film appreciation.
Robertson, Joseph F. *The Magic of Film Editing.* New York: Television/
Radio Age Books. Covers every aspect of professional film editing
from script to screen.
Shurtleff, Michael. *Audition: Everything an Actor Needs to Know to
Get the Part.* New York: Bantam Books, 1978. How to audition
successfully for stage and screen.

Professional Societies and Other Organizations of Interest to Film Professionals

American Film Institute Academy, Center for Advance Film Studies,
501 Doheny Rd., Beverly Hills, CA 90210; (213) 278-8777.
Internship program in feature-film production.
Artists Managers Guild, 9255 Sunset Blvd., Suite 930, Los Angeles, CA
90069; (213) 247-0628. Guild for Hollywood agents and man-
agers.
Association of Independent Video and Filmmakers, 625 Broadway,
New York, NY 10012; (212) 473-3400. Support services for
independent filmmakers.
Association of Motion Picture and TV Producers, 8480 Beverly Blvd.,
Los Angeles, CA 90048; (213) 651-0081. A trade association
representing producers and studios.
Astoria Motion Picture and Television Center Foundation, 35-11 35th
Ave., Astoria, NY 11106; (212) 392-5600. Internship program in
film.
Boston Film/Video Foundation, 39 Brighton Ave., Allston, MA 02134;
(617) 254-1616. Provides equipment and information to indepen-
dent filmmakers.
Career Planning Center, 1623 South La Cienega Blvd., Los Angeles,
CA 90035; (213) 273-6633. Offers a seminar in careers in the film
industry.
Contract Services Administration Trust Fund, 8480 Beverly Blvd.,
Hollywood, CA 90048; (213) 655-4200. Training programs in
film-related fields.

Directors Guild of America, 8480 Beverly Blvd., Hollywood, CA 90048; (213) 653-2200. Training program for directors.

Directors Guild of America, 1697 Broadway, Suite 405, New York, NY 10019; (212) 245-2545. Training program for film producers.

The Film Fund, 80 E. 11th St., Suite 647, New York, NY 10003; (212) 475-3720. Gives grants to producers of documentary and dramatic films.

Good People, 827 Hilldale Ave., Los Angeles, CA 90069; (213) 278-8221. Employment agency specializing in show business.

Institute of New Cinema Artists, 505 Eighth Ave., New York, NY 10001; (212) 695-0826. Training programs in technical areas of film and television for disadvantaged youth.

International Alliance of Theatrical Stage Employees and Moving Picture Machine Operators (IATSE), Local 659, 8480 Beverly Blvd., Hollywood, CA 90048; (213) 876-2320. Training program for film camera operators and special-effects assistants.

Motion Picture Association of America, 522 Fifth Ave., New York, NY 10036; (212) 840-6161. Trade association for large motion-picture production companies and distributors.

National Association of Broadcast Employees and Technicians (NABET), 135 W. 50th St., New York, NY 10022; (212) 757-3065. Union for movie and TV engineers and technicians.

Neighborhood Film Project, 3601 Locust Walk, Philadelphia, PA 19104; (215) 386-1536. Filmmaking workshops.

New School for Social Research, 66 W. 12th St., New York, NY 10011; (212) 741-5625. Courses in filmmaking.

New York Foundation for the Arts, 5 Beekman St., Suite 600, New York, NY 10038; (212) 233-3900. Placement program for artists in film.

New York University, Department of Cinema Studies, School of the Arts, 51 W. 4th St., New York, NY 10003; (212) 598-7777. Degree programs in cinema studies.

Northwest Film Study Center, Portland Art Museum, 1219 S.W. Park Ave., Portland, OR 97205; (503) 226-2811. Internships and courses in filmmaking.

Screen Publicists Guild, 13 Astor Pl., New York, NY 10003. Guild of film publicists.

Sherwood Oaks Experimental College, 6353 Hollywood Blvd., Hollywood, CA 90028; (213) 462-0669. Programs in filmmaking.

Society of Motion Picture and Television Engineers, 862 Scarsdale Ave., Scarsdale, NY 10583; (914) 472-6606. Professional organization for film engineers and technicians.

University of California, Theater Arts Department, 405 Helgard Ave.,
   Los Angeles, CA 90024; (213) 825-7891. Degree programs in film
   production, scriptwriting, and criticism.
*University of Southern California, Division of Cinema, School of
   Performing Arts,* University Park, Los Angeles, CA 90007; (213)
   741-2235. Academic program leading to a career as a film
   executive or independent producer.
Women of the Motion Picture Industry, International, c/o HOWCO
   International, P.O. Box 1805, Charlotte, NC 28201; (704) 375-
   6051. Publishes a newsletter for women in the movie business.
   Also offers career counseling.
Women's Interart Center, 549 W. 52nd St., New York, NY 10019;
   (212) 246-1050. Workshops in filmmaking.
Writers Guild of America, 8955 Beverly Blvd., Los Angeles, CA
   90048; (213) 550-1000. Labor union for film scriptwriters.
Writers Guild of America, 555 W. 57th St., New York, NY 10022;
   (212) 245-6180.
Young Filmmakers/Video Arts, 4 Rivington St., New York, NY 10002;
   (212) 673-9361. Film workshops.

Music

Ask the average person on the street to name five sculptors and he or she will come up blank. Five famous photographers? Again, a blank. Five painters? Most people won't get past two—Rembrandt and Picasso.

Now, ask a young person to name five rock groups or performers. He or she won't stop at *five*, but will give you names by the dozen: Boy George. Michael Jackson. Elvis Costello. Cyndi Lauper. David Bowie. Kiss. Queen. Huey Lewis and the News. The Eurythmics. Billy Joel. Lionel Richie. Duran Duran. The Cars. Genesis. Chicago. Prince. Talking Heads. Hall and Oates. Pat Benetar. Blondie. And the list can go into the hundreds.

Of all the commercial arts, popular music is the most widely enjoyed. A hardcover book is considered a best-seller if fifty thousand people buy it, but a record that sells fifty thousand copies is considered a flop. Top hits in rock and pop go gold (sell a million singles) every week; Michael Jackson's *Thriller* album has sold more than thirty million copies at the time of this writing. The media is fond of claiming that Johnny can't read, but he can sure buy and listen to records. Jim Miller acknowledges the boom in rock music in his introduction to *The Rolling Stone Illustrated History of Rock & Roll:*

> Today [rock] is an institution. A multi-billion dollar industry, it is welcome in Las Vegas and Hollywood, on the screen and over the air, in homes and theaters and supermarkets and elevators everywhere. It sells magazines, fills arenas, dominates radio. It is the music much of the world listens to much of the time.

The rock industry is a recent phenomenon, barely thirty years old. According to Carl Belz, author of *The Story of Rock,* the first rock record—the original version of "Sh-boom," by the Chords—was released in 1954 on the Cat label, a subsidiary of Atlantic. That same year, "Rock Around the Clock" by Bill Haley and the Comets became number one on the pop charts.

Things happened quickly after that. In 1956, Elvis Presley became nationally popular with the RCA release of "Heartbreak Hotel," and he remained the acknowledged king of rock-and-roll for more than ten years. The Beatles made their first visit to New York in 1964. And the next year the Rolling Stones released their big hit single "Satisfaction."

Millions of people today listen to rock. But almost none of them knows how the industry really works—how groups are discovered, how records are made and distributed, who earns the big money in the business. And without that understanding, you can't begin to look for a career in modern music.

This chapter is written to give you an overview of how the music business works and where the jobs are. Rather than focus on any one area, we show you where the opportunities are and help you decide which area is right for you.

We cover careers with record companies and music publishers, plus other related jobs, such as manager, producer, promoter, performer, and agent.

The good news is that the only prerequisite for most of these jobs is enthusiasm for and a love of contemporary music. Unlike such highly specialized fields as law, medicine, architecture, and computer programming, no special training is required to work in most of the jobs in the music business. Agents, managers, record-company executives, music publishers, and producers usually learn their profession through years of apprenticeship and on-the-job training, rather than academic courses or formal study.

The bad news is that the music business is highly competitive. It's tough to break in—especially if you have no more work experience or contacts than do the thousands of other people competing for the jobs.

By showing you where the jobs are, what they involve, and how to get them, this book will give you a competitive edge in your quest for a career in music.

"A VERY ROUGH BUSINESS"

Steve Scharf, an independent producer and former record-company executive, explains the competitive nature of the music business: "This is a very rough business. It takes an incredible amount of obsession. It's a full-time commitment. If you're meant to be in this business, you will be. If not, you'll get a lot of signs and you'll be thrust into something else.

"Music is a business and it's run like any other business. It is built on selling creative arts. The only business more difficult than this is the acting business, where it costs more and the cliques are tighter.

"There's very little middle ground. Either you're down in the dumps or you're up on top. You have to really want it, you have to love it, and you have to want to be in it all the way. You *can* make a lot of money in this business . . . but there are easier ways to make money.

"You've got to be meeting people and getting to the right people. Hustle is the key. You've got to *make* yourself become lucky. Most of the things that happen happen out of the blue. You're there, and something happens, and it clicks.

"A record deal doesn't mean you're going to make it. It's just the beginning of your troubles! A record deal is just a turn at bat.

"You have to dream. But you have to be realistic, too. Not everybody makes it. . . ."

"Everybody started somewhere," adds agent Dick Fox. "Most of us started at the bottom. You've got to crawl your way out."

Martha Reeves began her career as a $35-a-week secretary at Motown. Her group, Martha Reeves and the Vandellas, became one of the company's hottest acts. We asked one aspiring singer if she thought *she* was wasting time working as a secretary. She replied, "You're never wasting time when you're getting where you want to get."

Most successful agents, producers, and executives we interviewed agreed that unless you're a singer or songwriter, talent in music is second to luck, timing, persistence, hard work, and the ability to get along with people. "Music is a very people-oriented business," says Steve Scharf. "Everything you do is a personal contact."

Dick Fox agrees: "Half this business is relationships—*who* you know rather than *what* you know."

In 1979, records weren't selling, and the business was in a slump. Now, revitalized by music videos, the business is better than ever. But some observers say it has gotten tighter, more corporate, more businesslike.

The real money in the music industry is made in deals and percentages—not straight salaries. These days, a performer with a hit single can quickly grow wealthy. And the people who own a piece of his or her career—the agent, the personal manager, the songwriter, the music publisher, the publicist, the promoter—also profit from the star's success.

Songs earn money on many fronts, and each feeds into the other. Air play of a song on the radio promotes the sale of the single. The single helps sell the album. A music video also sells the album. And the album sells the live concerts, the *real* moneymakers of the business.

With so many hit songs bursting onto the scene every week, people get the false impression that rock-and-roll's superstars spring up overnight. But most "overnight successes" struggle for many years before getting their big break.

The question we hear most often from people is "What if I'm not a musician or experienced producer or promoter? How can a beginner—someone with no experience, contacts, or music background—get a job with a big record company or music publisher?"

There are no easy answers, no magic formulas to give job-seekers a guarantee of success. We did, however, ask top record-company executives to give us their advice on getting started. Here are their tips and tactics for getting that first big break:

1. **Start as a secretary.** In the major talent agencies, such as William Morris, men who aspire to be agents have traditionally been hired as secretaries and trained on the job.

   In record companies, secretaries are mostly women in the *A&R (artist and repertoire)* department; however, the

number of men starting as secretaries in all phases of the
business—including A&R—is on the rise.

To you, this may seem too humble a beginning, especially if you've already achieved some level of success in
the business world. But in a glamour field such as music,
getting in is the key. Take any job to start; it doesn't
matter which. Once you're in, you have the opportunity
to learn the business, to make contacts, and to move
around and up.

2. **Know music.** You wouldn't apply for a job as a computer
salesman and then go to the interview not knowing a
Kaypro from a Compaq. Similarly, you can't talk with
music people and convince them to hire you if you don't
speak their language.

This doesn't mean you have to be able to read music or
play lead guitar. But you should be up on what's happen-
ing in the business—the trends, the hits, the hot artists
and record labels, the "in" clubs and discos.

Learn to speak the jargon of music. Know the difference between *A&R, R&B,* and *P&D.* Be at ease with such
terms as *mix, master,* and *multitrack.*

You also need a basic grasp of how the industry works:
how artists are discovered and signed; where rock stars
find the songs they sing; how records are recorded,
manufactured, distributed, and marketed; how the business is organized; and where the jobs are. This chapter
provides you with an overview of the field.

3. **Transfer business skills from other industries.** As one
executive told us, "Business is business." On the business
and financial side, all industries are pretty much alike.
Working in the sales, marketing, distribution, publicity,
financial, or legal department of a record company is not
much different from holding the same position with a
bank, insurance company, manufacturer, or software
firm.

Yet it's far easier for a beginner to get a staff position in
these less competitive industries than it is in music. So
one career strategy might be to take a job in another field
(such as electronics, steel, automobiles, or packaged

goods), develop your skills in a particular area applicable to music as well (corporate law, finance, marketing, promotion), and later apply for a similar position at a record company. You'll be a much more attractive candidate than an applicant without your years of valuable "real world" experience.

4. **Make contacts.** Music is a people business, so the more people you know, the better your chances are of being hired. Don't be shy about getting a job through a friend, relative, or acquaintance in the business. What's important is getting hired, not how you do it.

   "But I don't know anyone!" you protest. Think again. Don't limit yourself to your immediate circle. Even a friend of a friend of a friend may wield enough influence to get you an interview or move your résumé from the bottom of the pile to the top.

   In his book *How to Sell Anything to Anybody,* Joe Girard estimates that the average person knows 250 people. Chances are that one of these 250 people may have an in at some record company or music publisher.

5. **Become known.** A more direct approach is to make yourself known to the important people in the business. Steve Scharf suggests going to music clubs in your area—clubs in which A&R people, agents, and producers may hang out in the hopes of discovering the next Blondie or Laura Branigan. Spotting these people is easier than you think, because they often sit at reserved tables with place cards showing their name and company affiliation.

   You might object that you can't just walk up to a stranger while he or she is enjoying a night on the town and introduce yourself. But you can. And it's that kind of aggressive, forward personality that employers in the music business are looking for.

6. **Use tapes.** If you're a songwriter, performer, manager, or producer, you're probably sending tapes of your act to A&R people, agents, and music publishers on a regular basis. After receiving your tapes repeatedly, these people get to know you, even if they're not particularly inter-

ested in signing your act. So if you decide to trade a chance at stardom for more steady employment, you already have valuable contacts you can call on for a job.

Phone your contacts and tell them that instead of sending another tape, you'd like to work in their department. If they like you and respect your work, you've got a good shot at a job.

7. **Avoid the personnel department.** Personnel doesn't hire. They just screen the résumés that come in through the mail and select the ones to be sent on to top management for consideration.

You can eliminate this screening step by sending your cover letter and résumé directly to the executive in charge of the department you want to join. Getting his or her name and title is as simple as calling up the company and asking the receptionist for it.

Also, you'll have a better chance of being noticed if you're persistent. Don't just mail a single letter and résumé and let it drop. Follow up with more letters, an updated résumé, and phone calls. You may not get a response for many months. But if you're persistent and professional in your approach, you'll be someone the executive thinks of when a job does open up.

8. **Sell yourself.** A lot of job-seekers tell us, "I don't see how I can get a record company to hire me. I don't have any specific background in music, and there must be a lot of people more qualified than me."

Take heart. As we've mentioned, the music business, unlike many other professions, doesn't require a college degree, special background, or extensive technical know-how. And what you lack in experience and training you can more than make up for with enthusiasm, aggressiveness, and hard work.

A shy personality is not an asset in this field. So don't be modest—highlight your positive features and tell people that you *can* do the job if they'll give you a chance to prove yourself. Don't apologize for your lack of experience; instead, stress your qualifications for the job.

Let's consider the case of John, a recent college graduate. At first glance, John doesn't see what an engineering major with no job experience can offer the A&R department of a record company.

But wait a minute. What about John's two years as a DJ on the college radio station? That indicates he's up-to-date on the latest in music trends. And what about his engineering degree? All those electronics courses will help him learn the technical side of record production in a hurry.

What else? John took trumpet lessons and played in his high-school band. So the record-company VP knows that John can read music. And John worked in a Sam Goody record store for two summers, so he's seen the retail end of the business firsthand.

Suddenly, John's prospects look a lot more promising. But he won't succeed in selling himself to the VP unless he highlights all this in his résumé, cover letter, and interviews. If John just puts "engineering major" at the top of his résumé and lets it go at that, he'll appear to be a far less attractive candidate than he really is.

9. **Free-lance.** If you can't get hired, you can always go out on your own as an independent producer, publisher, manager, songwriter, performer, technician, or studio musician.

Now, the chances are that if you're a novice, you won't make a lot of money free-lancing. But you will gain valuable experience and exposure in the industry. You'll see firsthand how the business operates on a day-to-day basis. And you'll come in contact with people who are in a position to give you a full-time job.

After six months or so, you can begin to approach these people about the possibility of employment. Because they know you as a working music professional, you'll be a more attractive candidate to them than someone without your music-industry background.

10. **Be in the right place at the right time.** There's no way to guarantee that this will happen, of course. But the more time and effort you spend in your job search, the more likely you are to end up in the right place . . . at the right time.

Be persistent. Keep a contact sheet showing whom you

have written to, when you sent each letter, the dates of your follow-up letters and phone calls, and what responses you received.

Luck and timing can play a big part in when and whether you get hired. Steve Scharf got his first job offer out of the blue while he was munching on a Swedish meatball at a dinner dance. But you have to be "out there," mixing and making contacts, for these opportunities to pass your way. As Louis Pasteur said, "Chance favors the prepared mind."

CAREER OPPORTUNITIES WITH RECORD COMPANIES

Record companies represent the largest source of employment in the music business and offer the best opportunities for beginners. This is because the major record companies are large corporations, and large corporations traditionally have more entry-level positions than small or medium-size firms.

There are two types of record companies: *majors* (the big companies, such as CBS, RCA, Warner Brothers, and Atlantic Records) and *independents* (smaller firms, such as Tommy Boy, Prelude, and Profile).

Focus your job search on the majors. For one thing, they have more jobs and more diverse opportunities. Independents have limited openings; a typical independent may have a staff of only five.

Second, majors usually work with the top artists because these companies have better distribution and can sell more records. Although an independent may discover rock's next superstar, the only way to rub shoulders with established big-name acts is to work at a major.

Independents are a vanishing breed. As independents grow and become larger, they get gobbled up by corporate conglomerates. For example, RCA recently purchased 50 percent of Arista, one of the larger independents.

You'll find a list of major record companies at the end of this chapter. Below, we outline the career opportunities they offer.

- **A&R.** A&R stands for *artist and repertoire*. The job of A&R
people (and a large record company may have a whole
department of A&R people) is to discover new talent and
sign the act to the record label. A&R people are also
responsible for finding songs for the recording artists to
perform.

  Perhaps the most famous A&R man is John Hammond,
who produced more than four thousand albums during his
tenure at Columbia Records. His acts included Benny
Goodman, Bessie Smith, Billie Holiday, Bob Dylan, and
Bruce Springsteen. Columbia also employed an A&R man
who went on to become famous as a performer: Mitch
Miller.

  You don't need musical ability to qualify for a job as an
A&R person. All that's required is an aptitude for spotting
songs and performers with star potential. Because there
are no concrete prerequisites, A&R is the best entry-level
opportunity in the business. Unfortunately, there are
many more people looking for A&R jobs than there are
openings, so it's difficult to break in.

  Marcy Drexler, East Coast A&R for MCA Records,
started out by taking a job as a secretary and moving up.
She recommends the same tactic for other beginners:
Start at a clerical job, then take on some extra work. For
example, most record companies are swamped with a
backlog of tapes submitted by performers, agents, and
publishers; you can score points with the A&R department
by volunteering to screen this backlog for them.

  A large part of the A&R person's day is spent listening to
demos—cassettes of songs sent in by musicians hoping to
be discovered by the record companies and launched into
stardom. A&R people we interviewed said they received
between twenty and one hundred tapes a week; surprisingly, most attempt to listen to all the tapes that cross
their desks.

  As an A&R person, you can spend your career listening
to endless amateur efforts in the hope of finding one new
talent. It has to be done that way, because there's no
scientific method of predicting where the next hot act will

come from. Drexler says she has listened to twenty to thirty tapes a day for the past eight years and has never signed one of them. But she keeps on listening. And hoping.

Tapes are not the only source of new talent. Many A&R people regularly go to clubs, concerts, and showcases to hear talent. And that can involve putting in a long evening of live music after a day at the tape player.

A&R people look for new songs for their label's current stars as well as for new performers. So they deal with music publishers and songwriters in addition to managers, musicians, and agents.

The smaller the record company, the more diverse the duties of the A&R person. At a major, the A&R person's sole function may be to listen to tapes and find new talent. At a medium-size company, the A&R might also work with existing talent and act as a "project coordinator" for new records, overseeing the details of budgets, schedules, and production. At small companies, the A&R people often double as record producers.

As an A&R person, you make recommendations, not decisions. The record-company president—not the A&R person—decides whether to sign an act. The attorneys in the business-affairs department—not the A&R person— determine how much the company will pay for the act.

How do you get started in A&R? Many people in this field start in other departments of the company—as sound engineers, producers, musicians, publicists, promoters— and move to A&R once they're established with the firm. Others come in off the street and, with luck and timing, land an entry-level spot in the A&R department.

Do you need to be musical? Not at all. A musical background is helpful, to be sure, but not necessary; many A&R people cannot even read music. In fact, one former A&R man said the biggest mistake A&R people make is to judge acts on personal taste rather than by what will sell. You'll succeed if you can figure out what the public wants . . . and then go out and find it.

Are there opportunities for advancement? Yes. An entry-level A&R person can be promoted to take charge of East

Coast or West Coast A&R. The next step up is a promotion to head of the A&R department and the title of Vice President. In general, the larger a record company is, the larger its A&R department—and the more opportunities there are to advance.

● **Artist development.** The artist-development person's job is to develop each act's "image." And the right image is the image that will sell the most records and keep the act in the public eye.

The exciting part of this job is that you'll be working directly with star performers and their managers. You and the manager will help build the star's career by shaping his image—how he looks, how he acts, how he dresses, what he says to the press, how he handles himself in public, how he performs on music videos.

The two skills you need to bring to the job are an instinct for what sells and an ability to manage people. You must establish a rapport with managers and musicians and get them to respect you and see your point of view. Because this is an entry-level position, no formal sales or managerial training is required. However, some background in promotion, personal management, or general involvement in the music business is helpful.

This is a highly specialized position, and only the largest of the majors have employees with the title of *director of artist development.* Smaller companies can't afford to hire specialists for this task and leave artist development to the A&R people.

● **Business affairs.** "Business affairs" is a fancy term for the record company's in-house legal department. Most record companies employ staff lawyers who negotiate record deals on behalf of the company and also handle record-club deals, distribution deals, and lawsuits.

Lawyers are more than technicians; they hold much of the real power in the music business. For example, it is the business-affairs department—not A&R—that decides how much money the company will offer a new act. Many record-company presidents started their careers in business affairs.

As a lawyer, you can enjoy great success at a record

company. But you can make even more money as an independent music attorney. We'll cover that career possibility a little later on in the chapter.

Business affairs is one department that does require specialized training: specifically, a law degree.

- **Marketing.** According to one record-company executive, "The job of marketing is solely to sell units of vinyl—as many as you can."

  The only difference between a marketing position with a record company and the same job with another firm is the product you are selling. The marketing person at a record company sells albums and singles; the marketing person at Procter & Gamble sells soap and detergent. Otherwise, the jobs are much the same.

  The marketing department is responsible for all activities that move albums from the factory to the record stores to the consumer: distribution, sales incentives, packaging, point-of-sale displays, consumer advertising, trade advertising, sales, merchandising, promotions, pricing. In some companies, the sales function is handled by a separate department; salespeople work directly with distributors and retailers to get the records into the stores.

  The best way to break into record marketing is to work in a marketing position in a different type of company, then move into music. Spend a year or two learning marketing at a large consumer-product firm. Get experience and on-the-job training to enhance your value to a record company. Then offer your services to the music business. Chances for employment are better when you are already an experienced marketing person, because few record companies can afford to take on and train a total novice.

- **Producer.** The producer is the person who is in charge of the creation of a new record. This job involves many responsibilities, from hiring studio musicians and sound engineers, to conducting recording sessions and mixing soundtracks, to the mechanical production of a master recording disk.

  A few of the largest majors have staff producers, and at

some small companies, A&R people double as producers. But most record companies hire independent producers rather than staff, and 99 percent of all producers are self-employed. Again, we'll discuss the career of independent producer later in the chapter.

- **Product manager.** At a big record company, a musician and his manager deal with many departments—A&R, production, artist development, business affairs, publicity, promotion, marketing, sales. And if the number becomes too large, the manager can become frustrated with struggling through the layers of corporate bureaucracy.

  To avoid this frustration, large record companies hire product managers. The product manager acts as a liaison between the artist and manager and all the departments in the record company. Rather than having to track down a dozen different people, the artist's manager can go to a single person—the product manager—to handle all his dealings with the company and get answers to his questions.

  The job requires a high degree of tact and diplomacy. To satisfy the needs of the artist, you must depend on the cooperation of people in your company who work in other departments and have other things to worry about. You must balance the artist's needs with the amount of pressure and prodding your colleagues are willing to put up with from you. Other than that, no special training or skills are required.

  The position of product manager is not a common one. Only the biggest companies need or hire product managers.

- **Promotion.** The best way to ensure the sale of a record is to get it played on the air. And getting the company's records played on the air is the job of the promotion department.

  This task seems easy enough: You mail your new album or single to the radio stations. Wait a week or two. Then follow up by mail, on the phone, or in person to convince them to play it. It's simple in theory, but tougher in practice. Radio stations are *deluged* with new albums and singles. So, as a promotion person, you've got to be a superior salesman to persuade the station to play your particular song.

Because there are so many radio stations—7,800 AM and FM stations at last count—record companies hire a lot of promotion people to reach all these stations. As a result, there are more jobs in promotion than in any other department (A&R probably comes in second, with business affairs a close third). And because getting air play is the key to boosting record sales, many people consider promotion to be the most important department in the company.

Promotion people specialize. There are promotion people who handle singles and promotion people who handle albums. There are national promotion people who work in the home office and local promotion people who handle specific territories throughout the country. There are promotion people who deal with specific types of radio stations: top 40, disco, rhythm and blues, country and western, easy listening, hard rock. Radio stations are also classified by the number of listeners they reach: primary stations reach a large audience; secondary stations reach a medium-size audience; and tertiary stations reach a small audience.

Promotion involves persuasion. A background in sales, marketing, advertising, or publicity can help develop your persuasive skills. Promotion is a good entry-level area, however, because there are so many jobs available. And if you're a successful promoter, you can step up to one of several vice presidencies in the department.

● **Publicity.** The publicist's job is to gain media exposure for his or her record company, its records, and its performing artists.

At first, this job sounds like a snap. After all, few subjects are as naturally newsworthy as a rock star. But the problem is that there are thousands of records and performing artists. And unless yours is in the top forty, the press simply isn't interested. The publicist's challenge is to *get* them interested.

Publicists prepare biographies, press photos, press kits, news releases, and video clips. They also handle press conferences, public appearances, parties, and anything else that will gain favorable exposure in the media.

You can learn the required PR skills by working for a public-relations agency or in the public-relations department of a large corporation. Once you've been trained, you'll be more valuable to the PR department of a record company than a novice with no prior experience.

Most record companies have publicists on staff. But there are also many music-industry publicists who work as independents.

CAREER OPPORTUNITIES IN MUSIC PUBLISHING

The record companies make deals with performers to produce and distribute their records. The songs on these records are written by songwriters. Some performers write their own songs, but most don't.

All songwriters are represented by firms known as *music publishers*. In a sense, the music publisher acts as the songwriter's "agent" by selling the right to record his or her songs in return for a percentage of the money paid by the record company.

Music publishing is one of the most lucrative areas in the music business because income is based on *royalties*. The songwriter and the publisher earn a royalty for every record sold and for every time the song is played on the radio, in concert, or even on a jukebox. Publishing can pay even better than performing. Bob Dylan and Buddy Holly both made more money from publishing royalties than from the sales of their own recordings.

Warner Brothers is the number one music publisher in the world, with a catalog of more than six hundred thousand songs. A *catalog* is the list of songs the publisher holds the rights to. The publisher makes money by licensing the songs in its catalog for recording or performance.

Other big publishers include Chappel, MCA, CBS Songs, and MPL Communications. MPL is owned by former Beatle Paul

McCartney, who is probably the wealthiest songwriter in the industry. McCartney owns his own compositions, plus those of Buddy Holly and such Broadway hits as *Annie* and *Grease.*

The catalog of Beatles tunes, comprising nearly three hundred songs, has generated more revenue than any other. Number two is the Jobete Music catalog. Jobete is the publisher for Motown, and their catalog contains songs by Marvin Gaye, Stevie Wonder, Smokey Robinson, and other Motown giants. Most performers rely on publishers to supply them with songs to record. Many performers—including the Beatles, Elton John, and Sting (of the Police)—set up their own publishing companies as they became successful enough to afford it.

Publishers make their money from a number of sources. One is the *mechanical royalty.* This is a royalty paid for every recording of the song sold. The royalty is negotiable, but as of this writing, it is approximately 4½ cents per song. The publisher usually splits this fifty-fifty with the songwriter.

A second source of publishing income is the *performance royalty.* This fee is paid to the publisher every time the song is played on radio and TV, in concert halls and clubs, or on a jukebox.

The performance royalties can vary from station to station, depending on the size of the audience reached. In general, AM stations pay from 1 to 3 cents a play; FM stations, 1 to 2 cents per play; TV, 2 to 6 cents and up.

Pennies can add up quickly when a hit receives heavy air play. In 1977, one hit single earned its publisher $2 million in performance royalties within a three-month period.

A third source of income for publishers is the *sound copyright.* In addition to the lyrics and arrangement, the actual sound recording can be copyrighted. The record company holds the copyright and makes money by selling the right to use the recording. They might sell it to a movie producer for use in a soundtrack or to another record company for inclusion in a collection of hit songs. The income from this sale is shared with the publisher.

Music publishers also get a royalty on the sale of sheet music and folios containing the printed lyrics and score of the song. The print royalty is 5 percent of the sale price.

The three basic career opportunities in this lucrative side of the music business are administration, professional management, and songwriting. Let's take a brief look at each area.

- **Administration.** Administrators handle the paperwork of music publishing: licensing deals, sublicensing, subpublishing, and copyrighting of songs.

  The music publisher controls 100 percent of the copyright and "owns" the rights to the song for a period ranging from eighteen months to two years, depending on the agreement with the songwriter. If the record gets recorded and released, the company owns it for thirty-five years.

  Administration is a pretty routine clerical job, but it can be a stepping-stone to the more challenging position of professional manager.

- **Professional manager.** The professional manager searches for promising songwriters, signs them up with the publisher, and tries to sell their songs to performing artists, record companies, agents, producers, and managers. The goal is to get the songwriter a *cover*, which is industry jargon for having your song recorded and released by a professional recording artist.

  The professional manager does more than scout talent, however. He or she also works with songwriters to help them develop their songwriting abilities.

  So professional managers serve a dual function. In one sense, the professional manager is the songwriter's "agent." The manager tries to get the best deals for the writer, since the publisher's income is directly proportional to the songwriter's success. In another sense, the manager serves as the publishing company's version of the A&R man. Just as A&R people search for new performers, professional managers are always on the lookout for songwriting talent.

- **Staff songwriter.** If you've written just one or two songs, a publisher might buy them individually. But if you've written half a dozen or more songs and are producing a steady output, the publisher might offer you a job as a staff songwriter.

This title is somewhat misleading. Staff songwriters don't put on a suit and tie, board the commuter train, and write songs in an office from nine to five. They are not actually employees of the publishing company.

A staff songwriter is paid a yearly salary, usually $15,000 to $25,000. Some songwriters receive one lump sum; others draw a weekly paycheck. In return for the salary, the music publisher owns every song the songwriter writes during the year. Staff songwriters have to meet a quota—usually a dozen or so songs a year.

Even if you meet your quota, success is not guaranteed. If your songs don't sell, the publisher is likely to drop you after the year is up. But if your songs *do* sell, the publisher will keep you on. They may even elevate you to the position of *copublisher,* which means that you get to keep a bigger percentage of your mechanical and performance royalties.

To become a staff writer, you have to interest a music publisher in your songs. And that's hard to do, because there are so many songwriters competing in a limited market.

Like the performer, the songwriter must create a demo tape and send it out to music executives. Assuming your songs are good, having a publisher listen to your tape and sign you up is largely a matter of persistence, luck, and timing. There's no way to *force* a publisher to listen to your tapc. They already have more tapes than they can ever hope to hear.

One way to turn a no into a maybe is to include a cover letter with your tape. In the cover letter, say that you'd appreciate any comments and criticisms the publisher can offer on your songs. This feedback can help you improve your demo so the next publisher hears a better tape. And it can help you cultivate a friendly contact who will give special attention to you when you come back with your next batch of songs.

OTHER CAREER OPPORTUNITIES IN THE MUSIC BUSINESS

So far, we've focused on working for large established companies: record companies and music publishers.

But the richest people in the music business are the independents—agents, attorneys, managers, producers, and, of course, performers. The rest of this chapter is devoted to careers in which you can make it big in the music business *working on your own.*

- **Agents.** Simply put, agents make deals for performing artists. And get 10 percent of the gross for their troubles.

  The big agents make record and concert deals, and also handle books, movies, and other special moneymaking offers. Smaller *booking agents* book lesser-known performers into local clubs, showcases, concert halls, lounges, and tours. To make deals happen, the agent has to be shrewd enough to negotiate with a wide range of people: publishers, record-company executives, promoters, producers, TV and movie writers. The agent does everything but handle the final contract, which is created and approved by attorneys.

  The big agencies in the music business include William Morris, International Creative Management (ICM), and the Agency for the Performing Arts (APA). There are also dozens of successful smaller agencies, including many independents.

  Dick Fox, a successful agent whose client list includes Barry Manilow, Neil Sedaka, Melissa Manchester, and Robert Klein, started in show business at age eighteen as an actor. Disillusioned with that career, Fox asked himself, "Do I want to schlep around the country getting bit parts, or do I want a real job?" He decided he wanted the security of a real job.

  Fox went to secretarial school and became a secretary in the agent-trainee program at William Morris. He worked hard, going to clubs and listening to tapes seven nights a week. One of Fox's first discoveries was Barry Manilow, who was playing piano in the lounge of a New York restaurant. Today Fox runs his own successful show-business agency with clients in music, film, and television. What is the secret of his success? "Instinct," says Fox. "This whole business is based on instinct."

The best way to break into the agent business is to start as a secretary/trainee with a big-name agency, as Dick Fox did. Having the name of a William Morris or ICM behind you gives you more clout than you'd have as a novice self-employed agent with no track record. Once you discover and create a superstar, you can leave the big agency and start your own firm.

Independents make more money because they get to keep the 10 percent. Staff agents at big agencies receive a salary plus bonus; the agency keeps most of the profit from the deal.

- **Lawyers.** Independent music attorneys are among the richest and most powerful people in the music business today. "The lawyers have become the power behind the record deals," says agent Dick Fox.

  Everybody in the business needs a lawyer. So lawyers can represent a wide range of clients: performers, songwriters, publishers, managers, agents, producers, and record companies. Almost no deal is made in music today without lawyers profiting on both sides.

  Fee arrangements vary. Some music attorneys charge a monthly retainer. Others get a percentage of the deal. Still others charge an hourly rate ranging from $100 to $250 and up.

  You must, of course, have a graduate law degree to work in this field.

- **Business manager.** There are two types of independent managers in the music business: personal managers and business managers.

  The business manager is a financial adviser. He takes the money the rock star makes and invests it. His role is solely that of personal financial planner and investment counselor; he has nothing at all to do with the music business.

  Most business managers charge a fee equal to 5 percent

of the funds they handle. To qualify for the job, you have to be an accountant, lawyer, or professional financial planner or money manager. (See our chapter on "Finance" for career information in the financial planning field.)

- **Personal manager.** The personal manager handles all of the performer's business affairs and guides the progress of his or her career every step of the way.

These responsibilities were once handled by the agent. The job of personal manager came into being when agents took on so many clients that they became too busy to give performers the kind of personal attention they need. A typical agent may have dozens of clients; a personal manager has three or four at most. The agent concentrates on making deals; the personal manager "holds the artist's hand" day in and day out.

Agents are limited by law to a maximum fee of 10 percent, but personal managers can charge whatever they think is fair. In general, their fees range from 15 to 25 percent of the performer's income.

A personal manager doesn't have to have good taste in music or be able to spot a hit song; he just has to be able to spot business opportunities and make deals happen. The personal manager is part negotiator, part career counselor, part psychologist to his clients.

There are no entry-level positions in personal management. Most managers were already successful in the music business (many were agents) and decided to concentrate their efforts on managing the careers of a few hot prospects. If a star comes to you because of your reputation and says, "I'd like you to manage me," then congratulations—you've become an instant personal manager!

- **Producer.** The producer is the person with the creative control over the final product (the record). Unlike a movie producer, a music producer does not put up money; rather, he is paid for his services by the record company who hires him. A few producers work on staff at major record companies. But the majority are independents, and that's where the money is.

The producer is responsible for all phases of record

production: budgets, studio work, electronics, engineering, sound mixing, hiring of musicians, rehearsals, arrangements, selection of songs, and the technical production of record masters.

"Half my job is being a psychologist—holding the artist's hand to get the best performance," says producer Steve Scharf. "You have to have a good song sense, know how to pick songs, how to put together bands or pick studio musicians, find and work with arrangers."

Producers come from varied backgrounds, and their prior experience often dictates their approach to the job. For example, producers who come from an engineering background produce technically slick recordings with sharp sound but may miss the emotion and the sensitivity of the music. Producers who once wrote musical arrangements tend to produce records with lush orchestrations—plenty of French horns, strings, that sort of thing.

Some producers make the mistake of forcing an artist to conform to their preconceived notion of how a record should sound. But a good producer captures, develops, brings out, and puts on record the best of what the artist already has. "I try to take the artists and make them go places they wouldn't go themselves," says Scharf. "I try to capture their essence but make them sound ten times better . . . make it feel real and alive and relaxed."

What are the steps involved in producing a record? First comes rehearsal and preproduction. The producer and performers experiment with arrangements, concepts, performances, and sounds. And a few basic tracks—bass, drums, rhythm, possibly piano—are recorded on tape. (A standard two-inch tape contains twenty-four separate tracks; each can record a different instrument or vocal.)

Next comes the recording session in the studio. The group plays the song, which is recorded on the tape. Then the tape is *mixed*. The mixing process balances the tracks. The engineer can boost some sounds and make others more subdued.

Once the tape is mixed to perfection, the recording is *mastered* (pressed into vinyl). Copies are made, packaged, and distributed to the stores. But the producer's job is over once the master is finished. For his labors, the producer receives a flat production fee plus a royalty based on percentage of sales. On a full-length album, the producer's fee can range from $10,000 to $50,000. Producing the album can take two or three months.

On a single, he earns from $750 to $1,000, or even more. He may spend two or three weeks producing a two-sided single. Royalties on singles and albums average 3 percent of sales but can be as high as 5 or 6 percent.

Keep in mind that the producer's fee is only one of the expenses involved in producing a record. There is studio time, musician's and arranger's fees, physical reproduction, and packaging. It generally costs the record company anywhere from $150,000 to $250,000 to produce a first-class full-length album. So it's important that the producer make it come out right.

- **Promoters.** Promoters put on concerts. Being a promoter isn't a job; it's an entrepreneurial venture.

  Promoters don't get salaries. Their profit on a concert is the revenue from ticket sales minus the cost of staging the concert. These costs include everything from renting the concert hall and paying the performer to printing the tickets and paying for the advertisements.

  Promoters are the great risk-takers of the music business. Agents, managers, and performers put their time and egos on the line, but promoters also put up their money— sometimes tens (or even hundreds) of thousands of dollars. Concert promotion is a business for experienced entrepreneurs who can afford to gamble money to make money. It's not a game for beginners.

- **Performer.** Thousands of youngsters dream of becoming rock superstars. Certainly, performing on stage and on record is the most glamorous aspect of the music business. It's also the toughest to break into. At best, pursuing a career as a singer and performer is a long shot. If it's your dream, go for it. But realize at the beginning that of the thousands who want to be stars, only a handful make it.

  If, on the other hand, you realize you're probably not cut

out to take Elvis's place, but still want to be involved in music, we suggest you try for one of the many rewarding music careers outlined in this chapter.

Still want to take a shot at the big-time? Okay. First, you'll need talent. And even talent is no guarantee of success. Rather, it's the minimum requirement for even *considering* the pursuit of a performing career.

Next, you need to make a great demo tape to send to agents, managers, and A&R executives at the record companies. The tape should show you at your best—a great performance with hit material. Don't send out second-rate material; if the A&R people don't like your first tape, they're less likely to listen to a second. Lead with the very best you've got.

If you know the basics of sound recording and have access to decent equipment, you can make the demo yourself. Otherwise, you might want to hire an independent producer. Although producers are expensive, many will charge less for a demo than they would for a song commissioned by a record company.

A&R people use their instincts and personal taste to pick the acts they want to sign. Which means that you, as a performer, can never predict who will like your music and why. Don't be disheartened by rejection. Just about every successful performer experienced years of rejection before being "discovered overnight."

However, to be discovered, you have to be out there, playing "gigs" and sending your demo tapes to music executives. Stick to a regular schedule of mailing tapes to various record-company executives. Follow up by mail and phone. Keep track of the results.

Also, play the clubs, discos, and lounges. In many cities, there are showcases and cabarets where undiscovered groups and singers perform without pay in exchange for the chance to be heard by record-company executives, producers, and agents. Many young agents and A&R people make a habit of going to these places in the hopes of finding an act with star potential.

And remember: The only thing that's certain in the business is that you can't be discovered if people don't get to hear you.

Persistence, dedication, and a belief in your own abilities are vital to your success. "To make it, you have to have a major commitment to your craft," says Dick Fox. "The business is tough today. But there's a chance for everyone."

Some Companies with Outstanding Records

There are hundreds of small companies churning out obscure records by the dozen. But only the larger record companies consistently make the top 40, and they generate most of the revenue in the record industry. Here they are:

A&M Records, 1416 N. La Brea Ave., Los Angeles, CA 90028; (213) 469-2411. Barry Korkin, A&R.

A&M Records, 595 Madison Ave., New York, NY 10022; (212) 826-0477. Nancy Jeffries, vice president, A&R.

Aero Records, 141 E. 63rd St., New York, NY 10022; (212) 838-6565. Michael Gusick, president.

Arista Records, 6 W. 57th St., New York, NY 10019; (212) 489-7400. Abbey Knowitch, vice president, A&R.

Arista Records, 1888 Century Park E., Los Angeles, CA 90067; (213) 553-1777. Neil Portnow, vice president, A&R.

Atlantic/Atco Records, 75 Rockefeller Plaza, New York, NY 10019; (212) 484-6000. Aziz Goksal, A&R.

Bearsville Records, P.O. Box 135, Bearsville, NY 12409; (914) 679-7303. Ian Kimmet, vice president, A&R.

Buddah Records, 810 Seventh Ave., New York, NY 10019; (212) 582-6900. Art Kass, president.

Capitol Records, Inc., Hollywood & Vine Sts., Hollywood, CA 90028; (213) 462-6252. Don Grierson, vice president, A&R.

Capitol Records, Inc., 1370 Sixth Ave., New York, NY 10019; (212) 757-7470. Bruce Garfield, vice president, A&R.

Caytronics Corporation/Salsoul Records, 240 Madison Ave., New York, NY 10016; (212) 889-7340. Ken Cayre, vice president, A&R.

Chrysalis Records, 9255 Sunset Blvd., Los Angeles, CA 90069; (213) 550-0171. Jeff Aldrich, vice president, A&R.

Chrysalis Records, 645 Madison Ave., New York, NY 10022; (212) 935-8750. Brendan Bourke, A&R.

Columbia Records, 51 W. 52nd St., New York, NY 10019; (212) 975-4321. Mickey Eichner, vice president, A&R; Don DeVito, director of talent acquisition.

Columbia Records, 1801 Century Park W., Los Angeles, CA 90067; (213) 556-4700. Michael Dilbeck, vice president, A&R.

CTI Records, 46 West 11th St., New York, NY 10011; (212) 674-1111. Creed Taylor, president; Vic Chirumbolo, vice president, A&R.

Delite Records, 1733 Broadway, New York, NY 10019; (212) 757-6770. Gabe Vigorito, president.

Elektra/Asylum/Nonesuch Records, 962 N. LaCienaga Blvd., Los Angeles, CA 90069; (213) 655-8280. Roy Thomas Baker, vice president, A&R.

Elektra/Asylum/Nonesuch Records, 665 Fifth Ave., New York, NY 10022; (212) 355-7610. Bruce Lundval, president; Victor Chirel, A&R.

EMI America/Liberty Records, 1750 N. Vine St., Hollywood, CA 90028; (213) 461-9141. Rupert Perry, president; Gary Gersh, vice president, A&R.

EMI America/Liberty Records, 1350 Sixth Ave., New York, NY 10019; (212) 757-7470. Steve Ralbovsky, A&R.

The Entertainment Co. Records, 1700 Broadway, New York, NY 10019; (212) 265-2600. Linda Gerrity, A&R.

Epic, Portrait & Associated Labels, 51 W. 52nd St., New York, NY 10019; (212) 975-4321. Lennie Petze, vice president, A&R—Epic; Bob Feineigle, vice president, A&R—Portrait.

Fantasy Records, Tenth & Parker, Berkeley, CA 94710; (415) 549-2500. Ralph Kaffel, president.

Full Moon Records, 8380 Melrose Ave., Los Angeles, CA 90069; (213) 938-9117. Howard Kaufman, president.

Geffen Records, 9126 Sunset Blvd., Los Angeles, CA 90069; (213) 278-9010. Carole-Pinckes Childs, A&R.

Geffen Records, 75 Rockefeller Plaza, New York, NY 10019; (212) 484-7170. John David Kalodner, A&R.

GRP Records, 555 West 57th St., New York, NY 10019; (212) 245-7033. Larry Rosen, vice president and general manager.

Hannibal Records, 611 Broadway, New York, NY 10012; (212) 420-1780. Joe Boyd, president.

Kirshner Entertainment Corp., 1370 Sixth Ave., New York, NY 10019; (212) 489-0440. Don Kirshner, president.

Lifesong Records, 488 Madison Ave., New York, NY 10022; (212) 752-3033. Terry Cashman, president.

MCA Records, Inc., 100 Universal City Plaza, University City, CA 91405; (213) 985-4321. Irving Azoff, president; Tom Trumbo, vice president, A&R.

MCA Records, Inc., 10 E. 53rd St., New York, NY 10022; (212) 888-9700. Bob Feiden, vice president, A&R.

Mercury-Phonogram Records, 810 Seventh Ave., New York, NY 10019; (212) 399-7485. Peter Lubin, A&R.

Millennium Records, 1697 Broadway, New York, NY 10019; (212) 974-0200. Jimmy Ienner, president.

Motown Record Corporation, 6255 Sunset Blvd., Los Angeles, CA 90028; (213) 468-3500. Steve Barri, vice president, A&R.

Nemperor Records, 888 Seventh Ave., New York, NY 10019; (212) 541-6210. Patrick Clifford, A&R.

Network Records, 9200 Sunset Blvd., Los Angeles, CA 90069; (213) 859-1220. Al Coury, president.

Polygram Records/Polydor & Associated Labels, 810 Seventh Ave., New York, NY 10019; (212) 581-4890. Jerry Jaffe, senior vice president, rock division; John Stainze, vice president, A&R.

Prelude Records, 200 W. 57th St., New York, NY 10019; (212) 582-3555. Cory Robbins, president; Steve Plotnicki, vice president.

RCA Records, 1133 Sixth Ave., New York, NY 10036; (212) 930-4000. Gregg Geller, division vice president of music operations; Wendy Goldstein, A&R.

RCA Records, 6363 Sunset Blvd., Los Angeles, CA 90028; (213) 461-9171. Paul Atkinson, vice president, A&R.

RFC Records, 75 Rockefeller Plaza, New York, NY 10019; (212) 489-0240. Ray Caviano, president.

Roulette Records, 1790 Broadway, New York, NY 10019; (212) 757-9880. Morris Levy, president.

RSO Records, 1775 Broadway, New York, NY 10019; (212) 975-0700. Fred Gershon, president.

Sire Records, 165 W. 74th St., New York, NY 10023; (212) 595-5500. Seymour Stein, president.

Streetwise Records, Ltd., 25 W. 43rd St., New York, NY 10036; (212) 382-1476. Arthur Baker, president.

Tommy Boy Records, 210 E. 90th St., New York, NY 10028; (212) 348-4700. Tommy Silverman, president.

Vanguard Recording Society, 71 W. 23rd St., New York, NY 10001; (212) 255-7732. Danny Weiss, vice president, A&R.

Warner Brothers Records, 3300 Warner Blvd., Burbank, CA 91510; (213) 846-9090. Lenny Waronker, president; Ted Templeman, vice president, A&R.

Warner Brothers Records, 3 E. 54th St., New York, NY 10022; (212) 832-0950. Jerry Wexler, senior vice president, A&R.

WMOT Records, 1307 Vine St., Philadelphia, PA 19107; (215) 922-6640. Steve Bernstein, president.

Ze Records, 850 Seventh Ave., New York, NY 10019; (212) 245-7233. Michael Zilkha, president.

They Write the Songs. . . .

Record companies record the songs. But they *buy* the songs from music publishers. Here are the top publishers in the music industry:

Acuff-Rose Publishing, Inc., 2510 Franklin Rd., Nashville, TN 37204; (615) 385-3031. Wesley Rose, president.

Almo-Irving Music Publishing, 1358 N. La Brea Ave., Hollywood, CA 90028; (213) 469-2411. Lance Freed, president; Brenda Andrews, vice president and general manager.

Arista/Careers Music, 1888 Century Park E., Los Angeles, CA 90067; (213) 553-1777. Billy Meshel, vice president and general manager.

Arista/Careers Music, 6 West 57th St., New York, NY 10019; (212) 489-7400.

Asilomar/Dreena Music Co., 43 W. 61st St., New York, NY 10023; (212) 757-8805. Ron Beigel, vice president and general manager.

ATV Music Group, 6255 Sunset Blvd., Hollywood, CA 90028; (213) 462-6933. Steve Love, vice president and general manager.

ATV Music Group, 888 Seventh Ave., New York, NY 10019; (212) 977-5680. Jerry Teifer, vice president and general manager.

ATV Music Group, 1217 16th Ave. S., Nashville, TN 37212; (615) 373-2753. Byron Hill, professional manager.

Belwin-Mills Publishing Corp., 1776 Broadway, New York, NY 10019; (212) 245-1100. Robin Feather, professional manager.

Bourne Co., 437 Fifth Ave., New York, NY 10016; (212) 679-3700. Bonnie Bourne, president.

Three B Music Co., 437 Fifth Ave., New York, NY 10016; (212) 679-3700. Michael Berardi, president.

CAM-USA, 489 Fifth Ave., New York, NY 10017; (212) 682-8400. Artie Simon, professional manager.

CBS Songs, 49 E. 52nd St., New York, NY 10022; (212) 975-4886. Danny Strick, professional manager.

Chappell Music & Co., 810 Seventh Ave., New York, NY 10019; (212) 399-7373. Bob Cutarella, professional manager.

Chrysalis Music Publishing, 9255 Sunset Blvd., Los Angeles, CA 90069; (213) 550-0171. Ann Munday, vice president and general manager.

Chrysalis Music Publishing, 115 E. 57th St., New York, NY 10022; (212) 935-8754. Cherie Fonorow, professional manager.

Delightful Music Publishing, 1733 Broadway, New York, NY 10019; (212) 757-6770. Gabe Vigorito, president.

Famous Music Publishing, 1 Gulf & Western Plaza, New York, NY 10023; (212) 333-3918. Sid Herman, vice president and general manager.

Fourth Floor Music, P.O. Box 135, Bearsville, NY 12409; (914) 679-7303. Ian Kimmet, vice president and general manager.

Al Gallico Music Corporation, 9255 Sunset Blvd., Los Angeles, CA 90069; (213) 274-0165. Craig Aristei, professional manager.

Al Gallico Music Corp., 120 E. 56th St., New York, NY 10022; (212) 355-5980. Linda Landi, professional manager.

Hudson Bay Music Co., 1619 Broadway, New York, NY 10036; (212) 489-8170. Robert Bienstock, professional manager.

Intersong Music, 810 Seventh Ave., New York, NY 10019; (212) 399-7910. Mitchell Schoenbaum, professional manager.

Dick James Organization, 24 Music Square E., Nashville, TN 37203; (615) 242-0600. Michael Hollandsworth, professional manager.

Jobete Music Co., 157 W. 57th St., New York, NY 10019; (212) 581-7420. Iris Gordy, vice president and general manager.

Kirshner Entertainment Corp., 1370 Sixth Ave., New York, NY 10019; (212) 489-0440. Don Kirshner, president.

Koppleman/Bandier Music Co., 1700 Broadway, New York, NY 10019; (212) 265-2600. Joanne Boris, vice president and general manager.

Louise Jack/Sumac Music Co., 1697 Broadway, New York, NY 10019; (212) 246-0575. Susan McCusker, president.

E.B. Marks Music Co., c/o Hudson Bay Music Co., 1619 Broadway, New York, NY 10036; (212) 489-8170. Fred Bienstock, president.

MCA Music, Inc., 70 Universal City Plaza, Universal City, CA 91608; (213) 508-4550. Rick Shoemaker, vice president.

MCA Music, Inc., 445 Park Ave., New York, NY 10022; (212) 759-7500. Mike Millius, professional manager.

MCA Music, Inc., 1106 17th Ave. S., Nashville, TN 37212; (615) 327-4622. Jerry Crutchfield, vice president and general manager.

Robert Mellin Music Publishing, 1841 Broadway, New York, NY 10023; (212) 757-3287. Robert Mellin, president.

Might Three Music, 309 S. Broad St., Philadelphia, PA 19107; (215) 546-3510. Constance Heigler, professional manager.

MLO Music, 919 Third Ave., New York, NY 10022; (212) 758-0522.

Ivan Mogull Music Corp., 625 Madison Ave., New York, NY 10022; (212) 355-5636. Ivan Mogull, president.

E. H. Morris & Co., Inc., 39 W. 54th St., New York, NY 10019; (212) 581-1330. Lee Eastman, president.

O'Lyric Music Co., 1116 North Cory, Los Angeles, CA; (213) 506-5473. Jim O'Loughlin, president.

Peer-Southern Music, 1740 Broadway, New York, NY 10019; (212) 265-3910. Holly Green, professional manager.

The Richmond Organization, 10 Columbus Circle, New York, NY 10019; (212) 765-9889. Paul Richmond, professional manager.

Rothstein Music, Ltd., 720 E. 79th St., Brooklyn, NY 11236; (718) 444-8387. Sharon Rothstein, president.

Runnit Music Publishing, 250 W. 57th St., New York, NY 10019; (212) 541-7283. Tony Smith, president.

Screen Gems–EMI Music, 6255 Sunset Blvd., Hollywood, CA 90028; (213) 469-8371. Lester Sill, president; Ira Jaffe, vice president and general manager.

Screen Gems–EMI Music, 1370 Sixth Ave., New York, NY 10019; (212) 489-6740. Don Paccione, general manager.

Shapiro-Bernstein & Co., Inc., 10 E. 53rd St., New York, NY 10022; (212) 751-3395. Michael Brettler, professional manager.

Sherlyn Music Publishing Company, 495 SE 10th Court, Hialeah, FL 33010. Henry Stone, president.

Stallman Records, Inc., 333 E. 70th St., New York, NY 10021; (212) 988-2873. Lou Stallman, president.

Tree Publishing Co., P.O. Box 1273, 8 Music Square W., Nashville, TN 37203; (615) 327-3162. Buddy Killen, president.

United Artists Music Corp., c/o CBS Songs, 1930 Century Park W., Century City, CA 90067; (213) 556-4790. Mike Stewart, president.

United Artists Music Corp., c/o CBS Songs, 49 E. 52nd St., New York, NY 10022; (212) 975-4886. Danny Strick, professional manager.

Valando Music Publishing Corp., 1270 Sixth Ave., New York, NY 10020; (212) 489-9686. Tommy Valando, president.

Warner Bros. Music Corp., 9200 Sunset Blvd., Los Angeles, CA 90069; (213) 273-3323. Ron Vance, vice president.

Warner Bros. Music Corp., 75 Rockefeller Plaza, New York, NY
10019; (212) 484-6237.

Ten Percent of a Superstar

Maybe you don't have the musical talent to become the next Lou Reed
or Michael Jackson. But you can still make 10 percent of the millions
music's next superstar will earn—by discovering this unknown talent
and becoming his or her agent.

One way to start is to get a job as an agent, clerk, or secretary with
an established agency. Some of the top ones are listed below:

Agency for the Performing Arts, 888 Seventh Ave., New York, NY
10019; (212) 582-1500. Roger Vorce, vice president.
Albatross Productions, 14611 First Ave. S., Seattle, WA 98168; (206)
241-2320. Ken Kennear, president.
Alive Enterprises, 8600 Melrose Ave., Los Angeles, CA 90069; (213)
659-7001. Shep Gordon, president.
Alive Enterprises, 1775 Broadway, New York, NY 10019; (212) 977-
8780. Danny Markus, vice president, East Coast.
Buddy Allen Management, 65 W. 55th St., New York, NY 10019;
(212) 581-8988. Buddy Allen, president.
American Entertainment Management, 230 W. 55th St., New York,
NY 10019; (212) 957-4090. Peter Leeds, president.
American Talent International, 888 Seventh Ave., New York, NY
10019; (212) 977-2300. Jeff Franklin, president.
Dee Anthony Organization, 33 E. 70th St., New York, NY 10021;
(212) 249-1250. Dee Anthony, president; Vince Mauro, vice
president.
Apostol Enterprises, Ltd., 201 E. 61st St., New York, NY 10021; (212)
832-2980. John Apostol, president; Lenny Lambert, vice presi-
dent.
Peter Asher, Suite 100, 8430 Santa Monica Blvd., Los Angeles, CA
90069; (213) 273-9433.
Associated Booking Corp., 1995 Broadway, New York, NY 10023;
(212) 874-2400. Oscar Cohen, president.
Athena Artists, 9100 Wilshire Blvd., Beverly Hills, CA 90212. Chet
Hanson, president.
Aucoin Management, 645 Madison Ave., New York, NY 10022; (212)
826-8800. Bill Aucoin, president.
Barry Bergman Management, 2555 E. 12th St., Brooklyn, NY 11235;
(718) 332-8500. Barry Bergman, president.

Sid Bernstein & Associates, c/o The New York Music Company, 29 W. 57th St., New York, NY 10019; (212) 980-4649. Sid Bernstein, president.

Brighton Agency, 9885 Charleyville Blvd., Beverly Hills, CA 90212; (213) 278-2210. Nick Masters, president.

Carr Company, P.O. Box U, Tarzana, CA 91356; (213) 705-2717. Budd Carr, president.

Castle Music Productions, 923 Fifth Ave., New York, NY 10021; (212) 759-7294. Peter Casperson, president.

Cavallo-Ruffalo-Fargnoli Management, 2323 Corinth Ave., Los Angeles, CA 90064; (213) 473-1564. Bob Cavallo, president; Joe Ruffalo, vice president.

Champion Entertainment Organization, 130 W. 57th St., New York, NY 10019; (212) 765-8553. Tommy Mottola, president; Jeb Brien, vice president.

Roger Davies Management, 9229 Sunset Blvd., Los Angeles, CA 90069; (213) 850-0662. Roger Davies, president.

Day 5 Productions, 216 Chatsworth Dr., San Fernando, CA 91340. Marcia Day, president.

Ron Delsener Productions, 27 E. 67th St., New York, NY 10021; (212) 249-7773. Ron Delsener, president; Stan Feig, vice president.

Rick Derrickson Management, 315 W. 55th St., New York, NY 10019; (212) 247-2745. Rick Derrickson, president.

Paul Drew Enterprises, 2151 N. Hovart, Los Angeles, CA 90027; (213) 469-4100. Paul Drew, president.

Empire Agency, 401 Atlanta St., Marietta, GA; (404) 427-1200. Alex Hodges, president.

Norman Epstein Management, 644 N. Doheny Dr., Los Angeles, CA 90069; (213) 271-5181. Norman Epstein, president.

ESP Management, 1790 Broadway, New York, NY 10019; (212) 765-8450. Bud Prager, president.

Fast-Forward Management, 81 Bedford St., New York, NY 10014; (212) 243-3423. Ed Kleinman, president.

Frank Management, 375 N. Broadway, Jericho, NY 11753; (516) 681-5522.

Free Flow Productions, 1209 Baylor, Austin, TX 78703; (512) 474-6926. Michael Brovsky, president; Witt Stewart, vice president.

Frontier Booking, Inc., 1776 Broadway, New York, NY 10019; (212) 246-1505. Ian Copeland, president.

Frontline Management, 8380 Melrose Ave., Los Angeles, CA 90069; (213) 859-1900. Larry Solters, president.

Garlund Management, 132 Nassau St., New York, NY 10038; (212) 499-6384. Eric Gardner, president; Janice Lundy, vice president.

Bennett Glotzer Management, 7720 Sunset Blvd., Los Angeles, CA 90046; (213) 855-7056. Bennett Glotzer, president.

Marc Gordon Productions, 1022 N. Palm Ave., Los Angeles, CA 90069. Marc Gordon, president.

Bill Graham Productions, 201 Eleventh St., San Francisco, CA 94103; (415) 864-0815. Bill Graham, president.

Hartmann & Goodman, 1500 Crossroads of the World, Los Angeles, CA 90028. John Hartmann, president.

Fred Heller Associates, 211 W. 56th St., New York, NY 10019; (212) 265-1501. Fred Heller, president.

Jake Hooker Enterprises, 444 E. 75th St., New York, NY 10021; (212) 744-3504. Jake Hooker, president.

Kevin Hunter, c/o New Directions, Los Angeles, CA; (213) 550-7205. Kevin Hunter, president.

International Creative Management, 40 W. 57th St., New York, NY 10019; (212) 586-0440. Shelly Schultz, vice president.

International Creative Management, 8899 Beverly Blvd., Los Angeles, CA 90048; (213) 550-4000. Tom Ross, vice president.

Katz-Gallin Entertainment, 9255 Sunset Blvd., Los Angeles, CA 90069; (213) 273-4210. Sandy Gallin, president.

Kessler-Grass Management, 449 S. Beverly Dr., Beverly Hills, CA 90212. Danny Kessler, president.

Jon Landau, 400 E. 57th St., New York, NY 10022.

Landers-Roberts Entertainment, 9255 Sunset Blvd., Los Angeles, CA 90069. Hal Landers, president.

Larson-Recor Associates, 8732 Sunset Blvd., Los Angeles, CA 90069. Larry Larson, president.

Leber-Krebs, Inc., 65 W. 55th St., New York, NY 10019; (212) 765-2600. Steve Leber, president.

Buddy Lee Attractions, 1775 Broadway, New York, NY 10019; (212) 247-5216. Joe Higgin, vice president.

Michael Lippman Management, 333 N. Foot Hill Rd., Beverly Hills, CA 90210. Michael Lippman, president.

Miles Lourie Management, 314 W. 71st St., New York, NY 10023; (212) 595-4330. Miles Lourie, president.

Magna Artists Corp., 595 Madison Ave., New York, NY 10022; (212) 752-0363. Ed Rubin, president.

Management III, 9744 Wilshire Blvd., Los Angeles, CA 90212; (213) 550-7100. Jerry Weintraub, president.

Mecca Artists, 1650 Broadway, New York, NY 10019; (212) 489-1400. Stu Ric, president.

Mike's Management, 445 Park Ave., New York, NY 10022; (212) 759-7500. Michael J. Lembo, president.

Mismanagement, Inc., 3805 W. Magnolia Blvd., Burbank, CA 91505; (213) 849-7871. Dave Mergereson, president.

Monarch Entertainment Corp., 412 Pleasant Valley Way, West Orange, NJ 07052; (201) 744-0770. John Scher, president.

Monterey Peninsula Artists, P.O. Box 7308, Carmel, CA 93921; (408) 624-4889.

William Morris Agency, 1350 Sixth Ave., New York, NY 10019; (212) 586-5100. Nat Lefkowitz, president.

William Morris Agency, 151 El Camino Dr., Beverly Hills, CA 90212; (213) 274-7451. Stan Kamen, vice president.

Al Nalli, Management, 313 S. Ashely, Ann Arbor, MI; (313) 769-5454. Al Nalli, president.

Next City Corp., 2166 Broadway, New York, NY 10024; (212) 787-1900. Lew Futterman, president.

Nightmare Productions, 2728 Union, San Francisco, CA 94123; (415) 885-2561. Herbie Herbert, president.

Olympic Entertainment Group, Ltd., 211 W. 56th St., New York, NY 10019; (212) 664-0469. Abe Hoch, president; Barry Taylor, vice president.

Paragon Agency, 560 Arlington Pl., Macon GA 31208. Alex Hodges, president.

Premier Talent, 3 E. 54th St., New York, NY 10022; (212) 758-4900. Frank Barsalona, president.

John Reid Enterprises, 3459 Cahuenga Blvd., Los Angeles, CA 90069. John Reid, president.

Renaissance Management, 433 N. Camden Dr., Beverly Hills, CA 90210. Elliot Abbot, president.

Rising Artists Management, 1697 Broadway, New York, NY 10019; (212) 765-2053. Tina Ball, president.

The Howard Rose Agency, 9720 Wilshire Blvd., Beverly Hills, CA 90212; (213) 273-6700. Howard Rose, president.

Sanford Ross Management, 1700 Broadway, New York, NY 10019; (212) 245-8228. Sandy Ross, president.

Mark Rothbaum & Associates, 225 Main St., Danbury, CT 06810; (203) 792-2400. Mark Rothbaum, president.

David Rubinson & Friends, 827 Folsom St., San Francisco, CA 94107; (415) 777-2930. David Rubinson, president.

Sidney A. Seidenberg, Inc., 1414 Sixth Ave., New York, NY 10019; (212) 421-2021. Sidney A. Seidenberg, president.

Shenkman & DeBlasio Management, 185 Pier Ave., Main St. at the Pier, Santa Monica, CA 90405; (213) 396-3185. Ned Shenkman, president; Ron DeBlasio, vice president.

Sight & Sound Management, 119 W. 57th St., New York, NY 10019; (212) 541-5580. Bob Schwaid, president.

Brad Simon Organization, 445 E. 80th St., New York, NY 10021; (212) 988-4962. Brad Simon, president.

Sound Seventy, 210 25th Ave. N., Nashville, TN 37203; (615) 327-1711. Joe Sullivan, president.

Sutton Artists Corp., 119 W. 57th St., New York, NY 10019; (212) 977-4870. Larry Bennet, president.

Tentmakers Corp., 141 N St. Andrews Pl., Los Angeles, CA 90004; (213) 937-6650. Ron Nadel, president.

TWM Management Services, Ltd., 641 Lexington Ave., New York, NY 10022; (212) 421-6249. Gerald DeLet, president.

Jeff Wald Associates, 9120 Sunset Blvd., Los Angeles, CA 90069. Jeff Wald, president.

Norby Walters Associates, 1290 Sixth Ave., New York, NY 10019; (212) 245-3939. Norby Walters, president.

Weisner-DeMann Entertainment, 9200 Sunset Blvd., Los Angeles, CA 90069; (213) 550-8200. Ron Weisner, president.

Norm Winter Associates, 8532 Sunset Blvd., Hollywood, CA 90069; (213) 275-5988. Norm Winter, president.

Required Reading for the Musically-Minded

Periodicals

Billboard, Billboard Publications, Inc., One Astor Plaza, 1515 Broadway, New York, NY 10036; (212) 764-7300. Weekly. The Bible of the record industry.

Cashbox, 330 W. 58th St., New York, NY 10019; (212) 586-2640. *Billboard's* major competition.

Creem, 187 S. Woodward Ave., Suite 211, Birmingham, MI 48011; (313) 642-8833. Rock-and-roll magazine slanted toward a teen audience.

Down Beat, 222 W. Adams St., Chicago, IL 60606; (312) 346-7811. Monthly magazine covering jazz music.

Modern Recording & Music, Cowan Publishing, 14 Vanderventer Ave., Port Washington, NY 11050; (516) 883-5705. Monthly magazine on recording music. Written for musicians, soundmen, and recording engineers.

Record, 745 Fifth Ave., New York, NY 10151; (212) 350-1298.

Articles on the latest in rock groups, technology, music video, records, and tapes. Monthly.

Rolling Stone, 745 Fifth Ave., New York, NY 10151; (212) 758-3800. Feature articles on the rock scene.

Books

Belz, Carl. *The Story of Rock*. New York: Harper Colophon Books, 1972. Chronicles rock from 1954 to 1971.

Christgau, Robert. *Any Old Way You Choose It: Rock and Other Pop Music, 1967–1973*. New York: Penguin Books, 1973. Essays on rock and soul.

Cohn, Nik. *Rock from the Beginning*. New York: Stein & Day, 1969. A history of rock.

Davis, Clive. *Clive: Inside the Record Business*. New York: Morrow, 1975. An insider's view of the record business from the mid-sixties to 1972.

Logan, Nick, and Bob Woffinden. *The Illustrated Encyclopedia of Rock*. New York: Harmony, 1977. Comprehensive sourcebook of rock-and-roll information.

Marcus, Greil. *Mystery Train: Images of America in Rock 'n' Roll Music*. New York: Dutton, 1976. A study of rock.

Marsh, Dave, with John Swenson. *The Rolling Stone Record Guide*. New York: A Random House/Rolling Stone Press Book, 1979. Reviews and ratings of almost ten thousand rock albums.

Miller, Jim, ed. *The Rolling Stone Illustrated History of Rock & Roll*. New York: A Random House/Rolling Stone Press Book, 1980. Collection of articles on rock trends and performers.

Shaw, Arnold. *The Rocking '50s: The Decade That Transformed Pop Music*. New York: Hawthorn Books, 1974.

Shemel, Sidney, and William Krosoloski. *This Business of Music*. New York: Billboard Publications.

Sklar, Rick. *Rocking America: How the All-Hit Radio Station Took Over—An Insider's Story*, 1984. Rick Sklar, the disk jockey who originated the top 40 format, analyzes how rock radio has changed the record industry.

Spitz, Robert Stephen. *The Making of Superstars: The Artists and Executives of the Rock Music World*. New York: Anchor Press/Doubleday, 1978. Stories about rock stars and record company executives who've made it big.

Weissman, Dick. *The Music Business: Career Opportunities and Self Defense*. New York: Crown, 1979.

Music-Business Organizations and Professional Associations

AFTRA, 1350 Sixth Ave., New York, NY 10019; (212) 265-7700.

AGAC, 726 Fifth Ave., New York, NY 10001; (212) 686-6820.

American Federation of Musicians, 1500 Broadway, New York, NY 10036; (212) 869-1330.

ASCAP, One Lincoln Plaza, New York, NY 10023; (212) 595-3050.

Black Music Association, 1500 Locust St., Philadelphia, PA 19002; (215) 545-8600.

BMI, 320 West 57th St., New York, NY 10019; (212) 586-2000.

Canadian Recording Industry Association, 245 Davenport Rd., Toronto, Ontario, Canada MAR 1K1; (416) 967-7272.

Country Music Association, Inc., 7 Music Circle N., Nashville, TN 37203; (615) 244-2840.

Institute of Audio Research, 64 University Pl., New York, NY 10003; (212) 777-8550.

MIDEM, 30 Rockefeller Plaza, New York, NY 10020; (212) 541-8862.

MUSEXPO, 1414 Sixth Ave., New York, NY 10019; (212) 489-9245.

Music Performance Trust Funds, 1501 Broadway, New York, NY 10036; (212) 391-3950.

NARM, 1060 Kings Highway N., Cherry Hill, NJ 08034; (609) 424-7404.

National Music Publishers Association, 110 E. 59th St., New York, NY 10022; (212) 751-1930.

RIAA, 888 Seventh Ave., New York, NY 10019; (212) 765-4330.

SESAC, 10 Columbus Circle, New York, NY 10019; (212) 586-3450.

Photography

Whether you're a top New York City fashion photographer or the photographer of a wedding at the church down the street, there's a joy in the creation of a photograph. Even if you never get to take pictures of Brooke Shields or Yosemite National Park or an American president, you can still be a part of this glamorous field.

With the accessibility, relative low cost, and popularity of the single reflex camera, millions of Americans have become interested in taking quality photographs. Many of them fantasize about earning a living from their photography, but this is a road open only to the most dedicated and well trained.

This chapter will give you an idea of how some people have broken into the world of professional photography. It is not meant to be comprehensive, because there are just too many types of photography careers to cover in a short chapter. Instead, we'll enumerate just a few specialties open to you and talk generally about some fees that certain assignments pay.

We'll discuss tips for breaking into the field, suggest some places that provide good training, and present interviews with a wedding photographer, an animal photographer, and a still-life advertising photographer. We also include lists of photography magazines and professional associations, and provide a glossary of relevant terms.

We want to help you take the first step. We know that not all photographers aim at becoming the next Richard Avedon or Jacques-Henri Lartigue or Ansel Adams. Photography can be glamorous, but basically it is a craft, requiring dedication, hard work, patience, an ability to work well with a number of

204

different people, and a taste for experimentation. If you are willing to work your way up, to pursue commercial as well as artistic assignments, and to market yourself, you may just forge your own route to success in this highly competitive field. And whether you ultimately find work as a photographer's assistant, a wedding photographer, or a staff photographer for a nonprofit organization, you'll be a part of an exciting, rewarding profession.

TYPES OF PHOTOGRAPHY

We've mentioned that this chapter will touch on only two or three specific specialties within the wide field of photography, but we recognize that many people dream of exploring other photographic realms. Here, briefly, are a number of those specialties. And although we can only mention them, it's fair to say that the type of apprenticeship described later in this chapter is similar to that of fledgling photographers in almost all specialties.

- **Architecture.** The architectural photographer's job is to express in his or her own work the feeling in another artist's work. Bringing out a building's personality is a challenge, one that enmeshes the photographer in a study of a building's materials, lighting, environment—indeed, its very purpose.
- **Advertising.** One of the most important and widespread uses of photography is in print advertisements, and many photographers spend their lives trying to break into this lucrative and often exciting market. One problem, however, is that most of the available work is in two cities: New York and Los Angeles, where art directors hire photographers to record every conceivable product. Per diem rates are high, and the competition for each assignment is staggering.
- **Portraiture.** The desire to capture the inner personality beneath a person's outer appearance is what attracts many people to specialize in portraiture. Arnold Newman,

for example, in his book *Faces U.S.A.*, captures the spirit of America with his photos of people who collectively personify the spirit of the country. Although most portrait photographers aim to please—Richard Avedon's often stark, unflattering portraits are one exception—you need to have a curiosity about people's inner selves if you are to come up with anything beyond a superficial pose.

- **Travel.** Such publications as *Travel and Leisure, National Geographic*, the *New York Times* Travel Section, and *Travel/Holiday* are some of the many markets for high-quality travel photographs. To succeed in this specialty, you'll need a high tolerance for the unexpected and an ability to turn opportunities into great photographs. It's hard to avoid the clichés of travel photography, so we'd recommend that you study the work of the most successful photographers in this field and try to articulate what makes it unique.

- **Wedding Photography.** Every wedding needs a photographer. So do many other occasions. To be good, you need experience, a sense of discipline, and a great rapport with people. Later on, we interview a wedding photographer and find out how he built his business.

- **Catalogs.** Merchants sometimes hire photographers to shoot their merchandise—pens, lamps, bras, shirts, coffeepots, perfumes, foods, paintings, and numerous other products. Catalogs may not be the most glamorous showcase for photographic work, but the work can be quite lucrative, and there is a lot of it to be done.

- **Corporate/Nonprofit.** Organizations need photographers for a wide range of assignments, including photos for brochures, direct mail, annual reports, or documentation. Usually hired by in-house communications departments, corporate photographers must be versatile to flourish in the organizational world.

- **Landscape/Nature.** Calendar companies keep flocks of photographers busy shooting rolls of film detailing our parks, mountains, lakes, streams, forests, and cities.

- **Photojournalism.** Though not as popular today as in the glory days of *Look* and *Life* in the 1940s and 1950s, photojournalism still attracts those who "have camera, will travel." There are opportunities for both free-lance and staff positions at magazines, newspapers, and supplements, but to apply for such jobs, you must first build a substantial portfolio of high-quality action or celebrity shots. A photojournalist might be asked to illustrate almost any type of story imaginable—anything from a jailbreak to a cook-off.

A WORD ABOUT FEES

Throughout this chapter there are references to fees or per diems or salaries commanded by particular photographers. Just as a writer's fee for an assignment can vary from pennies to many thousands of dollars, a photographer's fee will vary greatly, depending upon experience, circumstances, negotiating talents, and the area of the country in which he or she works.

The American Society of Magazine Photographers publishes a guide to suggested photographer's fees and sells it to the public for $18.95. In it, they try to give a range of standard fees for a wide variety of assignments. A photographer must remember to take into account such expenses as the cost of the film and processing, all location and transportation expenses, assistants, insurance, special equipment, overtime, and the talent used in the shoot.

Here's a sampling of what professional photographers can expect to be paid for a variety of typical assignments:

Annual report.	$500–$2,500
Brochure:	$300–$1,250
Basic press kit:	$250–$800
Editorial illustration (fashion, home products, magazine and book covers, etc.):	$300–$1,200
Still-life catalog (per single product):	$100–$1,000
Color promotional poster:	$500–$1,250

Advertising

Consumer magazine (national):	$1,000–$2,500
Billboard (national):	$1,000–$1,250
Record-album cover:	$400–$1,500
Photographic portrait of a senior executive:	$300–$1,500

TIPS FOR BREAKING IN

One of the best ways to begin a career in photography is to become a photographer's assistant. As an assistant, you'll work long hours; you'll carry heavy cameras, lights, and equipment; you'll put in twelve-hour days in 106-degree heat or 10-below cold. You'll be expected to remain patient when asked to move a light for the eightieth time in an hour, or to go without lunch to keep from "missing the light." The important thing is to get the shot. And since it's expensive to have a crew standing around doing nothing, you can expect to be kept moving every minute. Only the creation of a great photograph justifies the expenditure of time, energy, and money—and that takes almost continuous work on everyone's part.

Jennifer Levy, a New York City photographer, describes the life of the photographer's assistant:

"A full-time photographer's assistant works about forty to seventy hours a week but usually earns only $150 to $250 a week. Here are just a few of the things the assistant does: take light readings, clean and maintain the studio, shop for props, and arrange for the rental of equipment. The assistant will also help on location, arrange interviews with models, makeup people, and stylists. You also set up lights, load the camera, and sometimes even help build the set.

"On a typical 'shoot,' you're there with the photographer, the art director, and the client—and sometimes a makeup person and a stylist. The stylist helps 'dress the set.' In one shoot, the stylist arranged to get evening wear for the models and picked out earrings and other accessories.

"Speaking of *accessories*, you need to be strong to be a photographer's assistant. You're always lugging things like strobes, heads (lamps that plug into power packs), tripods, light stands, and several cameras. And, of course, you wouldn't want to forget things like clamps, tape, light bulbs, and filters. You may also need to bring along a choice of cameras—maybe a 35 mm. Nikon, a 2¼ Hasselblad, a four-by-five Sinar."

How does a photographer's assistant know when it's the right time to go out on his or her own? According to Jennifer, "You'll know because you'll feel more confident on the set. You'll understand everything the photographer is doing—and why he's doing it. You'll be ready when you can handle the pressure of producing a usable photograph by the end of the day. You should also have learned a bit about gaining rapport with clients, and the 'protocol' of the shoot. Technically, you'll have to be competent to handle any unexpected situations that arise."

At the beginning of their careers, photographers scramble for any kind of work that will keep them close to photography. You can start by filing photographs for a magazine or photo service, or by helping a photographer capture images of a wedding, bar mitzvah, or birthday. You can shoot passport photos or volunteer to take pictures for your local newspaper.

The late Ruth Orkin started in photography by taking a bicycle trip around the United States at age seventeen. Throughout the journey, she took photos with a one-dollar Pilot single-reflex camera. She also worked as a messenger at MGM, ran a photo concession at a nightclub, and did some free-lance photojournalism. All the while, she kept increasing her experience and fattening her portfolio. She scrimped pennies to buy better cameras, replacing her Pilot camera with a Speed Graphic and later a 35 mm. camera. She became a top professional whose work has been shown at the Museum of Modern Art and the Metropolitan Museum of Art.

Photography, like other artistic careers, is highly competitive and offers no safe "managerial track" to assure you of steady progress toward a high position and salary. Many noted photographers became rich and famous in their twenties—such as Annie Liebovitz and Richard Avedon. Still others, such as André Kertesz and Jacques-Henri Lartigue, were unknown until late in life.

According to the *American Almanac of Jobs and Salaries,* ninety-three thousand people who work in photography are associated with commercial studios. Many other jobs for photographers are available in advertising, popular magazines, and trade-magazine work. *Magazine Market Place* (known as MMP), published by R. R. Bowker, gives comprehensive lists of magazines, as well as addresses, telephone numbers, and names of editorial and advertising managers. MMP also has a section on "Where to Sell Your Photographs."

The federal government is another good source of employment for photographers, offering some three thousand related positions. Other photography jobs are available in catalog production, billboard production, and even police work.

TRAINING

So what is the best way to train for a career in photography?

Cartier-Bresson, one of the world's finest photographers, takes an idealistic stance: "There should be a visual education emphasized from the beginning in all schools. It should be introduced just like the study of literature, history, or mathematics. With a language, everyone learns the grammar first. In photography, one must learn a visual grammar. What reinforces the content of a photograph is a sense of rhythm, the relationship between shapes and ideas."

Translating that philosophy into something practical, you should aim to get a good background in handling techniques and materials, while getting some on-the-job experience, too. We've spotlighted a few schools that offer a range of good photography courses (see pages 219-220), and we've recommended that you try to attach yourself to a local photographer. You might consult the extensive list of photographic studios in *The Professional Photographer: Developing a Successful Career* by Larry Goldman (Doubleday-Dolphin, 1983). Putting in years of training behind the camera and in the darkroom is essential. Listen to these successful photographers talk about how their careers unfolded:

Paul Strand, an early innovator in the field, studied photography in the first decade of the twentieth century with his biology teacher, Louis Hine, at Ethical Culture School in New York. (Hine himself later became a master photographer.) One day, Strand and the rest of his class went to the Photo Secession Gallery at 291 Fifth Avenue. Strand walked out of the building that day feeling, in his words, that "this is what I want to do in my life. From then on, it was a struggle to fulfill that dream." In Strand's opinion, it takes eight or nine years to develop into a good photographer.

Photographer Jennifer Levy shared with us a little of her own first wobbly steps into the field:

"I was originally interested in filmmaking but switched to photography for a number of reasons. For one thing, it allowed me to be involved in a larger part of the process than filmmaking. Also, I like the freedom of being self-employed, the creativity, and the prospect of travel.

"I started as an assistant by letting people know about my interest in photography, showing my photos to people, and gaining a sense of what people look for in photographs. I studied photography at New York University, learning how to print, gaining a sense of aesthetics and mastering some techniques. But the real learning came on the job, when I gained access to the equipment of a studio—different brands of strobe equipment—and learned how everything operates."

Charles R. Reilly, a seasoned advertising photographic pro, says of his own entrance to the field: "I lucked in, if you want to call it luck. I was taken in by a former teacher and established photographer who showed me the ropes. After I had blown up a few strobe packs, I free-lanced in a six-block radius. All the photographers knew each other, and I got work by word of mouth."

Reilly is one of many photographers who picked up the camera bug early in life. "When I was nine, I was the family photographer," he says with great pride. "I took pictures of the house and brothers and sisters on Easter Sunday. Much later, I took a hitchhiker's vacation—nine months in Europe. Thirty or forty rolls of Ektachrome later, I was hooked."

THE SPECIFICS: ADVICE ABOUT COURSES, PORTFOLIOS, AND ASSISTING OTHER PHOTOGRAPHERS

Let's take a moment to answer some of the basic questions that novice photographers ask about getting a solid educational background, putting together a portfolio, and approaching studios in search of an assistant's position. Our answers are based on discussions with a wide range of photographers; the advice is applicable to many fields of photography, not simply fashion or advertising or portraiture.

What courses comprise a solid photographic background? Although every photographer will answer this question differently, we suggest that courses include a basic black-and-white course, followed by an intermediate one (which covers the zone system and fine printing). A studio-photography course will give you some experience in using large-format cameras and strobe equipment. We also suggest studying the history of photography, as well as taking a course that shows you how to build a portfolio. Advanced courses could include one in documentary photography or portraiture.

What are some ways to get your feet wet in photography? A novice can try to get photos published in a high-school or college newspaper or sell photos to a local newspaper. You may want to give yourself an assignment to cover a local sporting event or a human-interest story. Then take the photos to an editor at your hometown paper. Even if you are not interested in pursuing photojournalism, this self-assignment is excellent training for almost any aspect of photography. There may be opportunities for you to cover events for your local newspaper, illustrate brochures for local businesses, or even help insurance companies document claims.

How would I approach a photographer if I wanted to become a photographic assistant? Hiro, one of the great advertising photographers, approached Richard Avedon by writing him a letter. Avedon invited Hiro to come to the United States (from China) and become his assistant.

Traditionally, assistants approach established photographers by writing to them, expressing interest in their unique qualities as a photographer, and asking for the opportunity to show them their own work. This means that you need to be very familiar with the work of the photographer you approach. You should be ready to present your own work not as that of an equal but as that of an apprentice who admires the master's work and hopes to broaden skills by working with him or her.

Remember: Show only what you're proudest of. Both your cover letter and your work should convey to a prospective employer the type of person you are, as well as what it is about the photographer's work that inspires you.

Is it best to go after full- or part-time work? Will I have to work for free? Many photographers advise working full-time as a photographer's second assistant, then working up to first assistant, and then to studio manager. While the pay may be low, you shouldn't work for nothing.

What if I don't have a lot of photographic credits on my résumé? By presenting yourself honestly to a potential employer, you can position yourself as "eager to learn," and no one will expect a résumé filled with published work. You can help your cause by listing any photography-related jobs you've held. Perhaps you've worked in a camera store or in the audiovisual department of your college. Maybe you spent a month or two at a slide-production house or assisting at a photo lab at school.

Do I call or write first? There's a split of opinion on this issue. On one hand, it seems more professional to send a letter and a résumé to a photographer *before* calling. The letter will establish your enthusiasm, your awareness of the photographer's needs, and the experience you'll bring to the job.

On the other hand, a phone call is direct and personal. But since photographers are busy, they may not speak with you the first time you call. In fact, a studio manager may take your call and keep you from talking to the photographer. If calls don't work, send a letter and then follow it up a few weeks later with a phone call.

Will I be expected to have darkroom experience? Not necessarily. A lot of photographers don't even do their own printing.

You won't necessarily be expected to know a great deal about color processing or color printing. As for black-and-white film, you should know how to process film up to 4 × 5 format (including 35 mm. and 2¼) and be a competent printer.

The reason you are taking a low-paying second assistant's job in the first place is to gain experience. So be honest. You are selling your eagerness to learn and, in doing so, to put in long hours.

Are there any guidelines for building a strong portfolio? You may not need a portfolio to land a second assistant's job, but you'll need one if you are to progress in any area of photography. A portfolio shows your talent and your sensitivity to the needs of the marketplace.

First, let's take the word *portfolio* literally. You'll need a vehicle for displaying your work: a case or an album that can show 8 × 10s and 11 × 14s. It can be almost any size or color, and it should, of course, be portable.

Most important is what goes inside this case. (The word *portfolio* refers to your work as well as to the album or folder that holds that work.) It will include the original chromes of any published work, which should relate to the marketplace you are aiming to enter. After all, the only history a buyer is interested in is your commercial track record and how suited you are to his needs.

Are there dos and don'ts as to what to include in a portfolio? Photographers are always upgrading their portfolios to represent their best work. Therefore, do not include examples of techniques you have not perfected. Include only those photographs that display your strongest stylistic techniques. The photos should reflect not only your professionalism but the professionalism of your models and stylists (if any). Although your portfolio will cover a wide range of subjects, it should present a *consistent photographic personality*—in much the same way a painter's work shows a consistent style. By the way, the average portfolio should have between twenty and forty photos.

Obviously, a portfolio for a fashion photographer will differ from that of a photojournalist or an architectural photographer, but these basic principles still apply.

AIMING FOR THE TOP

After gaining a foothold in the photography profession, you'll spend many hours developing your skills, discovering new equipment, becoming acquainted with professional reference books and magazines, and developing an individual approach to your craft.

Finding your next job is always a top priority. Jennifer Levy believes that it is "assumed" a photographic assistant will moonlight. "As a matter of fact," she says, "one of the tradeoffs in working long hours at low pay is that, generally speaking, you have access to the studio and its equipment.

"Since it is a 'given' that you'll be moving on, try to get a recommendation from your employer. Then, start working on your book—a portfolio of your photos to show off your technical competence, as well as the wide range of subjects you can handle. When starting out, it's best to specialize.

"You can start by calling on art directors at ad agencies, PR firms, graphics houses, or book publishers. It takes a while to get known. Many art directors won't return your calls. Others may breeze through your portfolio in a matter of seconds. Some will offer suggestions. Some may actually give you a chance."

Tom Okada, who has assisted such eminent photographers as the late W. Eugene Smith and celebrity portraitist Arnold Newman, decided to try to generate interest in his own photography by writing and circulating a press release about the opening of his studio. Of course, he used his prestigious past associations as part of the draw.

By circulating the release to local newspapers and magazines involved with photography, advertising, and the media, Okada was able to generate interest in his work and get some publicity. If his goals had been to gain recognition in purely artistic circles, he might have sent it only to "art" photography magazines. But his main goal was to stimulate business, so he selected magazines that reach people who have the power to hire photographers, such as fashion magazines, women's magazines, and advertising trade magazines (*Advertising Age* and *Adweek*, for instance).

Okada's familiarity with these magazines and other publications read by potential clients was essential to the success of his campaign. Photographers should know these valuable resources so they can use them to gain new ideas, develop skills, make contacts, and see what the competition is up to.

The four key resources that photographers should become familiar with are *The ASMP Business Practice Guide, The Creative Black Book, The Madison Avenue Handbook,* and *The Standard Directory of Advertising Agencies.*

Published by the American Society of Magazine Photographers, *The ASMP Business Practice Guide* contains information on standard rates for jobs, standard forms useful to the working photographer, and some legal information. This useful guide, available through ASMP (205 Lexington Ave., New York, NY 10016), costs $17.50, plus $1.50 postage, and is considered indispensable by many free-lancers.

The Creative Black Book is a geographical list of suppliers and services for the media, including photographers, ad agencies, stylists, illustrators, and more. A portfolio version contains photographers and illustrators' color pages and is available for $55 from the publisher (Friendly Press, 401 Park Avenue S., New York, NY 10016). The regular version, a two-volume set including extensive lists of people in photography, costs $90 (plus sales tax, if applicable). It's also available at libraries and some bookstores.

The Madison Avenue Handbook lists resources for the communications industry, also by area. It contains many color ad pages showing photographers' work as well and is available for $25 from Peter Glenn Publications, 17 E. 48th St., New York, NY 10017.

Finally, *The Standard Directory of Advertising Agencies* lists 4,400 advertising agencies here and overseas. For each one, the "Red Book," as it is known, reports agency income, number of employees, key accounts, and the address and phone number of its offices. This reference book is available from the National Register Publishing Company, Inc., 5201 Old Orchard Rd., Skokie, IL 60677.

In addition to these books, two major professional associations offer practical advice you may want to take advantage of. The Advertising Photographers of America (APA) has offices in

New York, Los Angeles, San Francisco, and Chicago. Membership entitles you to a monthly newsletter, mailing list, meetings, seminars, and discounts at certain photographic-supply stores. (Benefits of membership vary from one chapter to another.) Following are the addresses and phone numbers of all four offices:

45 E. 20th St.
New York, NY 10003
(212) 254-5500

823 N. La Brea Blvd.
Los Angeles, CA 90038
(213) 935-7283

1061 Folsom St.
San Francisco, CA 94103
(415) 332-8831

2478 North Orchard
Chicago, IL 60614
(312) 348-0490

APA dues for full members are $300; $150, if one has been in business for less than two years. Photographic assistants' membership is $75 a year.

The other major association for working photographers is the American Society for Magazine Photographers (ASMP). Membership in ASMP entitles you to a monthly newsletter, a monthly national bulletin, meetings, seminars, group insurance, listing in the membership directory, and an option to advertise in the *Black Book.* Assistant membership, available to photographic assistants, is only $75 per year and is a good way of meeting people in the field and generating business. No portfolio is required, but you must be sponsored by a member. Associate memberships cost $100 a year, plus a one-time $100 application fee. This membership, for professionals who have been working less than three years, does have portfolio requirements. General membership costs $175 per year. ASMP is headquartered in New York City (205 Lexington Ave., New York, NY 10016; 212-889-9144) and has twenty-three branch offices across the country.

By associating yourself with other photographers, you'll

gain an overview of the pluses and minuses of this diverse field, while getting some tips on how to structure your fees.

Charles Reilly says that the most interesting people he knows are those in related fields: "I get along with them best. They're all peculiar—like me. I meet more people through jobs than through any other situation."

For photographers, fees can vary from a hearty handshake to several thousand dollars per print. Says Charles Reilly, "I don't think most photographers should expect to make more than a decent living. It depends on what field you choose and how much you push." For a detailed account of all the major specializations within commercial photography, take a look at *Career Photography: How to Be a Success as a Professional Photographer,* by Linda Moser (Prentice-Hall, 1983). In most cases, fees for a job depend upon a budget, not upon some pre-acknowledged amount.

But, money aside, photographers often allow their emotions to dictate terms when faced with the possibility of handling a project that's challenging. Charles Reilly has had memorable experiences shooting in the pit area at a rock concert in Detroit and at recording sessions. Ruth Orkin enjoys recording life from her Central Park West window. Annie Liebovitz earns both money and acclaim for her striking—some might say bizarre—portraits of such celebrities as Bette Midler, Mick Jagger, and Sylvester Stallone. Ansel Adams didn't need monetary motivation to capture the majesty of Yosemite.

Yousef Karsh gained worldwide recognition for his photographic portrait of Winston Churchill. Karsh seemed to capture the quintessence of Churchill's bulldog toughness after removing the cigar from Churchill's teeth and being rewarded with the scowl, the head thrust forward belligerently, and the hand on hip in an attitude of anger.

Richard Avedon's portrait of Rudolf Nureyev simply shows the great dancer's foot *en pointe.* A great photograph comes more from the heart and the brain of the photographer than from the camera.

Consider James B. Long of Fort Lauderdale. Long has gained a reputation for his stunning photos of space-shuttle launches and returns. In fact, he leads a whole team of photographers in his quest for the perfect photograph of a landing. At every launch, he's at Pad 39, armed with twenty-five cameras and two crews. For landings, he makes sure that his crews are on both sides of the runway. And since photographers must stand miles away from the actual launch site, he spends days positioning his camera so that he can take the photos on launch day by remote control. Says Long, "If one camera gets one good frame, that's all we care about."

Whether you're shooting the next Ralph Lauren spread, or covering a political contest, a space shot, or a rock concert, photography holds enough glamour to attract thousands of people who do everything from carrying lights to setting hair to choosing the clothes that models will wear.

Whether or not you soar to the heights of an Avedon, a Karsh, or a Liebovitz, you'll share in the excitement of this still-youthful art. For even the most jaded photographer knows that the next push of the button could yield an image that speaks to a generation.

Educating Your Eye: Schools for Future Photographers

Leaf through any photography magazine and you'll come up with the names of dozens of classes, workshops, and seminars on taking better photos. The following is a list of schools that have gained special prominence in the field and offer courses in both "art" and commercial photography:

East Coast

School of Visual Arts
209 E. 23rd St.
New York, NY 10010
(212) 679-7350

New York University
Photography Department
721 Broadway, 8th Floor
New York, NY 10003
(212) 598-3939

Pratt University
215 Ryerson St.
Brooklyn, NY 11205
(718) 636-3600

Rochester Institute of Technology
1 Lomb Memorial Dr.
Rochester, NY 14623
(716) 475-2505

Rhode Island School of Design
2 College St.
Providence, RI 02903
(401) 331-3511

Midwest

Chicago Art Institute
South Michigan Ave. and East
  Adams
Chicago, IL 60603
(312) 443-3600

The Minneapolis Institute of Arts
2400 Third Ave. S.
Minneapolis, MN 55404
(612) 870-3170

West Coast

San Francisco Art Institute
800 Chestnut St.
San Francisco, CA 94133
(415) 771-7020

The Art Center College of Design
1700 Lida
Pasadena, CA 91103
(213) 577-1700

Brooks Institute
School of Photographic Art &
  Science
2190 Alston Rd.
Santa Barbara, CA 93108
(805) 969-2291

Magazines and Publications

Photo District News, 167 Third Ave., New York, NY 10003; (212) 677-8418. Newspaper of current events in commercial photography, with features on photographers, technology, and business practices. Also has classifieds for job opportunities and equipment. $8.00 yearly. Published monthly. Available by subscription.

American Photographer, CBS Publications, Consumer Publishing Division of CBS, Inc., 1515 Broadway, New York, NY 10036; (212) 719-6000. Publishes photographers' portfolios; some technical information; good listings of schools, workshops, and exhibits across the United States. $17.95 yearly. Published monthly. Available on newsstands and by subscription.

Popular Photography, 1 Park Ave., New York, NY 10016; (212) 503-3700. (Subscription Address: Popular Photography, P.O. Box 2775, Boulder, CO 80322.) Similar to American Photographer, but concentrates more on commercial photography and has detailed technical information on current equipment. $7.99 yearly. Published monthly. Both Popular Photography and Modern Photography are available on newsstands as well as by subscription.

Modern Photography, 825 Seventh Ave., New York, NY 10019; (212) 265-8360. (Subscription Address: Modern Photography, P.O. Box 10786, Des Moines, IA 50340; 800-247-5470. Price: $13.98/ year.)

Alix Coleman, Photographer

Alix Coleman is one of a very small handful of people who make their entire living by photographing horses. And although she shuns competitions and thus does not have a wall of plaques or prizes to prove it, Alix is widely recognized as one of the very best horse photographers in the United States.

Perhaps it is because she knows her subject from the inside. "I've been riding ever since I can remember," she says. "I showed over fences when I was younger. I'm mainly into dressage now, though I'm not nearly as active as I'd like to be. I'm taking pictures all the time, and I haven't figured out a way to ride and take pictures at the same time."

Perhaps what elevates Alix Coleman's work to the level of art is the eye she developed as a painter. She graduated from the University of Pennsylvania Academy School and attended the Ecole des Beaux Arts in Lucerne, Switzerland. "After all that preparation, the gallery that was going to handle my work informed me that they would be teaching me how to paint all over again—in other words, how to be commercial. Painting was far too personal to me to become commercial, so I turned to photography," says Coleman. "It doesn't hurt as much to have an editor or an art director reject a transparency as it would to have them reject a painting."

Alix also wanted to be where the action is, not stuck in a studio. "I've stood right on the track at the Kentucky Derby, in the ring at the Olympics in Montreal, and ridden up on top of the wagon behind the Budweiser Clydesdales. I would never have done these things as a painter. Sometimes I'll be on a 727 waiting to take off for Portugal or South Africa, and I'll think to myself, My photography is taking me!"

Alix Coleman also brings to her work the mind of a writer. She was forced into that field in 1975 when she climbed off a plane from an exhausting shooting session at the Pan American Games and was asked by Classic magazine to write a story to accompany her pictures—and have it done by the next morning. It's gotten somewhat easier since.

She shot more covers for *Classic* than any other photographer, and later shot for *Centaur*. Her work has also appeared in *Geo, Town and Country, EquiSport,* and *The Horse Digest.* But she considers the pinnacle of her work a commemorative book on the Clydesdales called *All the King's Horses,* which Anheuser-Busch published in 1983.

Major Photography Museums and Galleries

Photographers are a great audience for other people's photographs, and in the past few decades, a handful of excellent museums and galleries have developed a keen interest in displaying high-quality photographs. Almost everyone is familiar with the Museum of Modern Art's leadership in establishing photography as an art, but below are a few other museums and galleries that photographers should know about:

East Coast

*International Center for
    Photography*
1130 Fifth Ave.
New York, NY 10028
(212) 860-1770

Light Gallery
724 Fifth Ave.
New York, NY 10021
(212) 582-6522

Robert Klein Gallery
216 Newbury St.
Boston, MA 02116
(617) 262-2278

The Witkin Gallery
41 East 57th St.
New York, NY 10022
(212) 355-1461

*International Museum of
    Photography at George
    Eastman House*
900 East Ave.
Rochester, NY 14607
(716) 272-3361

Midwest and Southwest

Minneapolis Institute of Arts
2400 Third Ave. S.
Minneapolis, MN 55404
(612) 870-3170

Center for Creative Photography
843 East University
University of Arizona
Tucson, AZ 85719
(602) 621-7968

Museum of Fine Arts
1001 Bissonet and Main
Houston, TX 77005
(713) 526-1361

New Orleans Museum of Art
City Park
New Orleans, LA 70179
(504) 488-2631

West Coast

Canon U.S.A.
3321 Wilshire Blvd.
Los Angeles, CA 90010
(213) 387-5010

*San Francisco Museum of
Modern Art*
Van Ness and McCallister
San Francisco, CA 94102
(415) 863-8800

Mike Buglio:
A Member of the Wedding

Mike Buglio started out in life as a photographer. He studied photography in school and worked in a succession of studios before World War II. After a stint in the service, he applied for a Christmastime position at the post office. He stayed for thirty-eight years. But his interest in photography never waned.

Now that his mail-carrier days are behind him, Mike has become a full-time photographer, specializing in weddings, bar mitzvahs, and other celebrations. We asked Mike for some tips on finding clients in his field:

"Well," says Mike, "most of my new work comes from past clients. People refer people to me. And, as a wedding photographer, you have to be able to promote yourself by letting people know of your availability, passing out your business card. Of course, you have to be discreet about it. I also advertise in my local "Shopper" and that pulls in a few people. Another good way to find clients is to contact clergymen. Let them know you're available for assignments, and be ready to talk with them about the work you've done—especially if you've just photographed a wedding for someone in their congregation. This is a business of referrals."

We asked Mike if he had any recommendations for gaining great results amid the joyful confusion of a wedding.

"Wedding photographers are benevolent dictators. They must be insistent, or they will neglect key shots. On the other hand, if you're pushy or abrasive, you turn off everyone and all you hear are complaints. I believe it's important to have a good rapport with the bride and the groom. Usually, they pave the way to your next job.

"A wedding photographer doesn't just record an event; he knows who to pose and how to pose them. He puts people in the right position, takes the right group shots. Preparation is very important. That's why I always try to get to the rehearsal at the synagogue or chapel or church. Once I get an idea of the area, I can work out a plan for the shots I need.

"Also, it helps to go to the rehearsal, because nowadays there are radical variations in the wedding ceremony. If you're not familiar with any changes they make in the traditional ceremony, you won't be prepared to get the best shot."

Although some wedding photographers take as many as two or three hundred shots at a wedding, Mike Buglio believes this is not wise. "It's amateurish," he says. "The bride and groom are only going to order two or three dozen pictures. By taking so many shots, you're simply displaying your insecurity. Also, you're probably annoying the people at the wedding. Also, you're adding to your overhead. Every roll of film costs you money and cuts into profits. And every roll you shoot will cost money to develop and print." The moral: Go to a professional. Don't entrust your wedding to a well-meaning friend or relative who is "into photography."

Tom Okada:
A Working Photographer's Perspective

Tom Okada is a young still-life photographer. Working at his mid-Manhattan studio, Tom shoots photographs for advertisements, catalogs, and a wide assortment of other commercial projects. Like most photographers, Tom is keenly aware of the delicate balance necessary to maintain aesthetics, remain idealistic, and still pay the bills. We thought it might be helpful to have his "real-life" view as to which trade magazines, directories, and photographic schools are the most valuable to a working photographer.

Although soft-spoken by nature, Tom makes sharp, uninhibited distinctions between what is aesthetically vital to a photographer versus what is vital to his business.

"Of the magazines you list," says Tom, "I find that *Photo District News* is most helpful. It gives me valuable business information and helps me shop for the best equipment. Although *American Photographer* has some nice photos and some interesting articles, and *Popular Photography* sometimes inspires the awestruck feeling of 'Gee, how did they get that shot?' I don't find them as useful as *Photo District News*.

"What is really helpful? Mailing lists of art directors, that's what! There's a mailing-list firm in Chicago called Creative Access that keeps tabs on art directors, design firms, and corporations that use commercial still-life photography."

We asked Tom about the helpfulness of various directories. According to him, *The Madison Avenue Handbook,* while a helpful source of suppliers and ad agencies, is updated too infrequently to be a reliable guide to *who* works *where.* People in this business change jobs constantly.

"*The Standard Directory of Advertising Agencies* helps the photographer by telling him or her which agencies have which accounts, and it does list the top managers of each company. The problem is that you don't necessarily want to reach the top managers; you want to reach art directors."

Tom was extremely positive about the American Society of Magazine Photographers because he feels that they are a good defense against would-be clients who balk at the high cost of photography. "By telling them that you can't go below ASMP minimums," Tom adds, "you give clout to your fee structure. Also, the ASMP gives you forms and formats for a number of the business and legal elements of your work. For example, they'll provide you with the form of a photo release [an agreement, signed by a model, allowing a person's photo to be used in the media], a written estimate, or a letter of agreement. They'll also give you a fee schedule that suggests a range of fees for every conceivable situation, every imaginable photographic assignment."

Finally, we asked for Tom's perspective on some of the nation's best photography schools. Tom prefaced his response by saying that he has not kept abreast of the latest trends in academic courses for photographers, but he did emphasize that it's important for would-be photography students to ask their instructors about the orientation of each school. Does the school stress aesthetics? Technical skill? Preparation to be a commercial photographer? This is the key question for anyone about to embark on a course of study.

Using that question as a yardstick, we asked Tom to go out on a limb and tell us his impressions of some of the schools we chose to include in our list of top photographic schools.

Tom believes that the School of Visual Arts, while it does offer photography courses, "is better known as a school that stresses advertising design and copywriting—just as NYU's photography courses are overshadowed by its reputation for video and film."

Tom has praise for Pratt Institute in Brooklyn and the San Francisco Art Institute. "They both have fine teachers, but both take an aesthetic orientation. In other words, you'll have to pick up your knowledge of the business of photography elsewhere. The same is true for Rhode Island School of Design. At the Rochester Institute, you'll pick up a tremendous amount of knowledge about the technical side of photography, since they have outstanding photographic equipment there.

"The International Center in Tucson is interesting because it has become a haven for photographic history and memorabilia. They have begun to buy prints from major photographers. For example, while Eugene Smith taught there, they bought much of his personal collection of prints. They catalog the prints and file the negatives. So I would imagine that serious photography students can benefit from having those photos so close at hand."

Building an Image: Words Photographers Know and Use

Aperture. The adjustable opening in a camera lens that controls the amount of light passing through to expose the film.

Backlighting. Light that comes from behind the subject toward the camera.

Bracketing. The technique of making several exposures of a single image, some higher and some lower than the meter reading. This allows for error in exposure time and permits selection of the best-lit exposure after development.

Cable release. Flexible cable attached to shutter release; allows photographer to take pictures without touching the camera body. Used when the camera is on a tripod, it reduces the risk of shaking the camera (and thus blurring the image) during long exposures.

Chrome. A transparency or slide.

Contact print. A photographic print made by sandwiching a negative between photosensitized paper and glass. Paper and negative are in contact during exposure; the print, therefore, is the same size as the negative.

Contact sheet. The print that is produced when all the negatives in a roll are cut into strips and printed on one piece of paper. Used to view all the photos on a roll at a glance and to help a photographer select images for enlargement.

Crop. To trim edges of an image, often in order to improve the composition.

Depth of field. The area between the nearest and farthest points from the camera at which anything photographed will appear in focus.

Development. The chemical or physical treatment that converts a photographic, invisible latent image on film into negatives ready to be printed.

Diaphragm. A device that limits the aperture of a lens to control the amount of light that passes through.

Diffuser. Any material that is used to scatter light. Softens the character of the light and eliminates hard shadow edges.

Electronic flash. Discontinuous artificial light source, balanced for use with daylight color film. The flash is created when an electric current is released across two electrodes contained in a gas-filled glass or quartz tube.

Exposure. The product of the intensity of light that reaches the film or paper, and the length of time this intensity of light is allowed to act, which is controlled either by the shutter or the enlarger timer.

Fill light. A light used to brighten specific areas, show details, and prevent them from appearing too dark in a photograph.

Film speed. A number indicating the film's relative sensitivity to light and thus influencing exposure time.

Filter. Any transparent material, such as acetate, colored glass, or gelatin, that modifies light passing through it.

Focal length. The light-bending power of a lens. In enlarging, focal length determines image magnification at a set column height.

F-stop. The number used to express the size of the opening in the camera's diaphragm.

Glossy. The characteristic of high sheen on the surface of a printing paper.

Key light. The main light used to illuminate a photographic subject.

Light meter. A device for measuring the amount of light falling on or being reflected by the subject. Also called exposure meter.

Polarizing filter. Colorless filter able to absorb polarized light. It is used over a camera lens or light source to reduce or remove reflections and to intensify color.

Print. An image produced by the action of light on paper or similar material coated with a photosensitive emulsion.

Proof. A contact sheet.

Reflector. Any material from which light can be reflected, usually a disk or bowl placed around a light source, or a white or gray card reflecting light from the main source into shadowed areas around a subject.

Shutter. The camera mechanism that controls that amount of time for which the film is exposed to the light to make an exposure.

Single-lens reflex camera. A camera with a built-in mirror that reflects the scene being photographed onto a ground-glass viewing screen. Views the image through the same lens that projects the image to the film.

Stop bath. Chemical bath that stops development by neutralizing the developer. This prevents active developer from contaminating further processing solutions.

Strobe. A light source that provides repeated rapid and powerful bursts of light.

Tearsheets. Clippings of magazine or newspaper pages in which a photographer's, stylist's, or model's work appears. Tearsheets are often used in portfolios to show that one's work has been published.

Telephoto lens. Any lens of a very long range of magnification.

Test strip. Strip of printing paper or film that is given a range of exposures or filtrations by shading to test for correct image density and color.

Transparency. An image set on a transparent base, such as film or glass, and viewed through transmitted light (e.g., a slide).

Tungsten-filament lamp. Artificial light source using a tungsten filament in a glass envelope. The tungsten (a metallic element) produces an intense light when an electric current is passed through it. This is the essential artificial light source used in photography.

Twin-lens reflex camera. A camera with two identical lenses, one on top of the other. One is for viewing, the other for making the exposure.

Zoom lens. A lens with an adjustable range of magnification.

Television

Television today is a big business—one that influences nearly everyone in the United States.

Ninety-eight percent of American homes have television. Eighty-five percent of them have color TV, and 55 percent have more than one set. The average home keeps the tube switched on for six hours and forty-five minutes every day of the year.

Three major networks, 750 commercial stations, and 300 educational stations keep these TV screens flickering with broadcasts of sports, news, weather, drama, comedy, and educational shows. That's an expensive proposition: A half-hour prime-time entertainment show can cost more than $400,000 to produce. And that cost is rising at a rate of 15 percent a year.

The right to broadcast a single NFL football game may cost the networks a million and a half dollars. The rights for the 1984 Olympics cost $225 million—more than $1 million an hour. Hundreds of millions of viewers watch all these expensive broadcasts without paying one penny to the networks or their local stations. The television industry's primary source of income is selling air time to advertisers. In 1981, these advertisers spent $13 billion to broadcast their commercials.

The viewing public has come to accept this as a way of life. According to one recent survey, 72 percent of television viewers say that having commercials is a fair price to pay for watching television.

The networks do a great deal of research to find out what type of audiences various shows attract. Advertisers plan their commercial schedules based on this knowledge, because they want their commercials to reach the right type of viewer.

The results of such research are often surprising. ABC, for example, discovered that almost 30 percent of all college students who watch daytime soap operas are *male*. And that nearly 70 percent of adults who watch the news actually look forward to the weather forecast.

Television is a complex business with a tremendous diversity in job titles and functions. There are thousands of entry-level jobs filled by beginners every year—beginners with no experience or qualifications other than a driving ambition to break into the business. Unlike many other fields, television's jobs rarely require special expertise. Rather, most knowledge is gained on the job as you work your way up from "gopher" to assistant to the executive suite.

On the other hand, breaking in is difficult because the field is so competitive. For each job opening, a network or local station may receive hundreds of résumés. And they are often more likely to promote from within than hire an outsider.

Breaking into television is tough. The aim of this chapter is to help shift the odds in your favor.

First, we'll look at how the industry works and how it is structured. Next, we'll cover a potpourri of entry-level positions—everything from researcher and assistant producer to secretary and production assistant. You'll learn that the key to breaking in is to take *anything* as a start. The first job is relatively unimportant. Getting into the business is what counts.

Finally, we'll discuss a number of job-hunting strategies revealed to us by executives, headhunters, and others in the business. These strategies will give you a competitive edge in your search for a career in the television industry.

A SHORT HISTORY OF THE TUBE

The term *television* was first used in 1907 in an article in *Scientific American* to describe early experiments in image transmission. But the industry didn't really form until two decades later.

In 1926, the first network was created when RCA purchased station WEAF from AT&T for $1 million and renamed it the

National Broadcasting Company. Although most people don't realize it, RCA still owns and operates NBC today.

In 1927, Herbert Hoover, then secretary of commerce, appeared in an experimental TV broadcast. The first broadcast of a drama, also experimental, was *The Queen's Messenger,* aired in 1928 by WGY Schenectady and produced by General Electric.

That same year, Philo T. Farnsworth created one of the first commercial television sets. Farnsworth was awarded the patent for "electronic television" in 1930 and made a fortune by licensing it to RCA and NBC. Two years later, NBC installed a television station in the newly built Empire State Building. One of the earliest shows was a TV pilot of the popular radio program "Amos 'n' Andy."

The pace picked up in 1939. Franklin Delano Roosevelt became the first president to address the nation on TV. RCA became the first company to mass-produce and sell television sets on a national scale. They manufactured five-, nine- and twelve-inch-diameter TVs, which sold for anywhere from $199.50 to $600. And CBS began telecasting that year.

World War II interrupted the growth of the industry. When it was over, TV continued its progress in full swing. Shows on the air in the late 1940s included Sid Caesar's "Your Show of Shows"; "Kraft Television Theater"; "Howdy Doody"; "Kukla, Fran and Ollie"; "Meet the Press"; "Camel News Caravan," with John Cameron Swayze; "Texaco Star Theater," with Milton Berle; and "Toast of the Town," with Ed Sullivan. In addition, a third network, ABC, had been formed to compete with NBC and CBS.

When RCA started broadcasting, there were perhaps one or two shows on the air a day. Today, broadcasts start in the wee hours of the morning and continue long after midnight. For most people, the day's viewing starts with the morning shows: "CBS News"; "Today," with Brian Gumbel and Jane Pauley; "Good Morning America"; or "Donahue."

If you're home during the afternoon, soap operas are standard fare. And there are a lot to choose from. Later, most of us come home from work or school and switch on a news program. First comes the local news, then the national.

From 8:00 P.M. until 11:00 P.M. is prime time, that part of the evening when the most people settle down in their easy chairs or sofas for an evening of TV viewing. Prime time offers the most variety. Some viewers choose dramatic series, while others opt for sitcoms or straight action/adventure.

The TV schedule is just one more contributor to most people's scheduled routine. The same shows air at the same time, week after week. As TV actress Diana Rigg points out, "People switch on to the familiar."

By nature, watching television is a passive act (although pursuing a career in TV or working in the industry is anything *but* passive). And many critics blame passive viewers for the mediocre quality of most programming. Les Brown explains it in his book *Television: The Business Behind the Box*:

> Since the business mission of broadcasting is to attract audiences and keep them happily tranquil, and since the viewership has demonstrated that it will abide mindless entertainment night after night, there is simply nothing of practical value to be gained from indulgences in programs that might be provocative or true to life.

> A good program executive always plays it safe.

AN OVERVIEW OF THE TELEVISION INDUSTRY

The TV industry is divided into four major areas:

1. **The networks.** As you know, there are three networks: ABC, CBS, and NBC. They are large corporations, and each has other business interests besides television. NBC, for example, is part of RCA, a company involved in many businesses, from rental cars and records to satellites and semiconductors. CBS also owns a record company and publishes many trade journals. ABC is a major publisher and a manager of several large leisure attractions. Profiles of the three networks appear at the end of this chapter.

   Network television is the big-time. Not that other areas can't be lucrative or rewarding, but most people view networks as holding the prestige and glamour in the TV industry.

Job-seekers should be aware that the hiring policies and job titles are different at each of the networks. The daily routine for an *assistant producer* working at one network may be very different from the tasks performed by someone holding the same title at another network.

In most areas of broadcasting, the networks prefer to hire from within. Each network regularly publishes listings of job openings in the company and circulates them internally to all employees—from the cafeteria cook to the chairman of the board. These listings are posted throughout the building in hallways, office areas, and elevators. If you can make contact with someone in the network and get them to supply you with these job listings, you'll gain a major advantage in your television career search.

2. **Local stations.** There are three types of local stations: those owned and operated by a network, those affiliated with a network, and independents.

Networks have complete control over those stations they own and operate. Each network owns five large stations; all network-owned stations are located in such major cities as New York, Los Angeles, and Chicago.

Affiliates are obliged to fill a large percentage of their broadcasts with network-provided shows. The remainder of the time is devoted to local productions (mostly news and community affairs).

Independents have no obligations to the networks. They can buy network programs if they choose but are not committed to broadcasting them.

Local television can, in many instances, provide as much career satisfaction and income as a network job. So if you're not dazzled by the lure of network glamour, you might pursue local television as your goal. Even if you prefer networks, starting at a local station is an excellent way to get the training and experience that networks look for when they hire. The best strategy is to make a series of small steps up. But don't expect to leap straight from hometown television to a network post—that's not likely to happen.

You could start with a small station in a backwater town, then move to a middle-size station. After some experience there, you could try for a large station, perhaps in Boston, San Francisco, or Washington, D.C. As you move to larger markets, your skills develop, your experience increases, and your chances of making it to a network improve.

3. **Educational television.** Choosing to work in educational television rather than network TV is similar to opting for a career as a college professor instead of a corporate manager. The work may be more meaningful and fulfilling, but the pay is lower, the pace slower, and it may seem less glamorous to many. But educational television can provide good experience and training for people who plan to move to the network side later on. And some people may even prefer this less hectic, more thoughtful type of work.

4. **Independent producers.** Networks almost never produce your favorite evening shows. Networks do produce their own news programs and soap operas. But prime-time comedy, drama, and action/adventure series are, for the most part, produced by independent producers and production companies.

If you want a job in production but don't like news or soaps, getting a job as a cameraman, producer, director, casting director, story editor, or film editor with an independent production company may be the way to go. Finding these companies is easy. Pick a show you like and watch the closing credits. The name of the production company is always listed. Some of the biggest are Lorimar, MTM, Twentieth Century Fox, and Norman Lear.

The production companies are not mere order-takers that produce what the networks order. Rather, a production company puts together a *package*, consisting of an idea for a series plus the *talent* (producer, director, actors) needed to make it a hit. Then they try to sell the package to the networks.

If a network is interested, they'll commission a pilot. If they like the pilot, the show gets on the air. (According to one TV writer, thousands of shows are proposed each year. About three hundred are made into pilots. Of these, less than ten get on the air.)

Be aware that the days of plenty for independent production companies may soon be over. Networks have traditionally gone to outside sources for shows not because they are incapable of creative work but because Justice Department restrictions currently limit the quantity of self-produced programs the networks can broadcast to two and a half hours each week. This restriction expires in 1990. When that happens, a lot of networks will pull business away from independent producers and beef up their in-house production operations. What this means for you is more opportunity for a production job at a network, less with an independent producer.

Business Week reports that all three networks already have plans to film their own series. And all three networks are hiring major producers.

BREAKING INTO LOCAL TELEVISION

There are 750 local stations scattered throughout the country. If you get a picture on your TV set, there's at least one in your area.

Finding local stations is easy. You can look them up in the Yellow Pages under Television Stations. (Local stations in twelve major cities are listed at the back of this chapter.)

The size of the city, or *market* (the number of people reached by the broadcast), determines the size of the station. And station size affects the prestige and salaries of its employees. The bigger the station, the more money you'll eventually make. The bigger the market, the more clout you'll have for breaking into network television.

One *disadvantage* of a large station is that the jobs are more specialized than at small stations. You'll handle one specific job—camera operator, researcher, producer, broadcast engineer. At a smaller station, where payroll budgets are more limited, people have to share the work and handle several jobs simultaneously. This makes for a hectic life, but it's great training for the TV neophyte, since it gives you a broader range of experience.

Local stations offer career opportunities in four major areas: programming, engineering, sales, and administration.

- **Programming.** The programming department is responsible for what is broadcast over the air. They plan the schedule of shows; produce local news, sports, and community affairs programs; and coordinate with the network the buying and scheduling of network-provided programs.

  The head of the department is the program director. Program directors and their assistants plan the daily schedule and oversee all programming activity. They also work with the station manager to set and carry out station policy.

  Some of the jobs in the programming department are: producer, director, announcer, art director, set decorator, makeup artist, graphic artist, wardrobe designer, music librarian, camera operator, film and tape editor, lighting director, floor director, sound-effects technician, researcher, property handler, and secretary. A separate staff for putting on the evening news includes news directors, reporters, writers, researchers, on-air personalities, producers, and assignment editors.

  The entry-level positions—secretary, researcher, assistant producer—require no special skill or training. An assistant producer, for example, might function as an administrative assistant to the producer. In doing so, he or she learns the producer's craft at the hands of a master. Training for the majority of careers in television is gained mostly on the job.

- **Engineering.** Engineering maintains, monitors, and operates the equipment that transmits programs over the airways.

  The engineering department is run by a chief engineer. The chief supervises technicians who deal with the various aspects of producing and broadcasting television—audio, video, lighting, equipment repair.

  Broadcast technicians work both in the studio and *on location* (shooting street scenes or any other scenes outside the controlled atmosphere of the studio). They must be familiar with such things as FCC regulations, equipment operation, and basic electronics. Stations hire only skilled technicians, so you must be trained before you apply for this job. You can learn what you need to know at a good trade or technical school, and a number of these are listed at the back of the chapter.

Some engineering jobs—such as operating microphones, tape machines, or cameras—don't require such a high degree of technical skill, but in any engineering job, the more technical knowledge you have, the higher you'll advance.

- **Sales.** The sales department sells local air time to spot advertisers, sponsors, ad agencies, and other buyers.

Selling is more than pushing thirty or sixty seconds on a buyer. Selling involves *service*: The goal is to sell the advertiser commercial time that will promote his business, product, or service most effectively, so that he will continue to buy time—or perhaps buy even more.

To do the job, you've got to know what type of audience each television program attracts and match the audience to the type of buyers the advertiser wants to reach. Saturday-morning cartoons are the best vehicle for advertising children's cereal or toys, but not for pushing business computers.

The sales manager sets the advertising sales policy, including rates, and supervises the salespeople. These salespeople, called *account executives* in TV jargon, work directly with local advertisers and agencies to help them plan their media schedules. The best qualification for an aspiring TV account executive is sales experience in some other business—perhaps radio, magazines, or newspapers.

For the inexperienced, the best entry-level position in sales is that of *traffic clerk*. The traffic clerk prepares a daily log of program activities and makes sure the advertisers' commercials are scheduled correctly. Another good entry-level job is *sales assistant*; although the responsibilities are mainly secretarial, you get a lot of valuable client contact.

Some stations also employ researchers in the sales department who conduct studies and viewer surveys to determine the characteristics of the audience watching the station at any particular time of the day. This information helps account executives and advertisers plan the most effective advertising schedule.

- **General administration.** General administration handles the business end of running a station.

General administration for a television station is much the same as managing any business. You have to worry about such things as leases, taxes, bookkeeping, payroll, credit and collection, legal matters, hiring and firing, promotions, pay raises, customer complaints, profitability, public relations, office equipment, and managing your personnel. What sets general administration of a TV station apart from other management careers is the exciting nature of the television business versus, say, accounting, law, or manufacturing.

The *station manager* (or *general manager*) is in charge of it all. He or she is responsible for the overall operation of the station, as well as the coordination of the other three areas (programming, engineering, and sales). General administration offers managerial positions in promotion and marketing as well as entry-level jobs for secretaries, typists, clerks, and bookkeepers. Since most people find programming more glamorous, you might have a better chance of breaking into television as a clerk or manager in general administration.

Obviously, one doesn't walk into a TV station and say, "Put me in charge." There are two ways to become the general manager. One is to start at an entry-level administrative position at a TV station—usually a small one—and work your way up. The other is to become a skilled manager in some other industry and transfer your managerial skills to television.

BREAKING INTO NETWORK TELEVISION

Network television is the toughest area to get into, because it's perceived as the most glamorous of all TV fields. Then, too, there are only three networks, compared to more than one thousand independent, affiliate, and educational local stations.

It's impossible to pinpoint every job in all three networks. To begin with, each network has different career paths, different job titles, and different job responsibilities. And the opportunities are constantly changing. A seven-person research team may be eliminated when a talk show is canceled. Or a dozen production-related positions might be created if the network decides to move a series from an independent producer to in-house.

The single best way to find out what and where the jobs are is to get your hands on the job listings for that week. As we mentioned, they are distributed to insiders only. So you need to cultivate a contact who is willing to pass the listings along to you.

This is difficult, but not impossible. Talk to friends, families, acquaintances, colleagues, teachers. Perhaps a great-uncle's second cousin or the friend of a friend of a friend knows someone who works at a network. Call on people until a contact pays off.

Read the trade journals listed in the back of this chapter. Check both the help-wanted ads and the news items. When you read about a network producing a new soap opera or news feature, you can be sure that jobs are opening up somewhere. Write to the network and try to get one of those jobs for yourself.

Understand that networks offer opportunities in three basic areas: news, soap operas, and corporate management. The first two involve producing specific types of shows, while the last involves the overall supervision, operation, and promotion of the network as a corporation. But don't let the word *corporate* put you off; the top corporate people are the ones who hold the real power in the industry and decide what appears on American television sets.

Rather than outline each area in detail, we've assembled brief descriptions of some of the most promising entry-level jobs—jobs that welcome beginners with little or no experience, skill, or training in TV. Some of these jobs are dead ends in themselves but are useful in that they get you in the door so you can move to other areas within the network. Other jobs are the first step in a career path in a specific area; where that's the case, we tell you where the entry position can lead to.

Here, then, are recommended entry-level jobs in network television:

- **Desk assistant.** This position is the television newsroom's equivalent of the newspaper copyboy. The desk assistant is a "gopher," handling a variety of clerical, administrative, and messenger-type tasks. As desk assistants take on more responsibility, they may do research or edit news copy.

    Starting pay is low: about $190 a week. But the job has potential and can eventually lead to such higher positions in the TV newsroom as writer, director, and producer.

- **Production assistant.** This position is a good entry-level spot if you want to become a director. Production assistants help set up the studio, organize the day's shooting schedule, and edit film or tape. Production assistants must join the Directors Guild once they get a job. (For more information, write to the Directors Guild. Their address is listed at the end of the chapter.)

    Production assistants should aim to become associate directors and—eventually—full-fledged directors. The director of a television show has a role similar to that of a movie director: He or she holds the main responsibility for the quality of the production.

    Television directors work with writers, actors, announcers, anchormen, reporters, camera operators, technicians, set designers, makeup artists, wardrobe designers, film editors, lighting technicians, and sound-effects experts to make sure the best show possible is broadcast.

    Production assistants start at $320 to $350 a week. Assistant directors earn between $450 and $600 a week, and directors make $700 a week and up.

- **Associate producer.** While the director is responsible for the creative aspects of production, the producer handles everything else, from researching feature stories to hiring personnel to keeping the show on schedule—and on budget. But producers don't start as producers. They start as *associate* producers.

The job title of associate producer is a catchall phrase designed to include any job imaginable that a producer might need help with. "Good Morning America," for example, has a staff of twelve associate producers known in the network as *bookers*. The sole responsibility of these bookers is to track down and sign up guests to appear on the show. Starting salaries can range from $300 to $400 a week.

- **Researcher.** Researchers look for ideas and information useful to producers of information-type shows: news, features, talk shows.

One example of this type of show is ABC's "FYI," featuring Hal Linden. "FYI" was a *filler*—a series of forty-five-second spots used to fill time between full-length daytime shows. The spots provided concise information on a variety of topics. To generate source material for "FYI," ABC employed a staff of four full-time writer-researchers and a producer, plus twelve consultants to verify the accuracy of the material.

Starting salaries for researchers are in the $400–$450 range, and there are frequent openings. However, the trend now is to hire combination researcher–associate producers—one person to do two jobs. Contact the producers of the shows you'd like to work for to find out their specific needs in this area.

- **On-air personality.** This term refers to anyone who appears on the air—talk-show hosts, anchormen, news correspondents, announcers, narrators, and series hosts.

Strictly speaking, this job doesn't belong in an entry-level list, because it's the toughest to break into; everybody wants to be on TV, but there just aren't that many opportunities.

Still, we include it for two reasons. First, the day of the stern, gray-haired "veteran" anchor is gone; more and more people in their twenties and thirties are getting high-paying on-air jobs (and their salaries are in the hundreds of thousands).

Second, for better or worse, you no longer need to have twenty years' experience as a foreign correspondent or newspaper reporter before TV will take you. Today,

younger people, with less journalism experience but personalities and appearances more appealing to the large
young audience, are dominating the news—at least on the
local level. And the trend may someday work its way to the
network side.

The problem with getting on the air is precisely that
there is no entry-level job. To get a job on-air, you've got to
be able to show a tape of your work. But to show a tape,
you have to have a job in TV (networks are not interested
in home videos or tapes from college TV stations).

There are three basic tactics for breaking in. One is to
simply start small. Get a job with a tiny station out in the
boonies and bug the manager until they let you do a
weather forecast or deliver the public-service announcements.

A second tactic is to start with radio and then move to
television. It's easier to get your voice on the radio than to
get your face on the tube. But if your goal is television,
make sure your appearance is as appealing as your voice is
golden.

The third tactic is to get a job in cable TV, build a great
reel of sample work, and pitch to local broadcast stations
or the networks. It may work. But be aware that many
people in broadcast television resent, fear, and look down
their noses at cable. (For more information on careers in
cable television, read our book *Dream Jobs*, also published
by Wiley Press.)

- **Account executive.** The network account executive performs basically the same function as the local station's
account executive: selling air time to advertisers.

  From late May through early July, network sales has
  what is known as their *upfront sales season*. During this
  six-week period, the network sells time in their fall schedule long before the programs actually hit the air. Major
  advertisers snap up anywhere from half to three-quarters
  of the available prime-time spots; the total commitment of
  this advertising money can run into the hundreds of millions of dollars.

  Network sales, though especially tough to break into, is

a good entry into television for people who have worked in such related areas as marketing, advertising, media, or selling in some other type of industry.

Strong sales skills are the most important prerequisite. The account executive must convince his clients that a dollar spent on his network will sell the advertiser's product better than a dollar spent with another network . . . or with newspaper advertising, magazine advertising, sales promotion, or direct mail.

- **Secretary.** Don't look down your nose at this one. This is one of the most practical, attainable entry-level positions for beginners who want to work in network television. In fact, a lot of people break in this way, so there's heavy competition for secretarial slots. Some supervisors at the networks look for candidates who blend the ambition and intelligence to rise out of the secretary slot with the typing, shorthand, and clerical skills to perform the job efficiently while they have it. So take your typing or word-processing skills seriously and sharpen them.

  Be honest about your ambitions. Some managers want to hire ambitious people; others prefer secretaries who stay secretaries. The right attitude to convey is "I want to move up to something in programming or production, but I'm willing to take anything to get in and work hard to prove myself."

  The secretary's pay isn't bad—$265 to $300 a week—but it's tough to live on that in New York City. Having a roommate can help cut your housing costs.

Some other positions good for beginners include work in these departments:

- **Station relations.** Jobs in this department involve handling relations with the network affiliates.
- **Guest relations.** In this area you would distribute tickets for shows with live audiences.
- **Program practices.** Here, you would act as a censor, reviewing everything that goes on the air—scripts of shows and tapes of commercials—to make sure they conform to federal and network guidelines.

- **Documentation.** A documentation clerk watches TV all day. He or she logs the exact time and date every program and commercial is aired.
- **Production.** Working as a production supervisor is a step up for production assistants. The production supervisor, also known as the *unit manager* or *production coordinator*, acts as a liaison between outside directors and the network. He or she provides directors with the people, facilities, services, and support they need to produce top-quality shows. Starting salary: $26,000 a year.
- **Production control.** A manager in this department makes sure that shows are produced within budget. The job involves a lot of bookkeeping, accounting, and paperwork.
- **Personnel.** A personnel scheduler coordinates the work schedules of technicians, set decorators, stage managers, camera operators, associate producers, and other people involved in the production of a show. He or she makes sure the right people are in the right place at the right time.

WHAT IT TAKES

What does it take to make it in television? Do you need a college degree in broadcasting? Good looks? An uncle in the business?

Start with a deep commitment to and love of the entertainment industry. "Television is a glamour industry, so it's very competitive, and very few people move up," says Marilyn Neckes, a former associate producer with WOR-TV in New York. "It was tough to find a job that I was interested in that two hundred other well-qualified people weren't also applying for."[1]

Next to the music business, nothing is as competitive as television. Not even advertising. So if TV is your dream, be prepared for a long, hard road to the top.

Job applicants come to networks and local stations from all walks of life. At a recent seminar on careers in broadcasting, the attendees included an actress, an attorney, a computer programmer, a magazine editor, a state-department employee, a singer, a teacher, a radio DJ, a nurse, a videotape editor, and a publisher's assistant. All wanted to move into television. All have a chance to succeed.

A word we kept hearing over and over from successful television people was *sacrifice.* You have to be willing to start in a dull job with long hours and low pay—and stick with it awhile—before you can move up. As Barbara Walters explains:

> Whether it's a woman or a man that's getting anywhere, if you are ambitious, you don't give up when the job is grubby and boring. I've had some boring jobs. If you really do want it, you've got to be available to work very long hours—women and men—you have to work longer and harder than anybody else. You have to be available that Saturday. You can't go home at five o'clock, especially in this business. If something comes up and you've got to travel you've got to be able to do it.[2]

In a survey made a few years back, television executives were asked to identify the primary considerations they took into account when hiring employees. Seven qualifications lead the list: experience, personality, attitude, ability to speak and write clearly, skill in operating station equipment, awareness of the station's relationship with its audience, and the ability to think.

If you're still in school, you might consider tailoring your studies to the television industry. Technicians should, of course, complete a course of study at an accredited trade school. (Technical courses in broadcast engineering are useful to everyone interested in the business.)

Does your school have a campus TV or radio station? Get involved with it as an extracurricular activity. And instead of slinging hash or sitting in a lifeguard's chair this summer, see if you can get an internship with a local station in your hometown or college town.

College isn't a prerequisite to working in television (a high school degree is), but we recommend it to anyone planning to go beyond the lower levels. Nowadays, many people in the higher network positions even have advanced degrees.

Pick the course of study that will best prepare you for your chosen career: English, history, journalism, or communications for television news; business administration for sales or corporate management. Most stations today use computers to manage sales, programming, and promotion, so computer courses can make you more marketable.

More than two hundred colleges and universities offer degrees in television broadcasting. Hundreds of others offer a wide variety of related courses. Check the schools in your area to see what they offer. If you're out of school and already working, a couple of courses at night school may fill in some of the gaps in your knowledge.

THE JOB SEARCH: GETTING STARTED

The first step in trying to get a job in television is the same as in any other business. You write a résumé, print copies, and send them out to potential employers with a cover letter. Then you follow up by phone and mail and hope someone is interested enough to give you an interview.

Unless you're an actor or an on-air personality, don't send your photo with the résumé. Don't use fancy borders, colored papers, or oddball designs. The résumé should highlight your experience—especially any experience in broadcasting, cable television, audiovisual production, sales, writing, marketing, or any other field related to the job you're seeking.

Use the simplest outline form possible. Avoid long sentences. Don't bore the reader with such meaningless trivia as height, weight, and health. Include hobbies and extracurricular activities only if they relate to the job at hand. Don't put an objective or goal at the top of the résumé. Save the objective for the cover letter, and tailor it to the specific job you want. Stress clerical skills, because if you're a beginner, starting as a secretary may be the best way for you to break in.

The résumé should describe your experience while the cover letter persuades the reader to give you an interview. A cover letter is your opportunity to sell yourself to the employer.

Here's a cover letter that was sent to network executives and resulted in interviews for the writer:

THE ONLY PROBLEM WITH WORKING AT THE CUT-
TING EDGE OF COMMUNICATIONS IS STAYING AHEAD
OF THE BLADE.

To stay ahead, you need aggressive people—willing to take
chances.
People who are confident, flexible, dedicated.
People who want to learn—who are not afraid to ask
questions.

I am one of those people—one of the people you should
have on your staff.
Let me prove it. Start by reading my résumé. It shows I can
take any challenge and succeed.

I want to succeed for you. But if you're looking for someone
comfortable with covering the same old ground, count me
out.
If you want to work at the cutting edge, call me.

I won't get cut.

The letter was printed on a tasteful gray stock. A picture of a
cutting knife was splashed across the top half of the page at a
forty-five-degree angle.

This letter is unusual and far from perfect. For one thing, it's
too vague, too general. It doesn't say who the writer is, what
job he wants, or why the network should hire him.

On the other hand, the tone is brash and bold without being
offensive. The writer's personality comes through, and he
seems a likable, aggressive, self-confident fellow—the kind of
guy a network would indeed like to hire. Perhaps that's why
this unconventional letter generated results.

Where do you send your letter? To local stations, networks,
independent producers, educational stations, cable television
. . . wherever you want to work.

The best source of names and addresses is *Broadcasting
Yearbook;* another good directory is *Television Factbook.* These
and other sources of information are described at the end of
this chapter. If you're in school or have recently graduated, the
campus placement bureau might be able to uncover additional
leads.

You can also learn where the jobs are by reading industry trade journals and by attending conferences and seminars. Even if a chance meeting at a reception or luncheon doesn't lead to work, you can make a contact that may pay off sometime in the future.

Be aggressive in your letter-writing campaign. If your response rate is one in twenty, you will get two responses if you send out forty letters, but five responses if you send out a hundred.

If you want to be a researcher, writer, or associate producer for a network-produced show (news, feature, or soap), don't go through personnel. Instead, write directly to the executive producer of the show, because the producer is the one who decides whom to hire. Personnel merely screens candidates. The producer's name will be listed in the closing credits of the show you're interested in.

If you want to get involved in the production of prime-time entertainment shows, go to the independent production company that produces the show, not the network that broadcasts it. Again, you'll find the production company listed in the closing credits.

When sending any cover letter, take the time to find out the name of the person you want to read it. Address your letter to that specific person. Never use a form letter or a letter that begins with "Dear Television Executive" or "Dear Sir." In job-hunting, personalized mail gets the best results.

Follow up by phone as well as by mail. The best time to call a potential employer is during lunch, because the secretary won't be there to pick up the phone and screen your call.

You can also talk to many hard-to-reach people by calling after five in the evening, when the secretary has gone home but the executive is still at work. Executives are more relaxed after five because the business day is officially over, and this can make them more receptive to your sales pitch.

When an employer doesn't have an opening for you, he'll write back a polite note saying that your résumé is being kept on file. This may be true, but it does you no good, because no one ever looks at this file. When a job opens up, the résumés that cross the producer's or executive's desk that day are the ones that get read. So be sure to develop a mailing list of key television people and regularly mail your résumé to them.

Your persistence will pay off and lead to interviews. The success or failure of the interview depends largely on the personal chemistry between you and the interviewer. "The first thing we look for is a good attitude," says Bruce Whigham, placement manager for CBS. "And during the interview we can tell. We want somebody who makes the company look good."

To Whigham, a good attitude means being willing to make sacrifices. "Somebody who has aspirations but is willing to make sacrifices—that's what gets my attention," says Whigham. He points out that at CBS "security guards, secretaries, and mail-room people have college educations in communications. They take these positions just to get in the door."

The hard part is getting in. Once you're in, it's easier—although still by no means easy—to move around and up. Insiders have access to those valuable listings of job openings. And the networks prefer to promote from within in many instances (one exception is technicians, who are often hired from outside for their expertise in a particular technical area).

If a full-time job eludes you, you might try for a spot with ABC's or NBC's vacation-relief programs. From March to October, these two networks hire temporary help to relieve vacationing staffers. The requirements for working vacation relief are less stringent than for full-time employment; a year's experience with a cable or educational station can qualify you to work vacation relief on a network news program or daytime soap opera. Best of all, CBS hires NBC and ABC vacation-relief people for full-time jobs because they have already been trained "free" by the competition.

Whatever the job, don't be afraid to start at the bottom. Take an entry-level position as a clerk or typist. Start at a small station and go on to bigger markets. Work at a job that doesn't thrill you if it gives you a chance to get the job of your dreams. "You don't make jumps from Butte, Montana, to New York," points out Whigham. "You make gradual moves from market to market."

Pay attention to the way your station or network operates—how things are done, who holds the real power, where the jobs are, how new openings are filled. Be aware that no two employers are alike in this industry. NBC does things differently than CBS. WPIX does things differently than WOR. "Every station has career *paths*—predetermined training and advancement procedures that follow a specific pattern," says Whigham. "You just have to know how they operate."[3]

If you have a chance to step in and help out when there's extra work, do so. It's a good way to get noticed and appreciated. By proving that you are able and willing to handle emergencies and work long hours, you will endear yourself to those who are in a position to promote you.

Television is as difficult to break into as any field in this book, yet you don't need greatly specialized skills or knowledge to succeed. Persistence, ambition, and aggressiveness are at least as important as experience, education, and technical know-how.

And if at first you don't succeed, keep at it, as did Ted Koppel, host of ABC's "Nightline." As Koppel explains:

> I couldn't get a job in broadcasting right away.... I looked extraordinarily young, and so people were able to overlook the great potential there. But I knew I was pretty good and would be able to do it. This industry never has been, and I guess never will be, overpopulated with brilliance.[4]

Suggested Reading List in Television

Periodicals

Action, The Directors Guild of America, 1516 Westwood Blvd., Suite 102, Los Angeles, CA 90024. Covers TV and film news relevant to industry professionals.

Back Stage, 165 W. 46th St., New York, NY 10023; (212) 581-1080. Weekly newspaper of the entertainment industry.

Broadcasting, 1735 DeSales St. NW, Washington, D.C. 20036; (202) 638-1022. The Bible of the television industry. Weekly.

Broadcast Engineering, Box 12901, Overland Park, KS 66212. For owners, managers, and top technical people at TV stations. Monthly. Technically oriented articles.

Broadcast Management/Engineering, 295 Madison Ave., New York, NY 10017; (212) 685-5320. For broadcast executives, general managers, chief engineers, and program directors of TV stations. Monthly.

Channels Magazine, Media Commentary Council, Inc., 1515 Broadway, New York, NY 10036; (212) 398-1300. Bimonthly magazine on television and radio communications.

Daily Variety, 1400 N. Cahuenga Blvd., Hollywood, CA 90028; (213) 469-1141. Reports daily on news and events in TV, theater, and film.

Journal of Broadcasting, Broadcast Education Association, 1771 N. St. NW, Washington, D.C. 20036. Quarterly.

Media Decisions, 342 Madison Ave., New York, NY 10017; (212) 391-2155. Monthly. Deals with the advertising side of the television business.

Promotion Newsletter, Radio and TV, Drawer 50108, Lighthouse Point, FL 33064; (305) 426-4881. Monthly newsletter covering the promotional activities of various television and radio stations.

Radio and Television Weekly, 254 E. 31st St., New York, NY 10001; (212) 594-4120.

Ross Reports Television, Television Index, 150 Fifth Ave., New York, NY 10011; (212) 924-0320. Detailed information on script and casting requirements of continuing television programs.

Television Digest, 1836 Jefferson Pl. NW, Washington, D.C. 20036; (202) 872-9200. Weekly.

Television International Magazine, Box 2430, Hollywood, CA 90028; (213) 876-2219. For management and creative members of the TV industry. Published every two months.

Television Quarterly, National Academy of Television Arts and Sciences, 110 W. 57th St., New York, NY 10019; (212) 586-8424. Quarterly.

Television/Radio Age, Television Editorial Corporation, 666 Fifth Ave., New York, NY 10020; (212) 757-8400. Biweekly.

TV Guide, Radnor, PA 19088; (215) 293-8500. Weekly TV listings plus articles about people and TV shows.

Variety, 154 W. 46th St., New York, NY 10036; (212) 869-5700. Weekly.

Books

Barnouw, Erik. *The Image Empire: A History of Broadcasting in the United States From 1953.* New York: Oxford University Press, 1970. A history of the television industry from 1953 to 1970. Comprehensive but rather heavy reading.

Brooks, Tim, and Earle Marsh. *The Complete Directory to Prime Time Network TV Shows.* New York: Ballantine Books, 1980. An alphabetical guide to every prime-time network show that aired from 1946 to the present. Must reading for trivia buffs.
Brown, Les. *Television: The Business Behind the Box.* New York: Harcourt Brace Jovanovich, 1971. Highly readable account of the television industry and the networks' competition to be number one in the ratings.
Quinlan, Sterling. *Inside ABC: American Broadcasting Company's Rise to Power.* New York: Hastings House, 1979. A history of ABC. Highly readable, with insights into the minds of top network executives.
Wurtzel, Alan. *Television Production.* New York: McGraw-Hill, 1979. Covers all technical and aesthetic aspects of producing television shows, including editing, special effects, remote operations, and digital equipment.

Directories
Broadcasting Yearbook, Broadcasting Publications, Inc., 1735 DeSales St. NW, Washington, D.C. 20036. Lists addresses and names of management personnel in TV stations, production companies, and ad agencies.
TV Factbook, 1836 Jefferson Pl. NW, Washington, D.C. 20037. Similar in content to *Broadcasting Yearbook.*
Twelve City Directory, Television/Radio Age, 1270 Sixth Ave., New York, NY 10020. Addresses and phone numbers of agencies, networks, TV stations, trade associations, and program syndicators. Contains over six thousand listings.

Organizations of Interest to TV Professionals

Alternate Media Center, 725 Broadway, New York, NY 10003; (212) 260-3990. Internship programs in commercial television.
American Women in Radio and Television, 1321 Connecticut Ave. NW, Washington, D.C. 20036; (202) 296-0009. Association for women in TV and radio.
Announcer Training Studios, 152 W. 42nd St., New York, NY 10036; (212) 221-3700. Training program for TV announcers.
Association of Motion Picture and TV Producers, 8480 Beverly Blvd.,

Los Angeles, CA 90048; (213) 651-0081. Trade organization of TV and film producers.

Boston Film/Video Foundation, 39 Brighton Ave., Allston, MA 02134; (617) 254-1616. Provides equipment and information to independent video artists.

Center for Media Arts, 226 W. 26th St., New York, NY 10001; (212) 929-6999. Seminars and career-placement services in television.

Communications Workers of America, 1925 K. St. NW, Washington, D.C. 20006; (202) 728-2300.

Contract Services Administration Trust Fund, 8480 Beverly Blvd., Hollywood, CA 90048; (213) 655-4200. Training programs in TV-related fields.

Directors Guild of America, 8480 Beverly Blvd., Hollywood, CA 90048; (213) 653-2200. Two-year internships with various TV programs.

International Brotherhood of Electrical Workers, Broadcast and Recording Department, 1125 15th St. NW, Washington, D.C. 20005; (202) 833-7000. Union representing technicians at CBS and some three hundred to four hundred independent TV stations throughout the country.

National Academy of Television Arts and Sciences, 110 W. 57th St., New York, NY 10019; (212) 765-2450. Trade association for television professionals.

National Association of Broadcast Employees and Technicians, 1776 Broadway, Suite 1900, New York, NY 10019; (212) 265-3500. Union representing film and tape personnel, broadcast technicians, and newswriters.

National Association of Broadcasters, 1771 N St. NW, Washington, D.C. 20036; (202) 293-3500.

National Association of Educational Broadcasters, 1346 Connecticut Ave. NW, Washington, D.C. 20036.

North American Television Institute, 701 Westchester Ave., White Plains, NY 10604; (914) 328-9157. Seminars in production, technical, and marketing techniques for the broadcast television industry.

Society of Motion Picture and Television Art Directors, 7715 Sunset Blvd., Hollywood, CA 90046.

Society of Motion Picture and Television Engineers, 862 Scarsdale Ave., Scarsdale, NY 10583; (914) 472-6606. Professional organization dedicated to the engineering and technical aspects of television.

Television Bureau of Advertising, 485 Lexington Ave., New York, NY 10017; (212) 661-8440.

Television Information Office, 745 Fifth Ave., New York, NY 10022; (212) 759-6800. Provides informational, promotional, and educational services to the television industry and to people with an interest in television (writers, job-seekers, and others).

Weist-Barron, 35 W. 45th St., 6th Floor, New York, NY 10036; (212) 840-7025. Courses in how to audition for a TV commercial.

Women in Communications, Inc., 8305-A Shoal Creek Blvd., Austin, TX 78758; (512) 452-0119. Career counseling for women in broadcasting and other communications industries.

Writers Guild of America, 22 E. 48th St., New York, NY 10036; (212) 575-5060. Labor union for TV and film writers.

Young Filmmakers/Video Artists, 4 Rivington St., New York, NY 10002; (212) 673-9361. Training workshops in TV-studio production for minority youth.

The Big Three: CBS, ABC, NBC

CBS, Inc.
51 W. 52nd St.
New York, NY 10019
(212) 975-4321

CBS is a broad-based entertainment and communications company. In addition to the television network, CBS owns two radio networks, five TV stations, thirteen radio stations, a toy company, a musical-instruments company, and the world's largest record company, CBS Records. They're also a major publisher of books, music, and magazines as well as a producer of feature films.

In 1983, CBS maintained its position as the number-one network in prime-time ratings for the fourth year in a row. One reason for the high ratings was the broadcast of the last episode of "M*A*S*H." This show reached 60 percent of all homes equipped with television and was the most watched program of all time.

CBS had a number of hit series in 1983, including "AfterMASH," "Simon & Simon," "Scarecrow and Mrs. King," "Magnum PI," "Cagney and Lacey," and "Dallas." The "CBS Evening News" with Dan Rather beat the competition's ratings by 20 percent every week of the year. And "60 Minutes" completed its sixteenth season.

The corporation's overall 1983 revenues were $4.5 billion, with $2.4 billion generated by the broadcast group. Sales and profits were up over the previous year, with CBS sports and news showing the healthiest gain.

ABC
American Broadcasting Companies
1330 Sixth Ave.
New York, NY 10019
(212) 887-7777
ABC describes itself as "a diversified communications, entertainment, and information company." Their businesses include broadcasting, TV and radio stations, magazine publishing, feature-film production, and tourist attractions.

ABC came in second in the ratings for the 1983 television season. But their ratings were up over the previous year. And they were number one in daytime ratings for the sixth year in a row—meaning that ABC is very strong in the soaps.

In 1983 ABC broadcast "The Day After," a film about the aftermath of nuclear war. This show reached one hundred million viewers and was the most watched made-for-television movie of all time.

Other successful ABC programs include the two miniseries "The Thorn Birds" and "The Winds of War," as well as "Good Morning America," the country's top-rated morning show. ABC broadcast a total of 4,167 hours of entertainment, news, sports, and information during 1983.

The corporation's revenue for the year was a record $2.95 billion. Eighty-six percent of this—$2.61 billion—was generated by ABC's broadcasting operations.

NBC
National Broadcasting Co.
30 Rockefeller Plaza
New York, NY 10020
(212) 664-4444
RCA owns NBC. RCA also owns Hertz and RCA Records and manufactures a variety of products including TV sets, satellites, video cassettes, integrated circuits, telex equipment, and defense systems.

NBC can rightly claim they're tops in quality if not in popularity. In 1983 NBC won thirty-three prime-time Emmy Awards—more than ABC and CBS combined—but came in last in the ratings.

Although they came in third, NBC improved their ratings over the previous year and narrowed the gap between them and their competitors. Broadcasting revenues were $2.09 billion, up 45 percent over the previous year. And profits were greater than ever before. Among NBC's more successful series were "Hill Street Blues," "St. Elsewhere," "Cheers," "Remington Steele," and "The A-Team."

TV Near Thee

The three major networks have their headquarters in New York City. But there are TV stations in just about every region of the country. And starting at a local station is a good way to get experience and prepare for a career in the big-time.

Here are the stations in twelve major markets (New York, Chicago, Los Angeles, San Francisco, Detroit, Atlanta, Dallas–Fort Worth, St. Louis, Philadelphia, Minneapolis–St. Paul, Boston, Washington, D.C.):

New York
WABC-TV, 7 Lincoln Sq., (212) 887-7777.
WCBS-TV, 51 W. 52nd St., (212) 975-4321.
WNBC-TV, 30 Rockefeller Plaza, (212) 664-4444.
WNEW-TV, 205 E. 67th St., (212) 535-1000.
WNJU-TV, 425 Park Ave., (212) 935-3480.
WOR-TV, 1440 Broadway, (212) 764-7000.
WPIX, 11 WPIX Plaza, (212) 949-1100.
WXTV, 24 Meadowland Pkwy., Secaucus, NJ, (201) 348-4141.

Chicago
WBBM-TV, 630 N. McClurg Court, (312) 944-6000.
WBBS, 5525 N. Broadway, (312) 271-7171.
WCIU-TV, 141 W. Jackson St., (312) 663-0260.
WFBN, 1922 John Hancock Center, (312) 751-0785.
WFLD-TV, 300 N. State St., (312) 645-0300.
WGN-TV, 2501 Bradley Pl., (312) 528-2311.
WLS-TV, 190 N. State St., (312) 750-7777.
WMAQ-TV, Merchandise Mart Plaza, (312) 861-5555.
WPWR-TV, 4255 Westbrook Dr., Aurora, (312) 851-7515
WSNS-TV, 430 W. Grant Pl., (312) 929-1200.

Los Angeles
KABC-TV, 4151 Prospect Ave., (213) 557-7777.
KCOP, 915 N. La Brea Ave., (213) 851-1000.
KHJ-TV, 5515 Melrose Ave., (213) 467-5459.
KMEX-TV, 5420 Melrose Ave., (213) 466-8131.
KNBC, 3000 W. Alameda Blvd., (213) 840-4444.
KNXT, 6121 Sunset Blvd., (213) 460-3000.
KSCI, 1950 Cotner Ave., (213) 479-8081.
KTBN-TV, 2442 Michelle Dr., Tustin, (714) 832-2950.
KTLA, 5800 Sunset Blvd., (213) 460-5500.
KTTV, 5746 Sunset Blvd., (213) 462-7111.
KWHY-TV, 5545 Sunset Blvd., (213) 466-5441.

San Francisco
KBHK-TV, 420 Taylor St., (415) 885-3750.
KCSM-TV, 1700 W. Hillside Blvd., San Mateo, (415) 574-6586.
KDTV, 2200 Palou Ave., (415) 641-1400.
KFTY-TV, 533 Mendocino Ave., Santa Rosa, (415) 788-1930.
KGO-TV, 277 Golden Gate Ave., (415) 863-0077.
KICU-TV, Box 36, San Jose, (415) 298-3636.
KNTV, 645 Park Ave., San Jose, (408) 286-1111.
KPIX, 855 Battery St., (415) 362-5550.
KRON-TV, 1001 Van Ness Ave., (415) 441-4444.
KSTS, 2349 Bering Dr., San Jose, (408) 946-3400.
KTSF-TV, 185 Berry St., (415) 495-4995.
KTVU, 2 Jack London Sq., Oakland, (415) 834-1212.

Detroit
CBET-TV, Box 9, (313) 961-7200.
WDIV, 550 Lafayette Blvd., (313) 222-0444.
WGPR-TV, 3140 E. Jefferson Ave., (313) 259-8862.
WJBK-TV, Box 2000, Southfield, (313) 557-2000.
WKBD-TV, P.O. Box 50, Southfield, (313) 444-8500.
WXON-TV, 27777 Franklin Rd., Southfield, (313) 355-2900.
WXYZ-TV, 20777 W. Ten Mile Rd., Southfield, (313) 827-7777.

Atlanta
WAGA-TV, 1551 Briarcliff Rd. NE, (404) 875-5551.
WATL-TV, 575 Ponce de Leon Ave., (404) 892-3636.
WGNX-TV, 1810 Briarcliff Rd. NE, (404) 325-4606.
WSB-TV, 1601 W. Peachtree St. NE, (404) 897-7000.
WTBS, 1050 Techwood Dr. NW, (404) 892-1717.

WVEU, 2700 NE Expressway #4, (404) 321-6969.
WXIA-TV, 1611 W. Peachtree St. NE, (404) 892-1611.

Dallas–Fort Worth
KDFW-TV, 400 N. Griffin St., Dallas, (214) 744-4000.
KNBN, 3333 Harry Hines Blvd., Dallas, (214) 760-8833.
KTVT, Box 2495, Fort Worth, (817) 738-1951.
KTWS, Box 470427, Dallas, (214) 637-2727.
KTXA, 1712 E. Randoll Mill Rd., Arlington, Fort Worth, (817) 265-2100.
KXAS-TV, P.O. Box 1780, Fort Worth, (817) 429-1550.
KXTX-TV, 3900 Harry Hines Blvd., Dallas, (214) 521-3900.
WFAA-TV, Communications Center, Dallas, (214) 748-9631.

St. Louis
KDNL-TV, 1215 Cole St., (314) 436-3030.
KMOX-TV, 1 Memorial Dr., (314) 621-2345.
KPLR-TV, 4935 Lindell Blvd., (314) 367-7211.
KSDK, 1000 Market St., (314) 421-5055.
KTVI, 5915 Berthold Ave., (314) 647-2222.

Philadelphia
KYW-TV, Independence Mall E., (215) 238-4700.
WAAT-TV, 15 South Shore Rd., Linwood, NJ, (609) 927-4440.
WCAU-TV, City & Monument Ave., (215) 581-5500.
WHYY-TV, 5th & Scott Sts., Wilmington, DE, (302) 569-9815.
WPHL-TV, 5001 Wynnefield Ave., (215) 878-1700.
WPVI-TV, 4100 City Line Ave., (215) 878-9700.
WRBV-TV, 4449 N. Delsea Dr., Vineland, NJ, (609) 691-6565.
WTAF-TV, 4th & Market St., (215) 925-2929.
WWSG-TV, 300 Domino La., (215) 483-4550.

Minneapolis–St. Paul
KMSP-TV, 6975 York Ave. S., Minneapolis, (612) 926-9999.
KSTP-TV, 3415 University Ave., Minneapolis, (612) 646-5555.
WCCO-TV, 90 S. 11th St., Minneapolis, (612) 330-2400.
WTCN-TV, 441 Boone Ave. N., Minneapolis, (612) 546-1111.

Boston
WBZ-TV, 1170 Soldiers Field Rd., (617) 787-7000.
WCVB-TV, 5 TV Place, Needham, (617) 449-0400.
WLVI-TV, 75 Morrissey Blvd., (617) 288-3200.

WMUR-TV, 1819 Elm St., Manchester, NH (603) 623-8061.
WNDS-TV, TV 50 Place, Derry, NH (603) 434-8850.
WNEV-TV, 7 Bulfinch Pl., (617) 725-0777.
WQTV, 390 Commonwealth Ave., (617) 267-1530.
WSBK-TV, 83 Birmingham Pkwy., (617) 783-3838.
WSMW-TV, 127 Beverly Rd., Worcester, (617) 852-0027.
WXNE-TV, 100 Second Ave., Needham Heights, (617) 449-4200.

Washington, D.C.
WDCA-TV, 5202 River Road, Bethesda, MD, (301) 654-2600.
WDVM-TV, 4001 Brandywine St. NW, (202) 364-3900.
WHAG-TV, 13 E. Washington St., Hagerstown, MD, (301) 797-4400.
WJLA-TV, 4461 Connecticut Ave. NW, (202) 686-3000.
WRC-TV, 4001 Nebraska Ave., (202) 885-4000.
WTKK, 9008 Center St., Manassas, VA, (703) 369-3400.
WTTG, 5151 Wisconsin Ave. NW, (202) 244-5151.

Source: Twelve City Directory (New York: Television/Radio Age, 1984–1985).

TV Training: Where to Find It

Even if you'd rather be an anchorman or producer, a technical understanding of how television broadcasting works is helpful. You should be familiar with the general operation of transmitting and receiving equipment, as well as with federal broadcasting regulations and practices.

Here are some schools that offer technical training in broadcasting:

Ballie School of Broadcast, 2108 E. Thomas Rd., Suite 130, Phoenix, AZ 85016; (602) 945-4245.
Ballie School of Broadcast, 420 Taylor, San Francisco, CA 94102; (415) 441-0707.
Ballie School of Broadcast, 11875 South Bascom, Suite 410, Campbell, CA 95008; (408) 298-7300.
Ballie School of Broadcast, 3045 S. Parker Rd., Suite 223, Building B, Aurora, CO 80014; (303) 825-3024.
Ballie School of Broadcast, 2517 Eastlake Ave. E., Seattle, WA 98102; (206) 328-2900.
Ballie School of Broadcast, The Flour Mill, W. 621 Mallong, Spokane, WA 99201; (509) 326-6229.

Columbia College, 925 N. La Brea Ave., Los Angeles, CA 90038; (213) 851-0550.

Elkins Institute in Dallas, 2603 Inwood Rd., Dallas, TX 79901; (915) 532-3737.

Miller Institute, Main Campus, 4837 E. McDowell Rd., Phoenix, AZ 85008; (602) 252-2331.

Miller Institute, Phoenix Branch Campus, 11062 N. 24th Ave., Phoenix, AZ 85029; (602) 861-2271.

Miller Institute, Spokane Extension Campus, 801 E. Second Ave., Spokane, WA 99202; (509) 535-2525.

National Education Center, Brown Institute Campus, 111 NE 44th St., Fort Lauderdale, FL 33334; (305) 772-0280.

National Education Center, Brown Institute Campus, 3123 E. Lake St., Minneapolis, MN 55403; (612) 721-2481.

Ohio School of Broadcast Technique, 1737 Euclid Ave., Cleveland, OH 44115; (216) 861-1111.

Professional Academy of Broadcasting, 1809 Ailor Ave., Knoxville, TN 37921; (615) 546-5717.

RETS Electronics School, 965 Commonwealth Ave., Boston, MA 02215; (617) 783-1197.

Specs Howard School of Broadcast Arts, 16900 W. Eight Mile Rd., Southfield, MI 48075; (313) 569-0101.

TESST Electronic School, 5122 Baltimore Ave., Hyattsville, MD 20781; (301) 864-5750.

Video Technical Institute, 1806 Royal La., Dallas, TX 75229; (214) 263-2613.

Source: Handbook of Trade and Technical Careers and Training: 1984–1985, published by the National Association of Trade and Technical Schools (NATTS), Washington, D.C. All schools listed are accredited by NATTS.

The Theater

My code of life and conduct is simply this: work hard; play to the allowable limit; disregard equally the good and bad opinion of others; never do a friend a dirty trick; never grow indignant over anything; live the moment to the utmost of its possibilities; and be satisfied with life always, but never with oneself.
—George Jean Nathan, drama critic

Gourmet food, photography, music, travel—not one of these intriguing fields can be said to have a center, a geographical hub of activity that casts an undeniable influence over the entire industry. But the theater does. It's a street: Broadway. And the epicenter is Shubert Alley, a narrow stretch of pavement between Broadway and Eighth Avenue, linking Forty-fourth and Forty-fifth Streets in New York City. Standing in Shubert Alley, you could easily pop in on a dozen theaters in a matter of seconds. The Booth, the Shubert, the Majestic, the Imperial, the Martin Beck, the Broadhurst, and a half-dozen others are less than half a block from Shubert Alley.

Although the theater has become decentralized in the past two decades, America clings to the myth of the stagestruck kid who gets a part in the chorus and then, overnight, becomes a star by understudying—and then appearing for—an established Broadway performer. But, like any other business, the theater is a mixture of the ridiculous and the sublime.

The "sublime" is working with talented, imaginative American producers who regularly bring compelling theater to Broadway, off Broadway, and off-off Broadway. It's working at one of the country's better resident theaters, children's theaters, or summer theaters. It's attaching oneself to a particularly productive theater artist and gaining an apprenticeship. Very few people get rich in the theater, and we certainly wouldn't try to tell you that you're going to become a star, a top director, or a big producer. But there are many related jobs for people who love theater, who value its twenty-five-hundred-year tradition, and who have the capacity for vicarious enjoyment.

First, a few definitions. *Broadway* is, as you may know, a misnomer; very few theaters are actually *on* Broadway. Most are located between Broadway and Eighth Avenue, from Forty-third to Fifty-second Streets. That area is known as the Broadway grid, within which theaters must pay Broadway-scale salaries to unions. And to have its resident plays be eligible for the Antoinette Perry ("Tony") Awards, a theater must have a minimum seating capacity of 499.

Now, where do *you* begin? You begin with preparation. No matter what specialty interests you, it's wise to gain an exposure to all facets of the theater. If you're an undergraduate, take courses in acting, directing, set design, lighting, playwriting, and theater management. Many theater people change courses as they grow: Dustin Hoffman was a stage manager; Lillian Hellman was a press agent; Walter Kerr was a professor; Clive Barnes was a dance critic; producer David Merrick was originally a lawyer.

You should also consider getting a master's degree, although it is not always essential. Recently, Yale Drama School has attracted a great deal of attention as being *the* place to study theater (Wendy Wasserstein, Christopher Durang, Sigourney Weaver, and Meryl Streep all went to Yale), but there are dozens of fine theater departments in the United States. Some of the ones you may wish to look into are those at the University of Texas, Boston University, Vassar, Carnegie-Mellon, the University of Illinois, the University of Michigan, the University of Washington, and the University of North Carolina at Chapel Hill.

Theater, of course, is not only acting and playwriting. This chapter will discuss the type of behind-the-scenes jobs that keep you close to the action, if not right in the limelight (we'll have a separate section on breaking into acting).

After achieving your formal education, you'll probably wonder about the wisdom of taking the next flight to New York. It seems to make sense. If you wanted to be in the film business, you'd go to Hollywood, right?

Not necessarily.

Broadway has been synonymous with American theater for almost a century, but with the growing expense of mounting a Broadway production and with the corresponding growth and popularity of resident theaters, Broadway is now only one of many spots where great theater is being created. (We've included a listing of resident theaters as well as of top children's theaters.)

Let's focus on New York first, though. We are examining legitimate theater—not ballet, puppetry, opera, the circus, magic, ice shows, or many other performing arts.

The Broadway theater has been steadily shrinking for more than fifty years, and no one feels the shrinkage more than the theater's most noticeable artists—the actors. Every year, throughout the country, about fifteen thousand actors find work. Unfortunately, at any given moment there are about thirty-four thousand actors looking for those jobs. In 1980, of the members of the Actor's Equity Association who *did* find work, 65 percent earned less than $2,500, and 30 percent worked less than fifty days that year. The off-off Broadway theater has blossomed, in part, because of the near-impossible odds against talented actors finding regular work on or off Broadway.

So newcomers to the field must keep up on casting by reading the "trades": papers such as *Show Business, Variety,* and *Backstage.* You should also try to make friends at one of the successful or up-and-coming theater companies. Be a "gopher" ("Go fer coffee"), a volunteer, or a student intern; do anything that gets you close to where the action is.

Where the Action Is

On Broadway, the "action" is with producers who are committed to bringing new musicals, comedies, and dramas to the stage. Here's a thumbnail sketch of some producers you may want to pursue. One strategy may be to write a catchy letter that details your specific interests and emphasizes your devotion, flexibility, and willingness to be of help. Say that you just want a place to *start* (Hal Prince's first job was as an assistant stage manager on *Damn Yankees*). We don't suggest that you just show up on their doorstep.

Keep in mind that *friends* are important when landing jobs in the theater. Stephen Sondheim, for example, found a mentor in his Bucks County neighbor, Oscar Hammerstein II. Joe Papp and his playwright protégé David Rabe formed a type of father-son relationship. Tommy Tune struck up a friendship with Agnes DeMille. So see if you have any friends or relatives who can introduce you to anyone with connections in the theater.

Robert Whitehead (1501 Broadway, New York, NY 10036; tel. 212-354-4774) is one of the most prolific producers in town. He's produced dozens of top plays, including the much-heralded Dustin Hoffman production of *Death of a Salesman*.

The Shubert Organization (Bernard Jacobs, Gerald Schoenfeld) 225 W. 44th St., New York, NY 10036; tel. 212-944-3790) is practically a theater monopoly. Started several generations ago by the Shubert brothers, this producing organization holds key theatrical real estate in New York as well as on "the road" (i.e. theaters west of the Hudson River). The Shuberts coproduced *Dreamgirls, The Life of Nicholas Nickelby,* and *Cats,* as well as *The Gin Game* and the off-Broadway hit *Little Shop of Horrors*.

Emanuel Azenberg (165 West 46th St., New York, NY 10036; tel. 212-382-0530) has produced all of Neil Simon's comedies of the past decade, as well as more serious drama, such as *Moon for the Misbegotten, Master Harold . . . and the Boys, Children of a Lesser God,* and Tom Stoppard's tragicomedy *The Real Thing*.

Harold Prince (1270 Sixth Ave., New York, NY 10019; tel. 212-399-0960) is the talented producer-director of most of Stephen Sondheim's musicals, including *Company, Follies, Pacific Overtures, Sweeney Todd, A Funny Thing Happened on the Way to the Forum,* and *Merrily We Roll Along*. He's also produced and directed such hits as *Zorba, Cabaret,* and *Fiddler on the Roof*.

Alexander H. Cohen (225 West 44th St., New York, NY 10036; tel. 212-764-1900), in addition to producing the annual Tony Awards show for television, has produced dozens of plays, including *Beyond the Fringe* and the production of *Hamlet* starring Richard Burton.

McCann & Nugent (1501 Broadway, New York, NY 10036; tel. 212-354-9570) are general managers as well as producers. Elizabeth I. McCann and Nelle Nugent have coproduced and managed such plays as *Amadeus, Mornings at Seven,* and *The Elephant Man.*

A recent American Express advertisement displayed a group photo of some powerful New York producers. As an addendum to the people we've spotlighted, here are the names of twenty other producers pictured in the American Express ad, along with the names of the outstanding plays they have produced or the theater companies they direct:

1. Morton Gottlieb—*Romantic Comedy.*
2. Theodore Mann—artistic director, Circle in the Square.
3. Harry Rigby—*Sugar Babies.*
4. Roger Beckind—*The Real Thing.*
5. Barry Brown—*La Cage aux Folles.*
6. Doug Urbanski—*Beethoven's Tenth.*
7. Arthur Cantor—*Ian McKellan Acting Shakespeare.*
8. Douglas Turner Ward—artistic director, Negro Ensemble Theater.
9. Wynn Handman—director, American Place Theater.
10. Fredd Zollo—*'night, Mother.*
11. Philip Smith—executive VP, the Shubert Organization.
12. Michael Stuart—*The Tap Dance Kid.*
13. Barry Weissler—*Zorba.*
14. Kenneth Waissman—*Torch Song Trilogy.*
15. Lucille Lortel—*The Beckett Plays.*
16. Norma Kean—*Oh! Calcutta!*
17. Eliot Martin—*Glengarry Glen Ross.*
18. Todd Haimes—managing director, the Roundabout Theater.
19. Francine LeFrak—*Nine.*
20. James Freydberg—*Baby.*

There are, however, many other alternatives to starting your theater career at a leading production company. Theater people have traditionally found rather untraditional way of breaking into the field. David Mamet, the Pulitzer prize–winning playwright, for example, got his start in theater on a religious TV show (his uncle was director of broadcasting for the Chicago Board of Rabbis). He then worked on- and offstage at Hull House, a community theater. He was also a busboy at Second City, a waiter, and a caption writer for *Oui* magazine. Mamet used his connections and persistence to work his way closer to mainstream theater, all the time cultivating his playwriting skills and showing his work to associates. He was also willing to accept low-paying, nonmanagerial jobs, which incidentally left him more psychic energy for playwriting.

Using contacts, as you may have gathered, is an important part of theater success. Morton Gottlieb, Stephen Sondheim, and Oscar Hammerstein would have had a much tougher time if they hadn't taken advantage of close friends and family. And don't forget your college classmates; we've already commented on Yale Drama School as being a one-stop shopping center for future actors as well as for directors. Undergraduate theater departments can also provide instant networking. Northwestern is alma mater to Cloris Leachman, Charlotte Rae, and the late Paul Lynde. Princeton's Triangle Club forged a lifelong friendship for many theater folk, including Joshua Logan and Henry Fonda.

Theater lore is filled with examples of big talents emerging from virtual obscurity. Shirley MacLaine was a chorus girl in *The Pajama Game* when she went on for the star and became an overnight sensation. Gary Sandy was appearing in off-off-Broadway showcases less than two years before he was chosen to star in TV's "WKRP Cincinnati." Eugene O'Neill failed at jobs with three major companies before writing his first play. (Fortunately, his father, James O'Neill, was a rich and successful actor, giving O'Neill financial support to get him started.) Tennessee Williams was somewhere in the Southwest plucking squab when his agent, Audrey Wood, sent him a telegram notifying him that his first major play had been optioned for Broadway.

Lillian Hellman, S. N. Behrman, and Howard Lindsay were press agents; George S. Kaufman was a drama critic for the *New York Times;* and Neil Simon, long before his first hit, was a comedy writer for Phil Silvers and Sid Caesar.

One of the most exciting positions you can aspire to in the theater is that of producer. Being a tireless fund-raiser, like Joe Papp, is one talent you'll need. Of course, it helps to have the imagination of a Hal Prince, the negotiating skills of a David Merrick, and the flair of an Alexander Cohen.

Even with the soaring costs for the simplest one-set play, there are always a few people ready to bet everything that their show will be the next *Fantasticks*, the next *My Fair Lady*, the next *Odd Couple*, the next *Amadeus*.

Two such blithe spirits are Louis Scheeder and Howard DeFelice, two young coproducers who are, at this writing, prying cash from potential backers to launch a musical revue called *Diamonds*.

Here's how they found their way to producing on Broadway:

Scheeder: I got into the theater because it rained for a week in high school. So, instead of trying out for a sports team, I tried out for the school play. I auditioned for and got a part in *Richard III*.

As a classics major in college, I auditioned for a musical and was cast. Later, I started directing plays. After college, I went to Columbia graduate school for a semester. Then I found a job as an apprentice stage manager at the Arena Stage in Washington, D.C. That was fifteen years ago. I earned ninety dollars a week; I got to take home eighty. Eventually, I used my stage managing credentials to get my first directing assignment.

Between 1973 and 1981, I ran the Folger Theater Group. I left in 1981 to free-lance. In 1982, my partner, Howard DeFelice, and I produced our first show, *How I Got That Story*. It won an Obie, got fabulous reviews, and ran several months. There are about twenty different productions that sprung from ours.

Now my partner and I are producing a musical revue called *Diamonds Are Forever*. Harold Prince has agreed to direct. Right now, we're searching for backers. In fact, we start backers' auditions next month. We've raised seventy thousand dollars in front money. In other words, that money covers such things as the legal expenses involved in filing with the SEC and giving advances to the authors, directors, and so on. (Our musical actually has forty-five different authors.)

To launch a play, you have to talk to lots of people; inviting them to backers' auditions is only one relatively glamorous part of the dreary process of raising money. We think this show is worthwhile. The time we're spending on it attests to our belief in it.

Originally, when we started working on this show, we went to Hal Prince just for some advice, but he became enamored with the project himself. He has some free time coming up in six months, so we plan to get the show launched by then so he can direct it.

How do we survive while waiting for our show to open? We do some teaching, some directing, some consulting. When we go into production, we'll actually have our own apprentice assisting us: Columbia is sending us a graduate student in theater. He or she won't be paid but will help out and get to see how a Broadway production takes shape. One generation of theater people learns from the previous generation.

DeFelice: I started in the theater by directing Jules Feiffer's *Little Murders* at Yale. Then I directed Samuel Beckett's *Happy Days*. I became friendly with the Brusteins [Robert Brustein is a former dean of the Yale Drama School], and that helped confirm my theatrical ambitions.

From Yale, I went to Williamstown, where I put in eight summers as associate director, working with such actors as Frank Langella and Blythe Danner. After that, I went to London and worked as an assistant director on several shows. Somehow, one day, I found myself at a nonprofit theater in Milford, New Hampshire: the American Stage Festival. And now I'm in commercial theater—probably because I got fed up with dealing with the boards of nonprofit theaters!

Louis and I produced *How I Got That Story* at Chelsea. Carol Rothman directed (she just directed *Painting Churches*). The thing that makes this business so exciting is working with material from the very beginning. Many producers see a show that works and bring it over from London, or from some resident theater. But, to me, that's like being a landlord, not a producer. The George Abbotts of the theater helped create their own material, shaping each musical's book and lyrics as well as raising money. It's one thing to pick up a known property and bring it to Broadway . . . and another to create your own show.

Another thing that could only happen in New York: the opportunity to work with Hal Prince. He's the finest director working in the theater today, and both Louis and I feel thrilled just to be working with a man who has shaped the course of American musical-theater history.

We've emphasized production jobs and general assistant jobs that pay little but keep you close to the action. But when you are ready to step into the professional ranks—as an actor, stage manager, designer, electrician, property person, choreographer, or director—you will probably have to join a union (see our rundown of unions).

For now, we'll define a few of the job categories open to you. For example, you may wish to be a stage worker and be among the scenery movers, painters, electricians, and carpenters who work behind the scenes.

The International Alliance of Theatrical Stage Employees (IATSE) represents more than sixty thousand stage workers throughout the country. Union wages for general stagehands and lighting crew is at least $12.80 per hour. The sound crew may, typically, earn between $450 and $475 per week. Assistant department heads in carpentry, props, and electrical work can earn upward of $475 per week, while department heads generally earn a minimum of $539. (Minimum rates vary from region to region.)

- **Stage Managers.** Stage managers make sure that everything runs smoothly backstage as well as onstage. They do everything from assisting at rehearsals to supervising the hiring of the crew. The stage manager takes over the director's function on opening night, making sure that the actors, electricians, and sound people are doing their jobs. All Broadway and off-Broadway stage managers represented by Actor's Equity Association can expect to be paid about $800 per week; first assistant stage managers earn slightly more than $600 a week, while second assistant stage managers can make more than $550 working on a musical. The pay for work on dramas is from 15 to 20 percent less. (See also our section on acting, since stage managers and actors face similar hurdles in joining Actor's Equity.)

- **Designers.** Stage designers create the scenery, lighting, and costumes for plays and musicals. They have usually been trained in special schools or universities, or through apprenticeships. Like other people in the theater, they usually start out working at a small theater and work their way up to Broadway or to a major resident theater.

  Most Broadway and off-Broadway designers are represented by the United Scenic Artists Union. Set designers, for example, earn a minimum of $2,700 for their work in creating a single set; multiset dramas bring in upward of $4,000. The scale rises to the peak of a multiset creation for a musical. Here, even a beginner on Broadway will receive more than $7,000. Top names can command more money, enjoy royalties on their designs, and even command a percentage of the show's weekly gross. In regional theaters, set designers earn wages scaled in proportion to the size of the theater. They may earn only $500 for creating a set for a theater seating 199 people or less, but they can earn more than $1,600 at a theater that seats more than 1,000 people.

- **Costume designers** plan the wardrobe for the play or musical's characters—an awesome task when you consider that many characters may have numerous costume changes in the same play. Costume designers can, as union members, earn between $1,500 and $7,000 per play, depending on the number of characters in the play (a bonus is paid for creating period costumes, which require extensive research for authenticity). Costume designers who create for Broadway—such as Ann Roth, who designed the costumes for *The Best Little Whorehouse in Texas*—earn more than $10,000 per musical.

- **Lighting designers** plan the lighting, decide where lights will be hung, and generally try to enhance the play's theme and mood by using appropriate lighting. Minimum pay rates for beginning lighting designers range from $1,700 for a single set drama to $4,500 or more for a musical's lighting design. Off Broadway, a single set design may bring in between $660 and $1,000, while a large regional theater pays about $1,100 for a lighting design.

(Such top pros as Tharon Musser and Jules Fisher command much more, of course.)

You'll probably start as a design assistant for a small theater—summer stock, resident theater, or off Broadway. Broadway design assistants earn between $350 and $450 a week.

When it comes to *directors* and *choreographers*, there are no well-established career paths, and salaries range widely from one theater to another. Top directors may get a fee plus a percentage of the weekly gross. As members of the Society of Stage Directors and Choreographers, Broadway directors can command fees beginning at $6,000 per show, but they usually get much more for musicals; off-Broadway directors earn at least $2,000 per play (plus a percentage) and the fee increases when combined with choreography. (See our rundown of unions for more information.)

Again, the trick is to combine training, experience, and connections to keep advancing to better theaters, more challenging plays and musicals, and opportunities to work with top professionals. We've already profiled some of the top production houses on Broadway; now let's talk a bit about off Broadway.

Theater critic John Simon has written, "There is more interesting, daring, literate—in short, good—theater every year, without exception, Off Broadway than on, as virtually everyone involved with the theater who has an ounce of intelligence and honesty knows."

What theaters are the stand-outs of off Broadway, the places where theater people dream of working? We'll tell you. But remember that these theaters are among the most competitive. Yalies, fresh from MFA programs and brimming with good connections, are happy to work at these places for little or no money. Keeping that in mind, you're free to explore these theaters, in addition to the one hundred or so other off-Broadway and off-off-Broadway establishments sprinkled throughout Manhattan.

The major theaters are: Playwrights Horizons, Circle Repertory, New York Shakespeare Festival, the Manhattan Theater

Club, La Mama Experimental Theater Club, and the Roundabout Theater—each is a production company that owns its
own theater space.

Playwrights Horizons (416 West 42nd St., New York, NY
10036; tel. 212-564-1235) has emerged as a leading theater
troupe. They're the ones who have produced such successes as
*The March of the Falsettos, Gemini, Sister Mary Ignatius Ex-
plains It All for You, Isn't It Romantic?* and *Vanities.* You'd have
to consider yourself lucky just to answer phones or do typing
for Playwrights Horizons, because it is a hub of theatrical
activity. You might find a place for yourself as part of their
newly emerging theater school. They've recently joined with
New York University to offer a complete theater curriculum
taught by members of the company. They offer courses in stage
direction, stage design, dramaturgy (the study of a play's
structure), theater management, costume design, and lighting
design. For more information, contact Mrs. Helen Cook, Administrative Director, Playwrights Horizons Theater School,
c/o Playwrights Horizons at above address.

The New York Shakespeare Festival (425 Lafayette St., New
York, NY 10003; tel. 212-598-7100) probably employs more
theater people than any other off-Broadway theater group.
Known for its flamboyant producer, Joe Papp, the "Public
Theater" (as it is commonly called) has forged a reputation
with such inventive experimental fare as *That Championship
Season, Hair, Two Gentlemen of Verona, Sticks and Bones,* and *A
Chorus Line.*

It was Papp who conceived of performing Shakespeare in
Central Park; of casting Linda Ronstadt in *Pirates of Penzance;*
of funding *A Chorus Line;* and of creating a multitheater
facility on Lafayette Street, far-removed from the boom-or-
bust financial pressures of Broadway. Right now, Papp is
spending increasing amounts of time developing the talents of
very young playwrights—some as young as eight. So if bold,
contemporary plays of the Papp stripe put a glint in your eye,
you should be ready to sharpen pencils just to be a part of this
troupe's fortunes.

Set designer Marjorie Bradley Kellogg got her first break at the New York Shakespeare Festival during her freshman year at Vassar. Hired as a summer production assistant, Kellogg met set designer Ming Cho Lee, who became her teacher. When she graduated in 1967, she became Ming's assistant. In 1969, she took her qualifying exams and joined the United Scenic Artists Union, which gave her carte blanche to work in any theater. Within several years she was designing her own sets and is today one of the few set designers in the United States who actually makes a living free-lancing in the theater.

Circle Repertory Company—known as CRC, or "Circle Rep"—is located at 99 Seventh Avenue South, but its executive offices are at 161 Sixth Ave., New York, NY; tel. 212-691-3210. Marshall W. Mason, the artistic director, has been largely responsible for making this theater a testing ground for new American comedies and dramas. Along with managing director Richard Frankel and dramaturg (play analyst) Milan Stitt (also playwright of *The Runner Stumbles*), Mason has produced works of John Bishop (*The Harvesting, The Trip Back Down*) and Lanford Wilson (*The Hot L. Baltimore, Talley's Folly*).

The Manhattan Theater Club (321 East 73rd St., New York, NY; tel. 212-288-2500) has become identified with its innovative and hardworking artistic director, Lynne Meadow. In her twelve-year tenure at Manhattan Theater Club, Meadow has made this establishment a hub of theatrical activity, producing the work of playwrights from Beth Henley to Harold Pinter to Samuel Beckett. Such top pros as lighting designer Ian Calderone and set designer David Jenkins work frequently at MTC.

Another female powerhouse in New York theater is Ellen Stewart, artistic director of **La Mama Experimental Theater Company** (aka Café La Mama). The La Mama (74A East 4th St., New York, NY 10003; tel. 212-475-7710) is, as its name suggests, a home for the avant-garde.

Diametrically opposite La Mama in style is the **Roundabout Theater Company** (333 West 23rd St., New York, NY 10011; tel. 212-924-7160). Devoted to lively productions of theater classics, the Roundabout is the place to be if you live to have the words of Miller, Shaw, Ibsen, Strinberg, Anouilh, or Molière ringing in your ears.

Here are a few other up-and-coming spots for solid theater, places that would be useful for training and connections:

Ensemble Studio Theater (549 West 52nd St., New York, NY 10019; tel. 212-247-4982). Curt Dempster is the artistic director. Known for their high-quality productions of short plays, they've staged such notable productions as *To Gilliam on Her Thirty-seventh Birthday*, by Michael Brady, and *Open Admissions*, by Shirley Lauro.

The American Place Theater (111 West 46th St., New York, NY 10036; tel. 212-246-3730) also produces interesting theater work, as does the **Hudson Guild Theater** (441 West 26th St., New York, NY 10001; tel. 212-760-9810). David Kerry Heefner is the artistic director of Hudson Guild.

ACTING OUT YOUR FANTASIES

To paraphrase a former president, we want to make one thing "perfectly clear": Professional acting is such a competitive career that it is unfair to suggest that people stand even a slight chance of succeeding (i.e., earning a living). But since we believe that it would be wrong to talk about theater jobs without at least mentioning how people become actors, we thought we'd sketch in the fundamentals.

There is such a glut of actors that very few—even those who are in Actor's Equity Association—can make acting a paying proposition. The college drama departments keep churning out dewy-eyed young would-be actors, and the market for their talents continues to shrink. There are more than one thousand college and university drama departments in the United States; add to that hundreds of conservatories, professional classes and coaches, community-theater workshops, and high-school teachers. While these people help teach actors their craft, few present their students with the facts: that actors are a product, a part of a business, and that their chances of success are frighteningly slim.

In his book *Acting Professionally*, Robert Cohen lists what it takes to make it as an actor; you need talent, a definable personality, certain physical characteristics, proper training, experience, contacts, the will to succeed, a healthy attitude, freedom from entanglements, good information, advice and help, and luck. Where do you even start to collect these exalted traits?

You should start by getting a good education. Look for a college or university where the faculty has had professional theater experience. Browse through college catalogs; visit several schools; sit in on both classes and productions; and talk with faculty and students.

Ask questions. Is there a professional theater nearby? Have any graduates of the program gone on to become major actors? Is the school's budget sufficient to ensure proper equipment and facilities? Will you have the opportunity to study classical acting as well as contemporary techniques?

In addition to college training, you'll need commercial training—this usually means studying at an acting school or with an acting coach in New York or Los Angeles. To find the names of reputable acting schools in Los Angeles, send for the Acting Coaches and Teacher's Association Directory (c/o P.O. Box 1482, Hollywood, CA 90028).

In New York City, any issue of *Backstage* or *Show Business* will give you lists of acting teachers and schools, but beware; many of them may not have substantial reputations. Get in the habit of asking colleagues for recommendations. You'll find that certain eminent schools, such as the HB Studio, will be mentioned repeatedly for their high-caliber training.

The League of Resident Theaters (LORT) consists of about one hundred good nonprofit professional theaters in major cities. LORT is good to know about, because they hold tryouts in New York to help actors find roles at these theaters. Casting is usually held at the office of Theater Communications Group, 355 Lexington Ave., New York, NY 10017.

Here are a few schools that have excellent reputations:

New York
The American Academy of Dramatic Arts
120 Madison Avenue
New York, NY 10010
(212) 686-9244

Herbert Berghof Studios
120 Bank Street
New York, NY 10014
(212) 675-2370

Lee Strasberg Theater Institute
115 East 15th Street
New York, NY 10003
(212) 533-5500

Neighborhood Playhouse School of the Theater
340 East 54th Street
New York, NY 10022
(212) 688-3770

Los Angeles
American Academy of Dramatic Arts/West
300 East Green Street
Pasadena, CA 91101
(818) 798-0777

Estelle Harmon Actors' Workshop
522 N. La Brea
Los Angeles, CA 90036
(213) 931-8317

The Lee Strasberg Theater Institute
6757 Hollywood Blvd.
Hollywood, CA 90028
(213) 650-7777

So, whether you just want to do a walk-on at your local community theater or play Broadway, you'll need to sharpen your skills through some type of training. You'll need to use contacts, charm, and determination to just get noticed in the crowd. And that brings us to the traditional way in which people get noticed: They start small. They appear in a summer stock or regional theater and invite people to see them. Or they get a role off Broadway and ask Broadway agents to take a look. If you continue acting and you learn to promote your talents, someone will eventually notice you and, if you're lucky, keep you in mind for the future. Since membership in the Actor's Equity Association is clearly no assurance of success, you should focus more on finding a good showcase (i.e., a production professional enough to invite agents to) for your work than simply striving to join the union. In time, if you're determined, you'll get a chance to join the Actor's Equity—the result of being cast in a professional or "Equity" production.

Your job is to get cast in shows, and then to see to it that influential people become familiar with your work. How do you do that? You send them a professional résumé with a good photo, and you invite them to watch you work. Below is an example of a typical cover letter to use when inviting a producer or agent to view you in a play. It's followed by a sample actor's résumé.

An Actor's Dossier

The Cover Letter

Mr. Albert Heyward
Jacqueline Productions
2101 Sixth Ave.
New York, NY 10610

Dear Mr. Heyward:

You are invited to attend, as my guest, a performance of *The Music Man* in which I portray Professor Harold Hill, under the direction of Gary Forman at the Fort Lee Playhouse.

Our show opens Friday, November 9, and closes on Monday, December 18, at the Fort Lee Playhouse (near Horizon House). Curtain rises at 8:30 P.M.

I have enclosed a photo and résumé, along with an addressed post card that will reserve a ticket for you and your guest at the performance of your choice, or you may call 987-0987, the Fort Lee box office, and reserve tickets by phone.

I hope you enjoy our production, and I look forward to calling you next week to follow up.

Sincerely,

Paul C. Porter

The Résumé

PAUL C. PORTER
(AEA)
(AFTRA)

Home & Serv.	Height: 6' 1"
(212) 555-0909	Weight: 188 lbs.
66 East End Ave.	Vocal: Bass-Baritone
New York, NY 10028	Hair and Eyes: Brown

Off Broadway
   EQUITY LIBRARY THEATER   Destry Rides Again (1977)
   CSC REPERTORY   The Changeling (1972)
   MERCER ARTS CENTER   The Zoo Story (1970)

Regional
   GUTHRIE THEATER   Loot (1980)
   A.C.T.   Tiny Alice (1981)

Off-Off Broadway
   West End Players   Born Yesterday (1983)

Film & Television
   ABC, New York   The Edge of Night (1982)

Training
   Curt Conroy, Marian Harper, Susan Schaefer, Sam Schuster, American Academy of Dramatic Arts, Bill Hickey, John Gielgud

---

A WORD ABOUT AGENTS

In addition to "making the rounds" of producers, casting directors, and casting calls, aspiring actors look for agents who will help them find work. Agents are often harder to find than acting jobs. The agent's job is to find you work. For that service, he or she receives a percentage—usually 10 or 15 percent—of what you earn. Therefore, agents have to be choosy or they wind up going hungry.

The agent is an important factor in most professional theater situations. They keep abreast of theater activity and submit the photos and résumés of their clients to producers and casting directors for plays, musicals, films, and TV shows. The best agents are those who are "plugged into" plays and films while they are still in the planning stage. Top agents think carefully about submitting the names of actors and actresses who will be right for a particular part. Poor agents flood producers with the names of all their clients—a big turn-off to producers who are already swamped with photos and résumés.

Agents can be the key to good roles, but there are some pitfalls to watch out for. Agents can ignore you, taking you on as a client without ever following through or helping you build your career. Or they can be overzealous, scaring producers by demanding too much money for your services. Also, they can give you bad advice, turning down the roles that they should accept and vice versa.

So you have to do everything you can to acquire the best possible agent for your own unique blend of talents and aspirations.

There are hundreds of agents, and the *top* agents aren't necessarily the best ones for a fledgling actor. For example, in the two huge, prestigious agencies International Creative Management (ICM) and William Morris, offices in New York and Los Angeles may hire as many as fifty agents to handle more than two thousand actors, many of whom are famous. So these agencies are reluctant to take newcomers. For beginning actors, it's often better to find a small, aggressive agency, with agents who regularly scout untried talent and have the time and patience to help build your career.

Where do you start to look for an agent? First of all, an agent must be franchised by the Actor's Equity Association. Equity will give you a list of their franchised agents. Franchised agents have a license on the wall. Another way to find the names of franchised agents is to go to wherever theater books circulate in your area—a library, a theater bookstore—and find a copy of *Geographic Casting Guide*; there's one for Los Angeles and one for New York (both published by Ramos Publications, P.O. Box 46423, Los Angeles, CA 90046). These directories (each

$3.00) give alphabetical listings of five hundred agents, casting officers, and producers in each city.

Another source of agents' names is *Hollywood Report Studio Blue Book* (6715 Sunset Blvd., Los Angeles, CA 90028), which offers a complete listing of talent agents and producers.

When you come up with a list of agents that you'd like to represent you, ask your colleagues and friends if they know anything about the reputation of each agent. Also, look at the published listing of actors and their agents that are available in both New York and Los Angeles.

In Hollywood, this is *The Players' Directory*, put out three times a year by the Academy of Motion Picture Arts and Sciences. In New York, the equivalent publication is *The Players' Guide*, and it is available at the publisher's office, 165 West 46th St., New York, N.Y.

These books help you gauge the competition. You should try to cull a list of fifteen to twenty agents who handle people like yourself and are possibly interested in taking on new clients. Then, write to these people (see sample letter) or try to get an introduction to them through a personal contact. Don't pop in unannounced.

EDUCATION

How useful is a graduate degree in theater? For an actor, the MFA degree adds a bit of prestige to a résumé. Going to graduate school can also supply you with a network of friends and contacts that may very well lead to your first acting job. The negative side of the MFA is that you could be spending that time trying out for shows. Besides, there are many people in the theater who feel that too much education is a bad thing—not only because it may mire you in theory, but because the world of the academic theater is so very different from the tough world outside it.

For a designer, however, an MFA is a necessity. Only on the graduate level can you accomplish the type of sophisticated design work that prepares you for planning and designing a professional production. Graduate school gives you the opportunity to experiment, to solve problems inherent in designing for plays from different eras and different countries that may require extensive research. Also, graduate school helps prepare you for the rigorous examinations you'll need to pass to be admitted to the union. It will also give you a taste of the long hours and backbreaking schedule that most of the people involved in technical aspects of the theater have to deal with: long technical run-throughs, round-the-clock hours when shows are in rehearsal, the ability to solve problems by putting crews to work for days at a time.

America's Best Resident Theaters

A recent study by the National Endowment for the Arts shows that the number of nonprofit professional theater companies in the United States has grown from a handful three decades ago to more than four hundred today. Attendance at some twenty-six hundred productions in the 1983 season exceeded fourteen million.

Resident theaters—regional theaters with resident production and acting companies—have attained a level of professionalism that is already the envy of Broadway. Many resident companies perform plays in repertory, which means that one night you might be watching a Beckett drama, the next night a Shakespearean comedy, and the next night a Greek tragedy. If this type of versatility and professionalism appeals to you, you may want to drop in and sample the productions at a few of the following long-established resident theaters:

Tyrone Guthrie Theater, Vineland Place, Minneapolis, MN 55403; box office, (612) 377-2224. The Guthrie, which opened its doors in Minneapolis in 1963, is the pioneer of America's resident theaters. Named for its noted British founding director, it is a handsome, thrust-stage theater, seating more than fourteen hundred, at which much fine theater is produced.

American Conservatory Theater (ACT), 450 Geary St., San Francisco, CA 94102; box office, (415) 673-6440. For first-rate theater in the land of cable cars and Fisherman's Wharf, there is a company known to theater buffs simply as ACT. Artistic director William Ball has made ACT the nation's largest and most active repertory company, having presented more than 150 major productions ranging from classics of world drama to contemporary works.

Actor's Theater of Louisville, 316 West Main St., Louisville, KY 40202; box office, (502) 584-1205. The theater complex, housed in a

Victorian warehouse structure and a beautiful Greek Revival building, has been serving its community for twenty years. The 641-seat Pamela Brown Theater and the cozy upstairs Victor Jory Theater have seen numerous premieres, among them D. L. Coburn's *The Gin Game* and David Mamet's *Reunion*.

Center Theater Group, 135 North Grand Ave., Los Angeles, CA 90012; box office, (213) 972-7211. Thanks to this group, Los Angeles is now a theater town as well as a film town. In the Music Center, the Mark Taper Forum 750-seat thrust-stage playhouse has offered premieres of many fine plays, among them *The Trial of the Catonsville Nine, The Shadow Box,* and *Ashes.* The Improvisational Theater Project and Forum/Laboratory presents work by new dramatists.

The Long Wharf Theater, 222 Sargent Dr., New Haven, CT 06511; box office, (203) 787-4282. Known for the vitality of its productions, New Haven's Long Wharf Theater has a reputation for spotlighting plays of international importance. They were the first in the United States to present David Storey's powerful *The Changing Room,* the South African drama *Sizwe Banzi is Dead,* and David Rabe's *Streamers.*

If you're interested in exploring other resident theaters, the following have also made names for themselves:

Pulitzer prize–winner *The Great White Hope* was first staged at the *Arena Stage* (6th and M Streets, S.W., Washington, D.C. 20024; box office, 202-554-7890), a theater whose dramas rival those of Capitol Hill.

At *Trinity Square Repertory Company* (201 Washington St., Providence, RI 02903; box office, 401-351-4242), artistic director Adrian Hall has gained a national reputation.

Paul Baker's *Dallas Theater Center* (3636 Turtle Creek Blvd., Dallas, TX 75219; box office, 214-526-8857) launched Preston Jones's *A Texas Trilogy,* which was subsequently produced on Broadway.

The Lone State's *Alley Theater* (615 Texas Ave., Houston, TX 77002; box office, 713-228-8421) managed to gain international attention with a production of *Echelon,* directed by Galine Volchek, the first Soviet director to stage a Soviet play for an American company.

Children's Theaters: A Selected List

If you love children as much as you love the theater, there may be a glamour job awaiting you in children's theater. Children's theater has long since outgrown the "Oh, how cute" phase of its development, and it no longer clings to syrupy productions of such standards as *Mother Goose* and *Peter Pan*. Today, children's theater takes many forms—urban satire, folklore, original musicals, puppets, pantomime, and tragedy—and adults are quite often surprised at the wit, imagination, and sophistication of these productions. Great children's theater can be found all over the country—in Seattle, Rochester, Albany, and Palo Alto, as well as in Chicago, Atlanta, Dallas, and Albuquerque. The following are among the oldest and best-established companies in America. Any may be open to hiring apprentices and nonacting personnel.

Fort Lauderdale Children's Theater P.O. Box 4779, Ft. Lauderdale, FL 33338; box office, (305) 763-6882. It may not yet rival Disney World as an attraction, but the FLCT is steadily building a reputation as Florida's most exciting children's stage. Classics, folk tales, musicals, and fantasies are aimed at children from the second grade through high school. Presentations are in either the theater's intimate 150-seat Studio Theater or the city's Parker Playhouse, which seats as many as 1,200.

Honolulu Theater for Youth, P.O. Box 3257, Honolulu, HA 96801; box office, (808) 521-3487. Although they don't have a theater they can call their own, the Honolulu Theater for Youth has built its national reputation through its high production standards as well as its dedication to touring. Now in its thirtieth season, HTY performs on Maui, Lanai, Molokai, Hawaii, and Kauai with a "story theater" type of presentation. Aimed at both children and adults, this company is the only professional troupe in Hawaii.

Louisville Children's Theater, 2117 Payne St., Lousiville, KY 40206; box office, (502) 895-9486. Stage One: The Louisville Children's Theater offers fast-paced and challenging productions aimed at "children of all ages," especially those between five and eighteen. Reservations are necessary for all performances.

The Nashville Academy Theater, 724 2nd Ave., S. Nashville, TN 37210; box office, (615) 254-9103 or 254-6020. Formerly the Nashville Children's Theater, The Nashville Academy Theater is the oldest and largest children's troupe in America, and it stages everything from *The Mikado* to *The Miracle Worker*. NAT's School of Dramatic Arts works with children aged eight to eighteen during an eight-week summer program, offering more than two dozen courses in all aspects of the theater.

The Paper Bag Players, 50 Riverside Dr., New York, NY 10024; box office, (212) 362-0431. Named after the source of their props and costumes, this inventive company is a New York tradition, casting

an unsentimental eye at such modern issues as family together-
ness, noisy cities, and the energy crisis.

The First All Children's Theater, 37 West 65th Street, New York, NY
10023; box office, (212) 873-6400. This company is comprised of
two high-spirited troupes: the MeriMini Players and The Tenn
Company, both of which serve as training centers for young
performers. Almost all of the First ACT's productions are original
musicals.

Palo Alto All-Children's Theater, 1305 Middlefield Rd., Palo Alto CA
94301; box office, (415) 329-2216. Entering its fiftieth season as a
municipally funded theater for and by children, the *Palo Alto All-
Children's Theater* presents ten productions each season, plus
many special events.

SUMMER THEATER: THE STRAW-HAT CIRCUIT

One traditional road into the glamorous world of theater is to
find an apprenticeship at one of the many active "straw-hat"
theaters that come alive in the summer. Like so many dinner
theaters, straw-hat theaters usually do a lot of advertising in
such trade papers as *Show Business* and *Backstage,* usually in
early spring.

Connecticut probably has more summer theaters and dinner
theaters (theaters that offer patrons a meal as well as a play)
per square mile than any other state. By July, barns, town
halls, and even churches are filled with the sounds of carpenters building scenery, actors rehearsing, and tanned audiences
taking their seats moments before curtain time. The following
summer theater groups are among the finest in the state; their
enthusiasm is high and their track records are excellent.

The long-established **Ethel Kweskin Sterling Barn Theater**
(Newfield Ave., Stamford, CT 06092; box office, 203-358-4999)
sits on the sprawling acreage of the Sterling Farm Recreation
complex. Commanding a beautiful view of Long Island Sound,
the Sterling—a proscenium stage set within the informality of
a barn—has a dedicated group of players.

Built in 1956, the **Sharon Playhouse** (Sharon, CT 06069; box
office, 203-364-5909) is a fully professional theater in a lovely
community at the foot of the Berkshire Mountains.

Located on eleven acres, the **American Shakespeare Festival** (Stratford, CT 06497; tickets, 212-966-3900 or, in Conn., 203-375-5000) overlooks the Housatonic River in Stratford. The beautifully landscaped grounds include a costume museum, an Elizabethan herb garden, and more than two hundred picnic tables.

No survey of summer theaters can ignore the **Eugene O'Neill Theater Center** (305 Great Neck Rd., Waterford, CT 06385; box office, 212-443-5378 or 443-1238). Idyllic in setting and close to where O'Neill spent his youth, the Eugene O'Neill Theater Center comes alive during its "miracle month"—mid-July to mid-August. During this time, the center is buzzing with twelve staged readings of new plays by fledgling playwrights. At the same time, the National Critic's Institute is in session, training a new generation of drama critics. The list of plays that have premiered at the O'Neill include *The House of Blue Leaves*, by John Guare; *The Indian Wants the Bronx*, by Israel Horovitz; and *Bent*, by Martin Sherman. An unusual feature of the center's productions is that the audience is invited to a "critique," usually held after the play's last performance.

Located in the land of country clubs and commuter trains, the **Darien Dinner Theater** (Tokeneke Rd., Darien, CT 06820; box office, 203-655-7667) is unusual in that it was built as a dinner theater, rather than converted from a structure with another function.

The **Westport Country Playhouse** (25 Powers Ct., Westport, CT 06880; box office, 203-227-4177) is an unimposing rust-colored barn at the back of a shopping center and adjacent to a wood-paneled restaurant-bar called Backstage. To look at the barn, you might not guess that it has long been renowned as one of the oldest and finest summer theaters in the United States. It was at Westport that *Come Back, Little Sheba* started on the road to Broadway; since then, many stars have welcomed the chance to mix country life with rehearsal.

There are plenty of other fine summer theaters to apply to besides the ones we've listed. For a complete guide to where the jobs are in summer theater, take a look at the *Summer Theater Directory*, compiled by Jill Charles, artistic director of Dorset Theater Festival in Dorset, Vermont, and a former theater teacher at Williams College. This annual directory lists opportunities in theaters and festivals from Alabama to Wyoming, and even in Canada. It's a comprehensive guide for both professionals and students. It includes information on internships, statistics on organizations, and advice on how to apply for combined regional auditions. The end of April is just about the latest you can still find jobs in summer theater.

The great acting teacher Stanislavski once said, "There are no small parts, only small actors." In the same way, every job associated with the theater, no matter how small it seems, carries with it the allure of rubbing up against the great and near-great.

For example, an usher in a Broadway theater may be as attracted to the limelight as an actor. Take Thelma Moore, an eighty-some-year-old usherette at Broadway's St. James Theater. A recent *New York Times* article described how she first became an usherette between theatrical engagements, then started doing it full-time. She has met Ann Miller, Tommy Tune, Gwen Verdon, Neil Simon, Kevin Kline, and Raul Julia. One of her biggest kicks is helping out-of-towners position themselves correctly to get an autograph following the show.

Even at a bookstore, the infectious enthusiasm for theater can make a bookseller's job exude glamour. Take the Theater Arts Bookshop on Forty-second Street in New York. The whole bookshop is devoted to the theater: albums, books, plays, anthologies, posters. Stars walk in on a regular basis; playwrights pop in to see how their plays are selling. You spend your day talking with theater buffs, passing opinions on the latest plays, trading quips with theater-lovers.

The Theater Arts Bookshop isn't the only New York bookstore specializing in theater. There's also Applause Theater Books (100 West 67th St.), Theater Books (1576 Broadway), the Drama Book Shop (723 Seventh Ave.), and Richard Stoddard Books (90 East 10th St.).

Broadway has been called a "fabulous invalid" because, although it often seems to be dying, it never actually dies. The number of plays produced every year has declined dramatically since the 1920s. Costs have skyrocketed; ticket prices have soared. Film, television, cable, and video games compete with increasing ferocity. Still, there is nothing that quite takes the place of actors performing live onstage. By allying yourself with the best that theater has to offer—as an actor, director, usher, bookseller, or "gopher"—you may not necessarily win a Tony Award or a Pulitzer, but you will be working in the theater and, in a way, contributing to the never-ending theater tradition. The theater never knows where its next George Abbott or Michael Bennett or Neil Simon or Tyrone Guthrie will come from; surprises are commonplace in the theater. Maybe that's what keeps so many people in theater hopeful.

Theater Bookshelf: Suggested Reading

There are hundreds of fine books about the theater, and few theater people would agree as to which are "essential" reading. The following books represent an amalgam of the popular and the scholarly, the theatrical and the literary aspects of theater. They should be read, as Aristotle might have put it, "to teach and to please."

Theater History/Reference
Aristotle. "The Poetics." In *The Pocket Aristotle*. New York: Washington Square Press, 1983. Influential work giving "rules" for playwriting. Shaped classic and neo-classic ideas of dramatic form.

Esslin, Martin. *The Theater of the Absurd*. New York: Penguin, 1983. Overview of the popular European and American movement of the 1950s and 1960s that spawned Beckett, Ionesco, Genet, Pinter, and Albee.

Hartknoll, Phyllis. *The Oxford University Dictionary of the Theater*. New York: Oxford University Press. An encyclopedic reference to all aspects of the theater.

Acting
Bolaslavski, Richard. *Six Lessons*. New York: Theater Arts Books. Acting lessons that imaginatively explore the techniques first elaborated by Stanislavski.

Hagen, Uta, with Haskel Frankel. *Respect for Acting*. New York: Macmillan, 1973. Top acting teacher Uta Hagen talks with actors about the acting profession.

Stanislavski, Constantin. *An Actor Prepares*. New York: Theater Arts Books, 1948. Cornerstone of the famous Russian director's "Method" acting techniques.

———. *Building a Character*. New York: Theater Arts Books, 1977.

Stresses realistic, natural way of building a character, which has influenced the theater worldwide.

Dramatic Literature

Archer, William, and Robert Loewe, eds. *Hazlitt on Theater*. New York: Hill & Wang, 1980. Compelling theater criticism of early eighteenth-century plays that featured such actors as Edmund Kean and John Macready.

Bentley, Eric. *The Life of the Drama*. New York: Atheneum, 1964. Outstanding theater scholar's synthesis of modern drama.

Brustein, Robert. *The Theater of Revolt*. Boston: Atlantic–Little, Brown, 1964. Former Yale Drama School dean discusses "revolutionary" aspects of such dramatists as Ibsen, Strindberg, and Shaw.

Gassner, John. *Dramatic Soundings*. New York: Crown. Overview of major twentieth-century drama by a top critic and teacher.

Goddard, Harold C. *The Meaning of Shakespeare*. Chicago: University of Chicago Press, 1951. Trenchant dissection of the patterns in Shakespeare's plays.

Playwriting, Producing, Directing

Brook, Peter. *The Empty Space*. New York: Atheneum, 1978. Brook's philosophy of directing.

Clurman, Harold. *The Fervent Years*. New York: Knopf, 1983. Written by the noted director and cofounder of the Group Theater, this book assesses the contribution of that company to acting, playwriting, and noncommercial theater in America.

Gibson, William. *The Seesaw Log*. New York: Atheneum, 1984. Written by the author of *Two for the Seesaw*, this journal of the birth of a Broadway hit stands as a monument to the fortuitousness of Broadway production.

Grotowski, Jerzy. *Towards a Poor Theater*. New York: Simon & Schuster. Description of production/direction techniques of the Polish director, famous for his stripped-down, ensemble theater productions.

Hart, Moss. *Act One*. New York: Random House, 1976. The late beloved director-playwright's apprenticeship—and love affair—with the theater.

Houseman, John. *Run-Through*. New York: Simon & Schuster, 1984. Autobiography of a popular producer-director associated with the Mercury Theater of the 1930s.

Jones, Robert Edmund. *The Dramatic Imagination*. New York: Theater Arts Books, 1941. A lyrical evocation of the designer's art.

A BRIEF GUIDE TO THEATER UNIONS

If you aspire to become a theater professional, you'll probably, at some point, join a union. Theater unions are quite strong and protect their membership from the intrusion of amateurs. They also help establish minimum pay scales, and they keep their members informed of activities within the profession. Aside from being powerful, unions are difficult to join. They usually require that you've put in a lengthy apprenticeship (been hired to work in a union-sanctioned production) or that you've passed rigorous examinations in your field.

Here's a brief rundown on four of the theater's largest and most important unions:

Actor's Equity Association
165 West 46th St.
New York, NY 10036
(212) 869-8530

Actor's Equity presides over all actors and stage managers in Broadway, off-Broadway, and most regional professional theater productions. We all know about the great catch-22 of the acting profession: You can't work until you join the union, and you can't join the union until you find work. This is Equity's way of protecting itself from being overrun by the thousands of amateur actors who fight valiantly to attain membership.

Professional acting is practically a closed shop. The Actor's Equity Association, with its twenty-five thousand members, sets minimum pay scales for actors in all types of professional productions, including professional children's theaters. You are free to work in as many amateur theatrical productions as you like, but you need more than just a list of amateur-production credits to join Equity.

Here are the ways most people join:

- **By being offered a job by a producer working under union auspices.** Obviously, this isn't easy, since most people who audition for professional productions have their Equity cards already. But if a producer or director saw you and wanted you, he or she could give you instant access to Equity by simply hiring you to appear in that show.

- **By enrolling in the Equity Membership Candidate Program.** This Equity-sponsored program offers you membership if you can secure fifty weeks of nonunion acting work with an Equity company. If you can, you get an Equity card. So you should file an application with Equity as soon as you start work.
- **By becoming a member of another actor's union.** A fully paid-up member of AFTRA (American Federation of Television and Radio Actors) or SAG (Screen Actors Guild), who has worked under either union's jurisdiction—usually for a year or more—can join Equity. So a year of unpaid spear-carrying with a professional film production or TV production, plus $1,000 in initiation fees, can give you the prestige of *AEA*, *AFTRA*, and *SAG* below your name on your résumé.

Among the benefits of Equity membership are: (1) it keeps the amateurs out; (2) it establishes minimum wages; (3) it provides information as well as audition opportunities; (4) it runs seminars and meetings for exchanges of information; and (5) it gives you a union card—your passport to audition for any Equity show in the United States.

Society of Stage Directors and Choreographers
1501 Broadway
New York, NY 10036
(212) 391-1070
If you think that Equity is difficult to join, try joining the Society of Stage Directors and Choreographers. This one-thousand-member union presides over directors and choreographers in professional productions across America—including all Broadway and off-Broadway productions.

Like Equity, you may join this union if a producer, working within the Society's jurisdiction, hires you to be a choreographer or director. To do this, of course, you usually have to have a background of work in nonunion productions. Then you have to convince a producer to hire you.

This Society does not sponsor any apprenticeship programs, not does it have reciprocal agreements with other unions. Aside from being hired to direct or choreograph a union-

sanctioned play or musical, you can attain membership by
presenting a list of "substantial credits" (e.g., numerous college, stock, and/or regional-theater productions you've directed). This is often a rare privilege granted to very few.

According to special projects director Jim Furlong, the Society of Stage Directors and Choreographers was founded twenty
years ago, when Bob Fosse refused to sign a contract to direct
Little Me. Before Fosse took his stand, directors negotiated
their own contracts. Now the union helps directors and choreographers gain a bit of leverage in their negotiations with
producers.

United Scenic Artists Union
575 Eighth Ave.
New York, NY 10018
(212) 736-4498
Founded in 1918, the USAU has jurisdiction over scenic designers, costume designers, lighting designers, and certain other
creative arts for the theater, opera, ballet, and motion pictures,
as well as for TV and industrial shows.

The union was organized to protect craft standards, working
conditions, and wages—essential in the theatrical industries
with their uncertainty of employment, limited time schedules,
and risky financial state.

Admission to the locals of this union is through the entrance
examination, which is given annually, generally in late May or
June. The union gives tests at this time for four categories of
membership: Scenic Design, Scenic Art, Costume Design, and
Lighting Design. Each examination tests the specific skills
required for that category. Experience in the field is the best
preparation for these tests—applicants with academic or fine-
arts backgrounds are encouraged to work in the field before
applying.

The annual examinations for Scenic Design, Scenic Art,
Costume Design, and Lighting Design are open to any and all
who file an application prior to April 1. The procedures of each
exam are under constant revision; the forms may vary from
year to year, but in general they reflect the conditions and
practical skills needed in each particular field.

The initiation fee for Scenic Designers and Artists is $2,500; for Costume Design and Lighting Design, $2,000. However, in consideration of the time and money normally expended for an applicant to successfully complete the examination, a credit is given. So the new members admitted upon the recommendation of the exam committee receive a credit of $1,500, so the total initiation fee for these members is $500 or $1,000; and for applicants in more than one category, it does not exceed $1,000.

International Alliance of Theatrical Stage Employees (IATSE)
1515 Broadway
New York, NY 10036
(212) 730-1770
IATSE represents more than six thousand stage workers, including carpenters, property masters, electricians, and painters. Like the USAU, this union allows people to join on the basis of passing an examination in one of the fields mentioned above. Usually, one thousand people take the test at the same time. Those with the top one hundred grades get put on a roster. These people become part of an apprenticeship program and are selected to work in the field. Eventually, as each person on the roster gets accepted into a position, new exams are given.

The initiation fee is $1,000. Examinations are given about every five years.

Keeping Up on the Theater

Ever since *Theater Arts* stopped publication more than a decade ago, the theater community has lacked a single, authoritative source of monthly information about the professional theater. In line with the trend toward specialization, theater publications have catered to a fragmented theater community. Here's a list of magazines, trade publications, and theater updates that range from mere lists of what's playing to serious journals on the theater art:

American Theater, Theater Communications Group, 355 Lexington Ave., New York, NY 10017; (212) 697-5230. Editor: Jim

O'Quinn. Comments on major productions, theater people, trends in commercial and noncommercial theater.

Backstage, 330 West 42nd St., New York, NY 10036; (212) 947-0020. Trade tabloid offering casting news, trends in theater, film, and TV production, and fillers about all aspects of preparing for work in the entertainment field.

Dramatists Guild Newsletter, The Dramatists Guild, 234 West 44th St., New York, NY 10036; (212) 398-9366. Informative update on Guild activities, including notes on members, seminars, and special events.

Entertainment New York, 250 West 57th St., New York, NY 10019; (212) 245-6046. Theater listings, highlights of the season, new productions.

New York On Stage, Theater Development Fund, 1501 Broadway, New York, NY 10036; (212) 221-0013. Listing of current Broadway and off-Broadway shows.

Performing Arts Journal, 325 West 44th St., New York, NY 10036; (212) 243-3885. Scholarly journal covering themes of modern serious drama, noncommercial theater events, books, playwrights, and directors.

Playbill, 100 Sixth Ave., New York, NY 10013; (212) 966-5000. Given free to all Broadway theatergoers, *Playbill* is now available at selected newsstands. Features articles on commercial theater, including reminiscences, behind-the-scenes looks at Broadway productions, and profiles of theater notables.

Show Business, 136 West 44th St., New York, NY 10036; (212) 586-6900. Trade tabloid covering theatrical casting news, as well as articles about breaking into show business.

Theater Crafts, 250 West 57th St., New York, NY 10019; (212) 677-5997. Emphasizing theater design, stagecraft, and regional-theater activity.

The Drama Review, 51 West 4th St., New York, NY 10003; (212) 598-2597. Scholarly articles on avant-garde, noncommercial theater production, trends, movements around the world.

Variety, 154 West 46th St., New York, NY 10036; (212) 582-2700. The Bible of show business; reports on the week's events in all aspects of show business. Reviews plays, films, Las Vegas shows, cabaret.

Travel and Tourism

For many people, the world of travel and tourism conjures up romantic journeys to faraway places; for the people actually in the travel field, however, the reality is a bit more mundane. Often low-paying, the travel industry has all of the routine pleasures and pains of other businesses. But dealing with a travel product can be rewarding and even exciting. And in many travel occupations, one has the chance to take trips that are beyond most people's budgets.

The travel field is vast. One could easily write a whole book about opportunities in hotels, and another one about opportunities within travel agencies. This chapter will try to briefly give you the basics of three interesting careers in the travel field: the travel agent, the tour operator, and the hotel manager. (Listings also sketch in some job resources for finding work on cruise ships and in the airline field.) All three of these specialized areas are healthy and growing; openings for travel agents, for example, are expected to increase by more than 40 percent in the next decade.

IN GENERAL

While you have every right to list "travel benefits" as high on your list of expectations in pursuing a travel career, you should keep in mind that most of your time will be spent in an office.

If you stay in the field long enough, you may well get to see areas of the world that would normally be difficult for other people at similar levels in other occupations to afford. A secretary for a travel firm might well get to tour Reykjavik for a weekend or play tennis at the Margaret Court Tennis Ranch in Tucson or spend a week on the beach in Cartegena. You probably won't travel in season—because that's when your clients travel, and the hotels are jammed—but you may get to see such off-season locations as Moscow in November, Paris in December, or Alaska in March.

Of all the glamour industries discussed in this book, travel is by far the largest. In fact, travel and tourism make up the world's second largest retail industry after food sales. In the United States alone, there are more than 250,000 travel-related firms, employing more than four million people. The travel-and-tourism industry accounts for more than $210 billion in sales—5 percent of the Gross National Product—and foreigners traveling to the United States spend an additional $13 billion. The growth of travel over the past three decades has been phenomenal. In 1973, for example, there were about twelve thousand travel agencies in this country; in 1983, there were twenty-two thousand.

According to the U.S. Travel Data Center in Washington, D.C., more than half of the population took at least one trip during the summer of 1984. Tourist spots such as Disney World—said to be one of the busiest attractions on earth—keep increasing in attendance, and Dee Minic, spokesperson for the American Society of Travel Agents (ASTA), called 1984's travel surge "much bigger than in past years."

How can you prepare for a career in travel? The first thing to do is to get a well-rounded education. It is not necessary to be college-educated to succeed in the travel business, but it helps. Among the courses we'd recommend are:

- **Foreign languages.** Especially helpful in the travel whole-saling business, foreign languages will give you an advantage if you apply to airlines, cruise lines, or hotel chains. Speaking French, Spanish, Italian, German, Japanese and/ or a Slavic language could make you useful to a tour operator or a charter airline company. Languages give you a taste of different cultures and help familiarize you with the customs of foreign lands.

- **Speech.** Your ability to speak clearly and express yourself articulately is important in the travel industry. Good pronunciation and enunciation are important when you are dealing with names, places, flights, dates, and times all day. Good interpersonal skills will help you land and keep a job in which service is all-important.
- **Geography.** Everyone in travel needs a bit of geography, but the leaders of the hotel, cruise, and wholesale travel industries rely on their knowledge of destinations, mileage, terrain, and routes.
- **History.** By understanding history, you'll learn some of the milestones of a society's development. Such knowledge can help you be aware of each country's important places, festivals, and landmarks. France, for example, is noisy on Bastille Day, and shopping in London on Boxing Day is impossible because all the stores are closed. A knowledge of ancient history will make you more valuable as you help clients prepare to visit Greece, Israel, or Spain. You will be able to explain why Pompeii is an important attraction. A knowledge of the Renaissance will give you a better feeling for Florence, Rome, and Milan.
- **Archaeology.** Few travel agents have an in-depth knowledge of archaeology, but studying this subject will better equip you to plan trips to such places as Cairo and Luxor. It will give you a perspective on the importance of the Mayan ruins of the Yucatan, the ancient Greek theaters, and the Acropolis of Athens.
- **Religion.** Courses in religion will round out your perspective on the Middle East, Ireland, Spain, and Italy, as well as Japan and Mexico. Much of the etiquette surrounding dress and culinary habits, for instance, is affected by religious custom in these countries.
- **Computer Studies.** The entire travel industry is computerized, especially airline ticketing and hotel reservations, so having a knowledge of computers will soon be essential. Also, it helps to have solid office skills—typing, letter writing, and telephone technique.

Since the 1970s, there has been steady growth in the number

of colleges, community colleges, and privately owned trade schools offering programs to prepare students for the travel industry and to equip employees for higher positions.

One school that offers both a bachelor's and a master's degree in travel and tourism is George Washington University. Among the subjects covered in its curriculum are marketing and sales management, data processing, tourism planning and development, and tourism operations.

At Niagara University, in Niagara Falls, New York, students work for a four-year bachelor's program in transportation, travel, and tourism. They take liberal-arts courses for half the program and career-related subjects (such as computer reservations and hotel management) for the other half.

We recommend that you explore all routes to a job you want. Review the schools offering appropriate courses, speak to people in the field, read the trade magazines, and get feedback on your résumé and cover letter. College graduates sometimes have to take low-level jobs to get into tourism, and industry leaders advise them to be patient. By getting into the industry, new employees will gain experience and be exposed to other travel-related opportunities.

Speak to hotel managers, travel agents, and tour operators about what their jobs are like on a day-to-day basis. Write to travel's major trade associations to see how others have entered the travel field. The rest of this chapter is devoted to mapping out a few of the opportunities available to you.

BEING A TRAVEL AGENT

The life of a travel agent is like that of many office workers, offering modest pay, an interesting array of colleagues and clients, lots of routine desk work; and requiring a head for details as well as managerial and interpersonal skills. What separates travel agents from other nine-to-five types is the opportunity—if only occasional—to take the kind of trips that most of us just fantasize about.

In 1980 there were approximately fifty-two thousand people in the United States working as travel agents. Most worked for one of the more than 19,200 travel agencies throughout the fifty states. Branch offices of large agencies accounted for only about 22 percent of these agencies, while almost 70 percent were agencies with single locations.

In 1981 American travel agencies helped clients book trips worth more than $31 billion in travel revenues (compared with $19 billion in 1978). Today 78 percent of travel agencies are automated. In travel, computerization is indeed the wave of the present.

In 1981 the average annual gross sales for a travel agency was about $1.7 million. Agencies with bookings worth more than $1 million accounted for more than 80 percent of the total amount booked through agencies. Of course, travel agents receive only a small percentage of the cost of each trip they sell—from 10 to 15 percent, depending on the nature of the transportation, wholesaler, hotel, and so on.

Most travel agents are paid employees, and the pay is generally low. Experience, sales ability, and the size and location of the agency determine the salary of a travel agent. (Average salaries of an agent ranged from $9,500 to $18,000 in 1980.) Salaried agents at large agencies may receive standard benefits—pension plan, insurance coverage, paid vacations—that self-employed agents must provide for themselves.

Despite the difficulties involved in running your own agency, it is probably the best bet for those who have initiative and dream of autonomy, potentially high income, and freedom to travel.

In general, travel-agenting is expected to grow faster than other occupations, according to industry sources, even though the field is wide open to the problems inherent in economic fluctuations. There is definitely a growing tendency for corporations to establish accounts with travel agencies; business travel has in fact grown faster than pleasure travel. Conventions and meetings provide agents with high volume for booking many people at once.

It takes a special person to succeed as a travel agent, because you need to be aware of the business trends as well as the geography; you need to be an accountant, a promotion person, and a ticket writer.

There are a number of schools with programs intended to train travel agents—Frommer's, Sobelsohn's, Travel Institute's and ASTA's come to mind—but don't rely on these schools to give you an instinct for the business. Veteran travel agents sometimes complain that graduates of these programs lack the logical frame of mind and the travel savvy needed to develop into fine agents. (Still, the ASTA correspondence course may prove useful; it consists of fifteen lessons, a bibliography, and a final examination, which, if passed, certifies you as competent in the field.)

So, then, what is needed to succeed? A good sense of geography, for one thing. If it takes you more than a few seconds to locate Brussels or Bogota on the map, you may need a refresher. Also, you need to be quick-witted; you must be able to listen to an airline quote five different fares for the same flight, and then know which one is the best one for your client. And *best* isn't always *cheapest*. You may be able to save a client a few dollars on a trip from Boston to San Francisco by first routing him to New York. But time and convenience may also matter. Is your client a paraplegic or an executive with a hectic schedule or someone who hates flying? Such a client is unlikely to want to change planes no matter how much money is involved.

YOUR FIRST BREAK

The best type of training is on-the-job training, but you must fight getting into a rut. After a while, you'll learn about air reports, sell a variety of destinations, get practice in using the *Official Airline Guide*, and perhaps even get your agency to pay for your training on the Sabre computer. While you're salaried, you can learn, make mistakes, and gain ideas on how you'd run your own shop.

The big break for a person hoping to land a spot as an *outside agent* (an agent who may work "outside" the agency's premises but who is affiliated with the agency as a salesperson) is the moment he or she convinces an agency owner to give him or her a telephone and a desk. Usually, outside agents are paid a percentage of the commissions on the sales they make. In other words, if an outside agent sells $10,000 worth of trips, the agency might receive 10 percent of that $10,000, or $1,000. The outside agent who brought in the business might receive a minimum of 25 percent of that $1,000, or $250. His commissions will probably be proportionate to the volume of business he sells.

Now, selling trips worth $10,000 in one week is very difficult. It would amount to selling $500,000 worth of travel a year. Frankly, if you're selling that much travel, you should be working for yourself and keeping all the commissions. So what you're doing at this point is serving an apprenticeship and building your client list. Therefore, don't expect to earn too much money your first year.

Make sales goals for yourself. You should also push your employer to give you as much as 50 percent of the commissions if you really start to attract a lot of business. Then your $10,000-a-week volume would be worth $500 to you. In addition, the agency should be picking up the tab for some of your secretarial and postage needs. Eventually, if you're productive enough, you should ask them to raise your allowance for letterhead, promotional mailings, and billing expenses.

If you're willing to start at the bottom and to accept low pay at first, you may well be able to convince an agency to hire you. Your training costs may come out of your pocket, or the agency may help fund you. Even as the owner of an agency, you may not make much money your first year in business. This is not just because the first year of any new business is a period of adjustment. Agencies cannot issue plane tickets until they gain formal approval from the various conferences that govern travel. Conferences are organizations of airlines, ship lines, and railroads. The International Air Transport Association, for example, is the conference of international airlines. To gain conference approval, an agency must be in operation, must be financially sound, and must employ at least one experienced travel agent.

Conference approval can take three to six months to obtain, so most self-employed agents make very little profit in their first year. Their income is generally limited to commissions from hotels and tour operators and to nominal fees for making complicated arrangements for particular clients. For those considering opening their own agency, a working capital of between $37,000 and $50,000 will be needed to carry the business through its first year.

There are no federal licensing requirements for travel agents. However, Rhode Island, Ohio, and Hawaii now have state licensing requirements. In California, travel agents not approved by a conference are required to have a license.

BECOMING A TOUR OPERATOR

The tour operator occupies a small but important place in the travel industry. Tour operators put together all the elements of a trip—transportation, ocean voyages, accommodations, meals, sightseeing. They work closely with all other segments of the industry, such as hotel companies, airlines, car-rental firms, and government tourism offices.

The satisfaction in being part of a tour operator's office is the challenge of solving problems, the knitting together of travel plans, and the excitement of dealing with the travel products produced by the firm.

An operator must keep a finger on the pulse of the traveling public. Such operators as TWA Getaway, American Express, Maupintour, and Lindblad create travel programs that will take you practically anywhere on the globe, from Seattle to the South Pole. We admit that the world of the tour operator is a small one, but tour operators often seem to have a monopoly on the truly creative, imaginative, and specialized travel packages that appeal to hobbyists, culture lovers, and connoisseurs of travel.

Robert Whitley, executive vice president of the United States Tour Operators Association, says that the tour-operations industry is welcoming increasingly specialized employees, including computer experts, telephone salespeople, and marketers. The USTOA's thirty member companies account for about 65 percent of the tour business in the United States. The biggest problem for job-seekers is that openings in the tour-operation business tend to be two extreme levels: clerical and executive. Middle-level jobs are difficult to find, unless you have a background as a travel agent.

A tour operator (sometimes referred to as a *wholesaler*, as opposed to the travel agent, who is a retailer) does not sell directly to the public but offers the packages to travel agents, who in turn sell them to the public. Like any manufacturer, tour operators think in large terms—a hundred rooms at the Nairobi Hilton, a hundred seats on the Concorde, two hundred transfers from the Madeira airport to Reid's Hotel in Funchal. The tour operator must have a broad knowledge of suitable hotels, restaurants, airlines, trains, car rentals, cruise lines, side trips, and local customs.

He or she must also be able to draw on a number of skills— planning, negotiating, and marketing, for example. The more specialized functions are typically reserved for a few key executives in the company. Entry-level jobs usually involve making reservations and are low-paying. However, there are often opportunities for moving up fast. Most companies try to promote from within, so someone who starts out writing tickets or filing can become a manager relatively quickly.

One of the most inventive tour operators, Four Winds Travel, offers expensive packages to people looking for new travel experiences. They market their trips through travel agencies. Here's a quick rundown of the areas in which positions are available at Four Winds and other such operators:

- **Reservations.** Called *travel consultants*, reps who make reservations need good telephone skills, enthusiasm, and a head for details. Although an employer may ask for a college degree as a means of screening applicants, you don't need the degree so much as the skills a degree represents. And enthusiasm for the job is always a prime requirement.
- **Operations.** Often the heart of a tour operator's business, people who work in operations plan and run the tours, try out new accommodations, and arrange all details of the package. They decide which hotels to use, which airlines to book, and which restaurants to recommend. They decide

which destinations are likely to appeal to the public and which ones will offer a combination of value and excitement to their clients. Operations people are usually required to have experience as travel agents or reservation agents.

From the position of *operations assistant,* one can progress to *supervisor of operations, assistant product manager,* and *product manager.*

Senior-level operations people are the ones who get to sample the accommodations, but even these top people only spend two to four weeks a year doing this most glamorous part of the job.

● **Marketing.** Almost every operator needs someone to handle the marketing, advertising, and public-relations side of the business. Usually, the entry-level job is that of *marketing assistant.* That doesn't mean you're a glorified "gopher," but it does mean you handle your own typing and correspondence. You may do anything from monitor the inventory of brochures to write copy for a direct-sales letter. The best background is a blend of copywriting, business administration, and sales experience.

These are the key areas in most tour operations. You may be selling such exotic packages as a thirty-one-day fully escorted Cairo-to-Capetown tour, meals and airfare included (price: $4,000 per person), but, alas, you won't be paid royally. In fact, Four Winds—and they are one of the best-established operators—pays all its entry-level employees $12,500 per year. Why? Because these jobs are in demand, as in most areas of the travel industry.

How do people find their way to Four Winds? "Help-wanted ads in the newspaper," says promotion director Risa Weinreb. There is no magical rite of passage to this industry, just a desire to be in it.

The United States Tour Operators Association (211 E. 51st St., New York, NY 10022; 212-944-5727) does not provide much help to people trying to join such firms, but it does offer some guidance to people trying to start their own operations companies. In addition to sending you their book *Ethics in U.S.*

Tour Operations, the USTOA will answer some preliminary questions about what you'll need to start a tour business. For example, they'll tell you that there is no organization that you need to affiliate yourself with in order to become a tour operator. Essentially, all you need is a business certificate. You can then begin dealing with carriers (airlines), cruise lines, and hotels.

Cosmos Tours, a U.S. subsidiary of one of Europe's largest tour companies, has found a ready market for budget-minded American travelers, so they are regularly on the lookout for reservations agents and escorts. In all, there are thirty staff members in the office, and about a hundred escorts. Most of the hiring is done in January.

According to owner Jeffrey Joseph, the tour business is designed for people who start their careers early—even part-time while at school. "We don't look for degrees; we look for personalities, good communications skills, friendliness, help-fulness, and a desire to please. If you start at the bottom, you can go straight to the top—if you put in the hours," says Joseph.

INFORMATION RESOURCES

By reading local editions of *TravelAge*, you'll become familiar with the names of active operators in your locality (*TravelAge* is mailed free to travel agents, so ask an agency for a copy, or ask them to request a subscription for you).

By writing directly to an operator, you can sell your skills, enthusiasm, and interest directly. Discuss your skills, flexibil-ity, and background. As you write, ask yourself, "What skills do I have that an operator would find immediately valuable?" Emphasize your own travel, educational, and business experi-ence.

By browsing through a typical issue of *TravelAge East*, you may discover, for example, that Tour Designs, based in Wash-ington, D.C., specializes in upscale tours to Eastern Europe that emphasize the history, music, and arts of each country. So if you speak Rumanian, or you're a devotee of Dvořák or an expert in Brechtian theater, you may be assigned to lead a tour to Rumania, Hungary or Berlin.

Another resource that will help you identify some of the more unusual tour operators in the field is the *Specialty Travel Index* (9 Mono Ave., Fairfax, CA 94930). This twice-yearly publication lists tour operators that specialize in everything from river-rafting and wine-tasting to archaeology and opera tours. Although the magazine is usually only available to travel agents, you can get a copy by writing to them at the address above. Make sure to include a check for $3 for each issue you want. (Also, check *The World Travel Directory*, published by Ziff-Davis, 1 Park Ave., New York, NY 10016.)

As a rule, the more exotic a trip is, the fewer people there are who will be interested; only certain travelers wish to see a rare blue whale off the coast of Baja California or explore the ancient tribal rites of a group of Indians on Pago-Pago. Nevertheless, you may wish to specialize in travel that is off the beaten path, even if it means less pay and a riskier future.

If your tastes run to such things, you might want to contact Sven-Olaf Lindblad, president of Special Expeditions. He creates adventures to satisfy the intellectually curious traveler. His New York–based company was originally founded as a division of Lindblad Travel, but it is now an independent company. As with so many of the other glamorous careers mentioned in this book, you lose the diversity of working with a large company when you seek a small, specialized company like Special Expeditions. But perhaps you'll be happier with a small, idiosyncratic tour operator than a larger one that might expose you to more facets of the travel business.

Also, such specialization doesn't necessarily mean you can't move back into the mainstream. Ilene Lowe, director of marketing for Isram Tours, says that "everyone in wholesaling would like to work for Lindblad, because of their reputation for creating original tours. Whenever we've interviewed people who've worked for them, we've snapped them up."

A final note: Check the "Changing Faces" column of *TravelAge* each week; it is a good source of prospective employers and shows you the names of decision makers and people on their way to the top.

So if you want to break into this field, you may wish to contact a tour operator. The major companies are listed in *The Travel Agent Personnel Directory*, an annual compendium of travel-industry personnel (published by Travel Agent Magazine, 2 West 64th St., New York, NY 10036; 212-575-9000), or you can get the membership list of the United States Tour Operators Association—write to request a copy. Here are the names, addresses, and phone numbers of nine tour operators with excellent reputations for offering exciting, quality tour packages:

Abercrombie & Kent
  International
1000 Oak Brook Rd.
Oak Brook, IL 60521
(312) 887-7766

Cortell Group
3 E. 54th St.
New York, NY 10022
(212) 751-3250

Four Winds Travel, Inc.
175 Fifth Ave.
New York, NY 10010
(212) 777-0260

General Tours, Inc.
711 Third Ave.
New York, NY 10017
(212) 687-7400

Hemphill/Harris Travel Corp.
10100 Santa Monica Blvd.
Los Angeles, CA 90067
(213) 277-2672

Lindblad Travel, Inc.
8 Wright St.
Westport, CT 06880
(203) 226-8531

Maupintour, Inc.
P. O. Box 807
Lawrence, KS 66044
(913) 843-1211

Tauck Tours
11 Wilton Rd.
Westport, CT 06880
(203) 226-6911

Travcoa Travel Corporation
  of America
875 N. Michigan Ave.
Chicago, IL 60611
(312) 951-2900

HOTEL MANAGEMENT

The hotel industry is a $30 billion field that offers worldwide opportunities, job security, good pay, and excellent potential for promotion.

There are more than fifty-three thousand hotels, motels, and resorts in the United States, employing more than a million people. The lodging business is one of the fastest-growing industries in the country today, and the need for qualified employees is growing as well. The U.S. Department of Labor predicts that hotel/motel industry employment will jump by 72 percent in the 1980s, creating more than seven hundred thousand new jobs for trained personnel.

This brief section on hotels will focus on defining the types of positions available and identifying the type of skills and training that are a prerequisite to becoming a part of hotel management.

Let's start by listing the types of positions available at hotels, motels, and resorts:

- **Front-office staff.** This is the "face" the hotel shows to the public. Here's where you'll gain visibility, meet the public, and progress to managerial rank. At the front desk, you'll make reservations and greet guests. Among the positions available in the front office are *front-office manager, assistant manager,* and *reservation clerk.*
- **Service Staff.** These people form the diplomatic corps. They cope with everything from greeting guests and handling baggage to assisting with travel plans. Positions often include *superintendent of service, concierge,* and *bell captain.*
- **Accounting.** This department generates financial information for management and provides operational support. Positions include *controller, credit manager, purchasing agent,* and *ADP systems supervisor.*
- **Food Service.** The food-service and preparation departments hold some of the best opportunities for advancement. Positions include *executive chef, first assistant, pastry chef,* and *pantry supervisor* (see the Gourmet Food chapter for more information).
- **Housekeeping.** This staff maintains the property and its rooms. Positions include *executive housekeeper, floor supervisor,* and *room attendant.*
- **Sales.** This department promotes and handles special

group arrangements, such as meetings and banquets. Positions include *sales director* and *banquet manager*.

You can start work in this field while still attending high school by taking a part-time job at a hotel, motel, or restaurant. Or you can wait until you graduate from college or vocational school, since this extra education puts you in an even better position for working your way up the ladder. So let's take a look at the kinds of courses and opportunities offered at some of the schools that specialize in preparing people for hotel management.

TRAINING

At Cornell's School of Hotel Administration, graduates are awarded a bachelor-of-science degree after taking a four-year course, and the school also offers master's degrees and doctorates in professional studies. Subjects covered in the curriculum include administration, management, accounting, advertising strategies, computers, hotel and architectural design, and the principles of nutrition.

New York University has a four-year program in hotel management—as do Michigan State, Boston University, and the University of Michigan. NYU's program director, Joseph F. Durocher, believes that NYU offers students a type of preparation for "urban realities" that out-of-town schools lack. In conducting a nationwide survey to determine the skills most in demand by hotel executives, he found that, ideally, hotel managers should be adept at handling numerous banquets at once; supervising large staffs of skilled and unskilled employees; handling marketing, energy management, and computerization. Durocher also found that hotel managers must, of course, be good with people. That's why NYU and other schools across the country offer psychology courses to hotel-management students. NYU also offers their students the opportunity to visit New York City's hotels and see firsthand how they operate.

At NYU, students spend two semesters working in hotels while taking a reduced courseload. This program allows hotel managers the opportunity to see the students in action before offering them permanent employment. Students, in turn, get a chance to look at various hotels before they accept a job. These internships pay $6 to $8 an hour.

The program provides fifty-two credits of liberal arts, including a speech course, a writing course, and a language— either Spanish, French or German.

Other required courses include chemistry, food preparation, marketing, mathematics, computer science, and economics. Graduates of the program receive a B.S. in hotel management and tourism. They can expect to earn starting salaries ranging from $18,000 to $24,000.

GETTING LEADS

Lack of experience or education is not a barrier to employment in the lodging industry; it only determines where your career begins. Once you have entered the field, the pace at which you move upward depends on your willingness to work hard and your eagerness to advance. On-the-job training programs are plentiful, and excellent correspondence courses are available through the Educational Institute of the American Hotel and Motel Association. Fees for vocational training courses are often reimbursed by your employer.

Managers are chosen for their experience as well as for their interpersonal skills. As a high-school graduate, you could expect to be employed in any of a number of entry-level positions: bellperson, room attendant, steward, busperson, waiter or waitress. In many cases, part-time employment can be arranged while you are still in school.

Junior-college graduates who earn an associate degree in hotel and restaurant management will find a wide range of jobs open to them. These programs are generally oriented to the technical or supervisory aspect of the job, and will prepare students in administrative or supervisory capacities, respectively.

Those who graduate from a four-year degree course in hotel and restaurant administration have undergone a thorough training in all aspects of the industry. They can expect to begin their careers as assistant managers in smaller hotels and motels, or in assistant managerial and supervisory positions in larger establishments. Westin, Hyatt, Marriott, Radisson, and Hilton are five hotel chains that offer exceptional management-training courses for their employees. They are among the many large hotel chains that encourage managers to grow within their jobs and to advance within the organization. They train managers to use initiative and to organize and direct the work of others. They help managers learn to solve problems and concentrate on details.

Some of these hotel chains offer programs that enable trainees to rotate among various departments and receive a thorough knowledge of the hotel's entire operation. Other hotels may help finance outstanding employees in acquiring the necessary training in hotel management.

Most hotels promote employees who have proved their ability—usually front-office clerks, who can be promoted to assistant manager and eventually to general manager. Brand-new hotels, particularly those without well-established on-the-job training programs, often prefer experienced personnel for managerial positions. Hotel and motel chains may offer better opportunities for advancement than independent properties, because employees can transfer to another hotel or motel within the chain or to the central office if an opening occurs.

Employment of hotel managers is expected to grow throughout the 1980s. Some job openings will occur as additional hotels and motels are built and chain and franchise operations spread. However, most openings will occur as experienced managers die, retire, or leave the occupation. Applicants who have college degrees in hotel administration will have an advantage in seeking entry positions and later advancement.

Here are two places to write for more information about trainee programs and career opportunities in the hotel management field:

The Educational Institute of the American Hotel
    and Motel Association
1407 S. Harrison Rd.
East Lansing, MI 48823

Council on Hotel, Restaurant and Institutional Education
11 Koger Executive Center, Suite 219,
Norfolk, VA 23502

The Council offers a directory of colleges and other schools
offering programs in hospitality education.

HOTEL LIFE: NEVER A DULL MOMENT

At Rancho Mirage in California, everyone on staff wears a rose.
It's just one more lovely detail—like the chocolates on the
pillow, the toiletries in the bathroom, and the robe left in every
guest's closet.

At the Atlantic Terrace in Montauk—one of New York's most
popular oceanside motels—owner-manager Frank Brill also
puts his guests' needs first. Brill supervises a staff of twenty-
four, half of whom maintain the rooms. We asked Frank to
share a few of his thoughts on the pleasures and responsibilities of running a small motel. Although he is the owner, Brill
can be seen at any hour of the day or night fiddling with such
details as cleaning the barbecue grills to draining the whirl-
pool.

- **On Staffing:** "Everyone here is part-time. We're also seasonal; we close down on October first. Everyone is on
  salary. Of course, the housekeepers also make tips. There's
  also the opportunity for extra work—like baby-sitting.

  In this business, you rely on a good maintenance person.
  Someone who can fix air conditioners, leaky faucets, and
  backed-up toilets. When people leave their shower cur-
  tains out, the floor gets wet, and that usually means that
  the room below suffers. A good maintenance person takes
  emergencies in stride.
- **On Reservations:** "Reservations people don't have to have
  experience. We'll train them. We always have three people
  at a time watching the reservations desk, answering
  phones, and checking people in and out.

  It takes quick thinking to get one hundred people

checked out by 11 A.M. and one hundred others checked in by 3 P.M. What do you do when a person shows up at nine o'clock and wants to get into his room? Or what about when a person arrives and claims that he sent you a check (which hasn't yet arrived)? You have to be careful about overbooking, and careful that people are checking in on the day they said they would.

Here's where most managerial people start. It's good experience keeping track of reservations—who has sent in the check, who has requested a particular room. You don't need a formal education to succeed in the hotel business, but horse sense helps. If a person does claim that he mailed in a check but you haven't received it, don't just let him into the room. Ask him for another check, and tell him that you'll happily refund the first check when (and if!) it arrives.

- **On Advertising:** "I spend about $10,000 a year advertising the Atlantic Terrace. Although that doesn't compare with the hundreds of thousands of dollars spent on advertising by the Atlantic City hotels, it's quite high for a small operation's ad budget. Advertising includes ads in the major newspapers on Long Island, in Westchester, and in New York City. I even advertise in the *Philadelphia Inquirer* and spend $1,000 each year on an ad in the local chamber of commerce directory. The chamber sends me a lot of inquiries each year."

Frank Brill lives at the Atlantic Terrace during the season— May through October. He works hard, but a look at the working conditions tells you that there are rewards for his toil: the half mile of beachfront, the rolling lawns and gardens, the friendliness of coworkers and neighbors. Frank derives a great deal of satisfaction from helping guests find a good restaurant for soft-shell crabs, or telling them where to find the best pieces of driftwood. Like Long Island itself, the Atlantic Terrace seems to be an island—and Frank Brill is its Robinson Crusoe, overseeing the self-contained world of his motel as efficiently as the manager of a vast resort would watch over his own.

Grand Hotels: A Selective List

Great hotels, like great baseball teams, exude pride, teamwork, quality. They are used to giving more than 100 percent, and they revel in providing guests with those little extras that separate a great hotel from the crowd. Great hotels combine an experienced staff, fine food, superior service, and exquisite living space. Here are a handful of the world's best hotels—glamorous places to work as well as stay.

The Carlyle
35 E. 76th St.
New York, NY 10021
(212) 744-1600

Caeser Park Hotel
Rua Augusta 1508
01304 São Paulo,
Brazil
(011) 285-6622

Four Seasons Hotel
21 Avenue Rd.
Toronto M5R 2Gl,
Canada
(416) 964-0911

Hotel Hassler
Villa Medici
Piazza Trinite Dei Monti, 6
00187 Rome,
Italy
(67) 82-651

The Mansion on Turtle Creek
2821 Turtle Creek Blvd.
Dallas, TX 75219
(214) 559-2100

Hotel La Mamounia
Avenue Bab Idiel
Marrakech,
Morocco
(04) 32381

Oriental Hotel
48 Oriental Ave.
Bangkok 10500,
Thailand
(2) 234-8620

Hotel Plaza Athenée
25, avenue Montaigne
75008 Paris,
France
(01) 723-7833

The Regent Hong Kong
Salisbury Rd.
Kowloon,
Hong Kong
(3) 721-1211

Reid's
9006 Funchal
Madeira,
Portugal
(91) 23001

Hotel Ritz
15 place Vendôme
75001 Paris,
France
(01) 260-3830

Le Richmond
1201 Geneva
Geneva,
Switzerland
(022) 311-400

Hotel Chains: Your Passport to the World

People used to say, "Join the army and see the world." However, you'll have an easier time of it if you join a hotel chain. Leading hotel chains offer great opportunities for advancement. And a new hotel assignment can well mean working in another country. Here's a list of some of the more prominent hotel chains—including address and phone number for each one's corporate headquarters:

Hilton Hotels
9880 Wilshire Blvd.
Beverly Hills, CA 90210
(213) 278-4321

Holiday Inns
3742 Lamar Ave.
Memphis, TN 38195
(901) 362-4001

Hyatt Corporation
1 Hyatt Center
9700 West Bryn Mawr Ave.
Rosemont, IL 60018
(312) 860-1234

Marriott Corporation
Marriott Dr.
Washington, D.C. 20058
(301) 897-9000

Meridien Hotels
1350 Sixth Ave.
New York, NY 10019
(212) 956-4398

Quality Inns
10750 Columbia Pike
Silver Springs, MD 20901
(301) 593-5600

Ramada Inns, Inc.
3838 E. Van Beuren
Phoenix, AZ 85008
(602) 273-4000

Sheraton World Headquarters
60 State St.
Boston, MA 02109
(617) 367-3600

TraveLodge
1973 Friendship Drive
El Cajon, CA 92090
(619) 448-1884

Trusthouse Forte
24-30 New St.
Aylesbury, Bucks,
England HP20 2NW
(011) 4429632861

Hotels: Where to Go for Education

Write to the Council on Hotel, Restaurant and Institutional Education for details about lodging-industry career training at colleges and universities offering two- and four-year programs.

Sources for information about training:

Bureau of Labor Statistics
U.S. Government Printing Office
Washington, D.C. 20402
"Employment Outlook—Hotels"
"Employment Outlook—Restaurants"

Council on Hotel, Restaurant & Institutional Education
Henderson Human Development Building, Rm. 12
Pennsylvania State University
University Park, PA 16802
(814) 863-0586

Culinary Institute of America, Inc.
North Rd.
Hyde Park, NY 12601
(914) 452-9600

Educational Institute of the American Hotel & Motel Association
1407 So. Harrison Rd.
East Lansing, MI 48823
(517) 353-5500

National Restaurant Association
One IBM Plaza, Suite 2600
Chicago, IL 60611
(312) 787-2525

There are a number of scholarships available to those pursuing a lodging-industry career, varying from cash awards to tuition payments at a particular institution.
For a list of these scholarships, contact:

American Hotel Foundation
888 Seventh Ave.
New York, NY 10019
(212) 265-4506

National Institute for the Food Service Industry
20 North Wacker Dr., Suite 2620
Chicago, IL 60606
(312) 782-1703

National Restaurant Association
One IBM Plaza, Suite 2600
Chicago, IL 60611
(312) 787-2525

Compiled by the American Hotel & Motel Association, 888 Seventh Ave., New York, NY 10019.

AIRLINES: FLIGHTS OF FANCY

Although the airline industry conjures up adventure to many people, the greatest adventure for some airlines has been learning to live with fare deregulation. Many airlines have cut back on flight personnel; others have instituted pay cuts. Continental, Braniff, Air Florida, National, Republic, and Allegheny have all folded, reorganized, or merged with other companies. Capitol Airlines recently suspended operations.

The ray of hope is in the new budget airlines, the most famous being People Express, which grew from a small, tentative business a few years back to the booming nationwide airline it is today. Smaller airlines, such as Muse, are cropping up all the time and looking for employees. Not all are guaranteed to prosper, but for many the risks may pay off.

In brief. The 1978 Airline Deregulation Act made stark changes in the airline industry, which is now open to anyone who owns or leases aircraft. The large airlines have felt the squeeze of competition from fledgling regional and national airlines. Once there were sixteen major American airlines; now there are only ten.

Airlines recruit flight personnel who have excellent interpersonal skills, experience in working with the public, and a good head for details. A college degree is not necessary for the position of flight attendant.

Training. Airlines such as American recruit flight attendants from all over the country. In many large cities, people will simply walk in the door and apply directly to the airline. Most airlines run advertisements telling where and when they will be interviewing applicants.

As for salaries, $1,000 per month is typical base pay. Increases come with experience, night-flight duty—especially calling for long hours—or with the ability to speak a foreign language. Airlines look for flight attendants who are flexible—people who can cope with varied schedules, changeable weather conditions, and the possibility of working weekends, nights, and holidays.

American Airlines sends its recruits to a six-and-a-half-week course at its learning center in Dallas. There, the recruits are taught beverage service, food preparation, and, most importantly, what to do in a variety of medical and flight emergencies. When they start work, flight attendants automatically become members of their union, the Association of Professional Flight Attendants. Most airlines are unionized (with the exception of Delta).

These days, more and more flight attendants are staying on the job longer. Some have put in twenty years or more. The reward for long service is decreasing one's number of trips and hours spent working. (Also, as one gains seniority, one can choose more interesting or convenient destinations.) As with other airline positions, flight personnel and their immediate families can fly anywhere practically free (they pay only a service charge).

If you'd prefer to stay on terra firma, however, you might want to explore the position of reservations agent. This job will hone your skills in solving problems and in dealing with the public. You'll need a pleasant speaking voice and calm disposition. You'll also need a high-school diploma; clear, grammatically correct speech; and good writing skills. Entry-level pay for airline-reservations representatives ranges from $16,000 to $25,000, according to Susan Starrett Vannasse, owner of Travel People, a Boston personnel agency specializing in the travel industry.

Moving up. From reservationist, you can make the jump to airline representative. As an airline rep, you'll visit travel agencies, develop new commercial accounts, attend trade shows, call on tour and charter operators, and keep everyone abreast of your airline's latest fares, destinations, and packages.

As with other airline jobs, your family can fly free—paying only the taxes—to anywhere your airline flies (as well as on other airlines with reciprocal agreements).

From airline representative, you can progress to district sales manager and corporate management. Since airlines are struggling to survive, they are always on the lookout for fresh marketing talent. An airline's marketing department is generally most interested in someone with a business degree, an intense interest in marketing, and selling skills.

Major American Airlines

American Airlines
P.O. Box 61616
Dallas–Ft. Worth Airport
Dallas, TX 75261
(214) 355-1234

Delta Air Lines
Hartsfield Atlanta
   International Airport
Atlanta, GA 30320
(404) 346-6011

Eastern Airlines
International Airport
Miami, FL 33148
(305) 873-2211

Northwest Orient
Minneapolis–St. Paul
   International Airport
St. Paul, MN 55111
(612) 726-2111

Pan American World Airlines
Pan Am Building
New York, NY 10017
(212) 880-1234

Piedmont Airlines
Smith-Reynolds Airport
Winston-Salem, NC 27102
(919) 767-5100

Trans World Airlines
605 Third Ave.
New York, NY 10016
(212) 557-3000

United Airlines
P.O. Box 66100
Chicago, IL 60666
(312) 952-4000

US Air
Washington National Airport
Washington, D.C. 20001
(202) 783-4500

Western Airlines
P.O. Box 92005
World Way Postal Center
Los Angeles, CA 90009
(213) 646-2345

CRUISE LINES: THE DECK IS LOADED

The successful TV series "The Love Boat" has probably been an enormous public-relations boost to the cruise industry. The show emphasizes the glamorous aspects of cruising—travel, meeting interesting people, pleasant working conditions—and plays down the drawbacks—low pay, a sense of rootlessness, difficulty in moving up through the ranks.

The competition for challenging shipboard jobs is so intense that we don't want to arouse false hopes. So we'll very briefly survey the types of jobs available and ways of getting in.

In Brief. During the past twenty years, cruise lines have steered their business toward a younger clientele. They've created informal cruises that emphasize the interests and concerns of young adults.

We've listed some of the major cruise lines operating in the United States. Positions aboard ship fall into two distinct categories: crew and staff. *Crew* refers to the people who run the ship—everyone from the captain, purser, and engineers, to the maître d', waiters, and bartenders. *Staff* refers to people involved in the entertainment of the passengers: the cruise director, assistant cruise director, and hostesses.

Which Jobs? Most of the cruise lines operating in the United States are owned by foreign companies. Therefore, these ships tend to hire crews of their own nationality. However, the entertainment staff about these ships may include Americans as well. You can apply for these staff positions by contacting a cruise line and applying directly to their personnel department or to their concessionaire (a type of employment agency for cruise lines; most ship lines use concessionaires to fill on-board positions).

"The trick is to get your foot in the door," says Sue Suzell, assistant to the entertainment coordinator at Marine and Mercantile, a large Miami-based concessionaire. "If a ship has a number of American passengers, the firm is likely to hire Americans in a variety of capacities. For example, foreign cruise lines like Carnivale and Costa hire American women to serve drinks."

Suzell suggests that the most realistic on-board jobs to aim for are hostess and assistant cruise director. These people, in general, are entertainers, who have the flexibility and talent to help run simultaneous activities aboard ship. The job of hostess usually pays less than $15,000 per year (all salaries given are approximate, varying greatly among different cruise lines). Assistant cruise directors earn about $20,000 and help the cruise director (who makes between $25,000 and $50,000) oversee all of the ship's entertainment. When a ship has close to a thousand passengers, there's always need for additional help.

If you are interested in seeing whether you might qualify for a position on the crew, you can always fill out an application. Every cruise ship must hire engineers, maître d's, waiters, secretaries (sometimes called *purserettes*), and bartenders. There's also a need for room stewards, who supervise the housekeeping staff. You might have a chance at landing a job as a waiter or room steward these positions often have a high turnover. Most of the jobs we've described pay less than $30,000 a year, but the food and lodging are part of the perks of all shipboard jobs.

Making Yourself Useful. To get a staff job, you'll have to find an unusual way to "position" yourself. Don't be shy about discussing special skills that might gain the attention of a personnel director. For example, you may be a whiz at Trivial Pursuit or be a backgammon champion. You might be a sharpshooter at skeet or an expert on the commodities market. Any or all of these interests and skills could catch the eye of a person looking to find a well-rounded person to fill out the staff positions aboard ship.

Whatever your skills, you'll have to pitch in with whatever needs doing. To keep its staff productive, cruise lines expect all employees to help out in a variety of ways. For an assistant cruise director, that may mean anything from pulling the curtain during the evening show to running a table-tennis tournament.

Ships That Pass in the Night:
Cruise Lines Worth Exploring

Holland America Cruises (Dutch)
2 Penn Plaza
New York, NY 10001
(212) 290-0100

Cunard Lines (British)
555 Fifth Ave.
New York, NY 10036
(212) 880-7500

American Hawaii Cruise
1 Embarcadero Center
San Franciso, CA 94111
(415) 392-9400

Pacquet Cruises, Inc. (French)
1370 Sixth Ave.
New York, NY 10019
(212) 757-9050

Royal Viking (Scandinavian)
1 Embarcadero Center
San Francisco, CA 94111
(415) 366-2223

Bahamas Cruise Lines
61 Broadway
New York, NY 10006
(212) 696-2360
(305) 885-4722

Costa Cruise Line (Italian)
733 Third Ave.
New York, NY 10017
(800) 327-2537

Royal Caribbean Cruise Lines
903 South American Way
Miami, FL 33132
(305) 379-2601

Norwegian Caribbean Lines
   (Norwegian)
1 Biscayne Tower
Miami, FL 33131
(305) 358-6670

Princess Cruises (British)
2029 Century Park E.
Los Angeles, CA 90067
(213) 553-1666

Sitmar Cruises (American)
80100 Santa Monica Blvd.
Los Angeles, CA 90067
(213) 533-1666

Home Lines Cruises (Italian)
1 World Trade Center
New York, NY
(212) 432-1414

A Reader's Guide to Travel

General Interest Magazines

Frequent Flyer
888 Seventh Ave.
New York, NY 10019
(212) 977-8300

National Geographic
17th and M Sts.
Washington, D.C. 20036
(202) 857-7000

Signature
880 Third Ave.
New York, NY 10022
(212) 888-9450

The Sunday *New York Times* (Travel Section)
229 W. 43d St.
New York, NY 10036
(212) 556-1234

Travel: Trade Periodicals

ASTA Travel News
488 Madison Ave.
Room 1110
New York, NY 10022
(212) 826-9464

Business Travel
Travel Trade Publications
605 Third Ave.
New York, NY 10016

Pacific Travel News
274 Brennan St.
San Francisco, CA 94107
(415) 397-0070

Thomas Cook Business Traveler
352 Nassau St.
Princeton, NJ 08540
(609) 987-7200

Time Share Traveler
7000 S.W. 62nd St.
Suite 306
South Miami, FL 33143
(305) 374-3195

TravelAge East (West, Southeast)
888 Seventh Ave.
New York, NY 10019
(212) 977-8300

Travel & Leisure
1350 Sixth Ave.
New York, NY 10019
(212) 399-2500

Travel/Holiday
Travel Magazine, Inc.
51 Atlantic Ave.
Floral Park, NY 11001
(516) 352-9700

TravelAge Midamerica
Official Airline Guides, Inc.
Suite 2416
Prudential Plaza
Chicago, IL 60601
(312) 861-0432

The Travel Agent
2 W. 46th St.
New York, NY 10036
(212) 575-9000

Travel & Tourism Executive Newsletter
53 Church
Stonington, CT
(203) 535-3866

Travel Digest Magazine
342 Madison Ave.
New York, NY 10017
(212) 986-5700

Travel Guide
1085 Raritan Rd.
Clark, NJ 07066
(201) 964-3480

Travel Illustrated
2 Park Ave.
New York, NY 10016
(212) 340-9883

Travel Industry Monthly
342 Madison Ave.
New York, NY
(212) 661-0656

Travel Industry Personnel Directory
2 W. 46th St.
New York, NY 10036
(212) 575-9000

Travel Management Daily
888 Seventh Ave.
New York, NY 10106
(212) 977-8312

Travel North America
1 Park Ave.
New York, NY 10016
(212) 725-3600

Travelscene Magazine
888 Seventh Ave.
New York, NY 10019
(212) 977-8337

Travel Trade: The Business Paper of The Travel Industry
6 E. 46th St.
New York, NY 10017
(212) 883-1110

Travel Weekly
Ziff-Davis Co.
1 Park Ave.
New York, NY 10016
(212) 725-3600

Unique & Exotic Travel Reporter
P.O. Box 98833
Tacoma, WA 98499

Major Hotel/Motel Trade Publications

Hotel & Motel Management
545 Fifth Ave.
New York, NY 10017
(212) 888-2939

Hotel & Resort Industry
488 Madison Ave.
New York, NY
(212) 888-1500

Lodging
888 Seventh Ave.
New York, NY 10015
(212) 265-4506

Lodging Hospitality
122 E. 42nd St.
New York, NY 10017
(212) 867-9191

Deluxe Article Reveals 5-Star Truth of Travel*

By Richard Douglass
VP-Marketing for AHI International, a large travel concern in Des Plaines, Illinois. For over 20 years I have been subjected to a continuing barrage of travel magazines, Sunday travel sections, lurid brochures and jam-packed itineraries. Using these as reference, I have contributed to the confusion myself, cranking out hundreds of titillat-

*Reprinted from *TravelAge East* by permission of the author.

ing filmscripts and tantalizing full-color mailings, extolling the virtues of more destinations than I'll ever see.

Everything was going well until a few years ago. I started traveling, actually visiting places and experiencing first-hand the "never-to-be-forgotten adventure-of-a-lifetime in exotic. . . ."

My travels have opened my eyes. I confess I have been careless with the truth.

I'm sure you've seen work like mine. I'm the guy who told your clients how their transatlantic flight to Europe would end. "As the morning sun filters gently through the cabin window, awaken to the delicate aroma of freshly-brewed coffee being served by a smiling attendant." Something closer to the truth might have read: "Exhausted and queasy from too much liquor and too little sleep, fliers are startled into wakefulness by the blinding sun and the acid smell of coffee mixing with the brewery atmosphere of the cabin."

No more lies. No more ". . . racing the sun across the Atlantic" to describe the irreparable damage done to your client's body clock upon returning to the United States. No more "specialty of the house" to cover the fact that they can't order from the menu. No more "cozy" for tiny, "stately" for over-the-hill, or "relaxing" for boring.

Here for your edification, or to confirm your worst suspicions, are some most widely-used euphemisms in travel literature today, together with what I have determined to be their best approximate English translations. I offer them to you as a public service.

Beware the following:
- Old World charm—no bath
- Carriage trade—no kids or pets
- Sun-drenched—arid wasteland
- Tropical—rainy
- Majestic setting—a long way from town
- Authentic native dishes—inedible but cheap
- Options galore—nothing is included in the itinerary
- Secluded hideaway—impossible to find or get to
- . . . too numerous to mention—the writer has never been there
- Pre-registered rooms—already occupied
- Leisurely transfer—tedious bus ride
- Explore on your own—pay for it yourself
- Knowledgeable trip hosts—they've flown before
- Nominal charge—outrageous charge
- "Thieves' Market"—thieves
- Dare to be different—ignore your common sense
- No extra fees—no extras
- Steeped in history—old; backward

- Tipping is considered an insult—they love to be insulted
- . . . and much, much more—that's about all there is
- All the amenities—free shower cap
- Aristocratic—hasn't been renovated
- Gentle breezes—gale-force winds
- Picturesque—theme park nearby
- Airy—no air conditioning
- Brisk—freezing
- Carefree natives—terrible service
- Bustling metropolis—thousands of hostile locals
- Open bar—free ice cubes
- Plush—top and bottom sheets
- Spacious quarters—sparsely-furnished quarters
- Surprising bargains—save on hollowed-coconut birdfeeders
- Motorcoach—bus
- Deluxe—bus with windows
- Unique—no one else would do it like this
- Quaint—run-down
- Off-the-beaten-path—people have stopped coming here
- Standard—substandard
- Deluxe—standard
- Superior—free shower cap
- Undiscovered—not worth discovering
- Convenient—bring busfare
- Playground of the Stars—Eve Arden once stayed here
- If you like being pampered—you can get waited on
- Tree-lined boulevards—no sightseeing

Breaking Into Travel: A Selected Reading List

Hollander, Janet and Joe Hollander. *Your Career in Travel.* New York: Arco, 1981.

Lerner, Elaine, with C. B. Abbott. *The Way to Go: A Woman's Guide to Careers in Travel.* New York: Warner Books, 1982.

Morrison, James W. *Travel Agent and Tourism: A Manual of Travel Agency Operations.* New York: Arco, 1980.

Peck, Ralph H. *Travel Careers.* New York: Franklin Watts, 1976.

Stevens, Lawrence. *Your Career in Travel and Tourism.* Wheaton, Ill.: Merton House, Travel & Tourism Publishers, 1979.

Notes

Advertising
1. Karen Cole Winters, *Your Career in Advertising* (New York: Arco, 1980).

Finance
1. Michael W. Robbins, "Three Who Dared," *Savvy*, August 1984, p. 37.
2. Studs Terkel, *Working* (New York: Pantheon, 1972), p. 335. Reprinted with permission of Pantheon Books, a division of Random House, Inc., copyright 1972.
3. Leslie Wayne, "The Method and Magic of the Superbrokers," *The New York Times*, 29 July 1982, sec. 3, p. 6.

Television
1. Michael W. Robbins, "Three Who Dared," *Savvy*, August 1984, p. 32.
2. Leonard Probst, *Off Camera* (New York: Stein and Day, 1975), p. 145.
3. Westwinds Learning Center, October 1984 catalog, p. 145.
4. Nancy Collins, "The Smartest Man on TV," *New York*, 13 August 1983, p. 22.

Index

Agents
  literary, 57
  music, 183, 185-186
    listed, 197-201
  theatrical, 278-280
  travel. *See under* Travel/tourism
Airlines. *See* Travel/tourism
Ayer, A. W., 2

Book publishing. *See* Publishing
Brokers, 84-85, 91-96
  commissions, 91-92
  discount brokers, 93
  getting into the field, 95
  MBA not necessary, 91
  qualifications and training, 91
  retail vs. institutional, 93-94
  specialization, 94
  styles, 95-96
  superbrokers, 92-93
  test (NASD), 92
  training program, 92
  types of firms, 92-93
  typical work, 94-95
  See also Finance

Career changes, finance, 82-83
Catering, 114-126
  advertising and promotion,
    120-124
  business realities, 115
  capital, 118
  checklist before starting business,
    116-120
  costs, 118-120
  employees, 119
  equipment, 119
  fees, 117-118, 119
  getting into business, 116
  hot caterers, listed, 126
  interviewing clients, 124-126
  licenses and insurance, 115,
    118-119
  liquor, illegal to mark up price,
    116, 125
  location, 117
  skills, 117-118
  up-front payment, 117-118
  who enters business, 114-115
  See also Hotel management; Res-
    taurant management

Cone, Fairfax, 1
Contacts, importance of
  advertising, 28
  music, 171
  theater, 262
  TV, 239
Copywriter, publishing, 47; *See also*
  under Advertising; Writer

Direct marketing, 7
Directors Guild of America, 146

Finance, 74-111
  analyst, 83
  back office vs. front office, 76-77
  best jobs, 83-90
  brokers. *See* Brokers
  career changes, 82-83
  cash management, 89
  Citicorp, divisions of, 78
  deregulation, 75, 77-78
  financial writers, 85-86
  glossary, 106-108
  growth of field, 74-75
  headhunters, 108-109
  history, 76
  interviews, 80-83
    guidelines, 81-82
    typical questions, 80
  loan officer, 86
  major employers listed, 103-105
  marketing/product manager, 86-87
  MBA, 83
  money management, 87-88
  new entrants, career changes, 74
  operations manager, 88
  order clerks, 89
  personality, career choices, 77
  professional organizations, 102
  reading, 100-102
  résumé and cover letter, 78-79
  sales, 88-89
  trading, 89-90
  types of organizations, 77
  underwriting (investment bank-
    ing), 90
  venture capitalist, 90
  Wall Street, defined, 76
Financial planners, 86, 96-100
  business management, music, 187
  compensation, 98

ABOUT THE AUTHORS

Gary Blake is director of The Communication Workshop, a New York City communications consulting firm helping management improve business and technical writing skills. His clients include major insurance companies, manufacturers, and financial institutions. Mr. Blake is the author of *The Status Book.*

Robert W. Bly is an independent copywriter/consultant specializing in industrial advertising and promotion. He is the author of *A Dictionary of Computer Words.*

Together, Robert W. Bly and Gary Blake have written *How To Promote Your Own Business* (New American Library), *Technical Writing: Structure, Standards, and Style* (McGraw-Hill), and *Dream Jobs: A Guide to Tomorrow's Top Careers* (The Wiley Press).